Advanced Public Speaking

A Leader's Guide

MICHAEL J. **HOSTETLER**

St. John's University, New York

MARY L. **KAHL**

State University of New York, New Paltz

PEARSON

Boston   Columbus   Indianapolis   New York   San Francisco   Upper Saddle River
Amsterdam   Cape Town   Dubai   London   Madrid   Milan   Munich   Paris   Montréal   Toronto
Delhi   Mexico City   São Paulo   Sydney   Hong Kong   Seoul   Singapore   Taipei   Tokyo

Editor-in-Chief, Communication: Karon Bowers
Associate Development Editor: Angela Mallowes
Editorial Assistant: Megan Sweeney
Project Manager: Renata Butera
Marketing Manager: Blair Zoe Tuckman
Creative Art Director: Jayne Conte
Full Service Project Management: Chitra Ganesan/PreMediaGlobal
Composition: PreMediaGlobal
Cover Designer: Karen Noferi
Cover Photo: Colin Anderson, © Blend Images/Alamy
Printer: Courier Inc.

Library of Congress Cataloging-in-Publication Data
Hostetler, Michael.
   Advanced public speaking : a leader's guide / Michael Hostetler, Mary Kahl.
      p. cm.
   Includes bibliographical references and index.
   ISBN-13: 978-0-205-74001-7
   ISBN-10: 0-205-74001-4
  1. Public speaking.   I. Kahl, Mary L.   II. Title.
   PN4121.H67 2012
   808.5'1—dc23

                                       2011025436

1 2 3 4 5 6 7 8 9 10   14 13 12 11

ISBN-13: 978-0-205-74001-7
ISBN-10: 0-205-74001-4

To LH and ML

BRIEF CONTENTS

CONTENTS

INTRODUCTION: WHY ADVANCED PUBLIC SPEAKING?

If you are taking a class in advanced public speaking, you have probably already determined that communication skills are important and worth pursuing. Although communication occurs in a multitude of media, you probably also realize that public speaking is a foundational skill required in a host of civic, business, and personal situations. The advent of electronic communication has done little to diminish the ubiquity and everyday importance of public speaking. In fact, electronic transmission of speeches has exponentially expanded speech audiences. Even though live and mediated speeches are not the same communication phenomena, the reach of the mediated speech makes public speaking more, not less, important in the twenty-first century. The meteoric rise of Barack Obama, in which his extraordinary speaking skills played no small part, is evidence of the continuing importance of speech-making in contemporary politics.

Public speaking is an ancient art, imbued with mystique, an art that enacts a human instinct to reach out and connect with others. This mystique is admirably described by Peggy Noonan, a former presidential speechwriter, in her book *What I Saw at the Revolution:*

> A speech is part theater and part political declaration; it is a personal communication between a leader and his people; it is art, and all art is a paradox, being at once a thing of great power and great delicacy.
>
> A speech is poetry: cadence, rhythm, imagery, sweep! A speech reminds us that words, like children, have the power to make dance the dullest beanbag of a heart.
>
> Speeches are not significant because we have the technological ability to make them heard by every member of our huge nation simultaneously. Speeches are important because they are one of the great constants of our political history.[1]

Noonan's encomium to speaking is reminiscent of one given by one of the principal characters in Cicero's *De Oratore* (I, 30–32):

> ... there is to my mind no more excellent thing than the power, by means of oratory, to get a hold on assemblies of men, win their good will, direct their inclinations wherever the speaker wishes, or divert them from whatever he wishes.... For what is so marvelous as that, out of the innumerable company of mankind, a single being should arise, who either alone or with a few others can make effective a faculty bestowed by nature upon every man? Or what so pleasing to the understanding and the ear as a speech adorned and polished with wise reflections and dignified language? Or what achievement

so mighty and glorious as that the impulses of the crowd, the consciences of the judges, the austerity of the Senate, should suffer transformation through the eloquence of one man? What function again is so kingly, so worthy of the free, so generous, as to bring help to the suppliant, to raise up those that are cast down, to bestow security, to set free from peril, to maintain men in their civil rights?[2]

Obviously, the importance of public speaking is no recent phenomenon. In fact, it is rooted deeply in the European cultural tradition. Its appearance in *The Iliad* is instructive. This epic Greek poem is about the Trojan War, which may have occurred around 1200 BCE. Homer probably compiled or composed the work a few hundred years later. The story is well known. Achilles, the Greeks' greatest warrior, had withdrawn from the attack on the city of Troy because of a disagreement he had with the Greek king Agamemnon. Realizing that they could not prevail in battle without their champion, the Greek generals selected a delegation to appeal to Achilles to rejoin them. One of the men in the delegation was Phoenix, who was well known to Achilles. Phoenix had been hired by Achilles' father, Peleus, as mentor and trainer of the young man. In his appeal to Achilles to rejoin the battle, Phoenix said this (Iliad, 9, 533):

The old horseman Peleus had me escort you,
that day he sent you out of Phthia to Agamemnon,
a youngster still untrained for the great leveler, war,
still green at debate where men can make their mark.
So he dispatched me, to teach you all these things,
to make you a man of words and a man of action too.

Phoenix's words reflect a fundamental belief of classical culture that a leader must be a person of action and words. War is held up as the ultimate example of action, a viewpoint typical of martial societies. Of equal importance, however, is debate, the verbal action by which leaders "can make their mark." The privileging of verbal skill is common in other cultures as well as the European. The contemporary importance of being a person of words and the ubiquity of verbal performance in the world of leadership are seen in the day-to-day business of the United Nations where all the cultures of the world gather—to do what? Talk.

It is not surprising, given the importance and ubiquity of public speaking, that a variety of approaches can be taken to its study and practice. For example, some consider public speaking as a form of entertainment, an offshoot of acting. Not a lot of everyday public speaking, however, is intended to entertain. While there are some similarities between acting and speaking, they are not as numerous as you might suppose. In his classic work on rhetoric *De Oratore*, mentioned earlier, Cicero often refers to the noted delivery skills of Roscius, the most famous Roman actor at the time (ca. 55 BCE). While acknowledging Roscius' considerable talents, Cicero clearly believes that no one in his right mind would entrust Roscius to argue an important case before the judges or in the Roman Senate.

More commonly, many people assume that public speaking is primarily a job skill, something along the order of keyboarding. It is true that communication skills, including public speaking, are highly desirable in college-educated job applicants. In a survey of American employers conducted by the Association of American Colleges and Universities, 73 percent of respondents indicated they wanted colleges to "place more emphasis" on teaching "written and oral communication."[3] However, it is also true that it is virtually impossible for a college or university to provide job-specific communication training to students. The demands of the marketplace are too varied, and, besides, if you are an undergraduate, there is a good chance that the job you will have 20 years from now does not even exist today. When you finally land your dream job after graduation, be assured that your new employer will carefully train you in the communication practices of its own organization. University education in public speaking, therefore, is usually not job specific.

Instead of approaching public speaking as a form of entertainment or simply a job skill, the viewpoint of this book is that public speaking, just as Phoenix argued to Achilles, is a function of leadership. Think of it this way: leaders speak; speakers lead. People in leadership positions are usually expected to be the spokespersons both within their organization and to the outside world. Conversely, people who develop good speaking skills are often sought out to be the leaders of organizations. This means that advanced public speaking is not for everyone. A little over a quarter of American adults have earned bachelor's degrees. This minority is usually the group required or expected to speak—the leaders and the speakers. If you are reading this book, it is likely that you have already committed yourself to becoming a leader/speaker.

How should we study and practice public speaking? Like Aristotle, we can approach speeches according to speaking situations in which educated people (leaders) often speak. For example, speaking often occurs at American funerals, whether you are asked to "give a eulogy" or merely "to say a few words." In the workplace, leaders give business reports or briefings regarding technical information with which the audience of coworkers, clients, or customers is familiar. These, and other common speaking situations, can be practiced in the classroom. We can also study and practice certain processes and techniques of speaking that can be applied to a variety of speech situations. If you practice oral writing style by writing manuscript speeches, for example, you could apply your skill to any number of speech-making occasions.

In keeping with the classical approach to developing rhetorical skills, this book is designed around a variety of speaking situations frequently encountered by educated people. The format is quite simple. Each of the chapters in the first section focuses on a specific type of speech commonly encountered by educated persons. The chapters of the second section are about processes or techniques that speakers may adopt for a variety of situations. Every chapter begins with an assignment followed by a discussion of the chapter's theme. Classical Concepts in each chapter relate the theme to foundational classical ideas about communication. Each chapter (except Chapter 13) also features one or more sample speeches of the type under discussion. These speeches may be historical or contemporary examples. (Your instructor will probably omit some of these examples or choose others for you to study.) All the example speeches are unedited, complete texts. In addition, you will find discussion questions and bibliographic references at the end of the chapters. Your class will not have time for everyone to do all the speeches in the book, but if all of you do some of them, you will be able to learn something about all the types of speeches discussed. Finally, remember that all the information in the world will not automatically make you a better speaker. In fact, a person who knows everything in this book by heart could still be a poor speaker. Knowledge of speaking must be matched with your own enthusiasm, hard work, and diligent practice in order for you to become the speaker and leader you want to be.

---

[1] Peggy Noonan, *What I Saw at the Revolution: A Political Life in the Reagan Era,* New York: Ivy Books, 1990, p. 70.

[2] Cicero, *De Oratore,* I, 30–32.

[3] "Written and oral communication" ranked second of seven "intellectual and practical skills." It was tied at 73 percent with "critical thinking and analytic reasoning." The most desired skill, at 76 percent, was "teamwork skills in diverse groups." The study that generated these data was commissioned by the Association of American Colleges and Universities and conducted by Peter D. Hart Research Associates in late 2006. For the full report and findings, see www.aacu.org/leap

PREFACE FOR INSTRUCTORS

*A*dvanced Public Speaking: A Leader's Guide* is different from many textbooks you have used in the past, and we hope that you find it a useful and provocative answer to an unfulfilled need in communication pedagogy. What makes this text unique is its advanced focus, its emphasis on student engagement, and its notable flexibility.

First, *Advanced Public Speaking* aims to be advanced. It is not simply another public speaking book with all the standard chapters and topics revisited at a higher level of abstraction. Instead, our objective is to offer students opportunities to increase their speaking abilities across a variety of more specific and complex contexts. Whether you want your students to master the techniques for making a proposal presentation, learn how to deliver a eulogy, or speak from a manuscript, this text offers sound instruction to accommodate a variety of discursive situations. We assume from the outset that your students have already completed a basic course in public speaking or, at the least, a hybrid communication course in which public speaking was a major component. In selecting example speeches for the various chapters, we have avoided the inclusion of student speeches and celebrity commencement addresses in favor of offering substantive, real-life, and sometimes challenging full-text speeches.

Second, *Advanced Public Speaking* is designed to enhance student engagement. This text seeks to engage students by broadening the appeal of advanced public speaking to a wide range of student career interests. By emphasizing the importance of public speaking for leaders in all fields, our book reaches beyond its natural audience of communication, public relations, and marketing majors. Rather than connect public speaking to a predictable and narrow range of careers, we emphasize its importance for all college-educated people. The text accomplishes this by:

Opening each chapter with an assignment. One of the first things you will notice about this book is that it upends the traditional structure of textbooks in which application predictably follows theory. In this book, the assignment comes at the beginning of the chapter. This approach is informed, in the first place, by the fact that public speaking courses are usually driven by speech assignments, not by chapters in a text. Confronted with a specific assignment, students are often motivated to discover what experienced experts can tell them about the task at hand. While some professors may have a strong interest in theory and disciplinary pursuits, students are usually more focused on what they are supposed to do to fulfill the assignment and thus be successful in the class. They ask: "What am I supposed to do? When is it due? How will it be graded?" Our assignment-first format puts the students' work— and their concerns—front and center.

Grounding students in rhetorical theory. *Advanced Public Speaking* can help engage students in communication as an academic discipline, in general, and rhetorical studies in particular. We introduce classical rhetorical theory in small increments in every chapter. As much as possible, the Commentary sections in each chapter draw examples and illustrations from the discipline of rhetoric. The Discussion Starter questions, based on the sample speeches, can be used to offer a gentle introduction to rhetorical criticism. We have also deliberately drawn on rhetorical history, whether by citing Nixon's Checkers speech, for example, or by reproducing Acres of Diamonds. Advanced students are capable of finding their own way to texts that are connected to their own times and experiences. They need to be encouraged by their teachers to reach into unfamiliar history.

Providing examples for analysis rather than exemplars. A few observations need to be made about the example speeches and Classical Concepts provided in each chapter. The speeches are intended to be examples, not exemplars. Some of them obviously resist or deviate from the advice given in the chapter. So much the better. One of the most important lessons advanced public speakers should learn is that real-world speeches are complicated, surprising, and often exasperating. Just when we think we have the rhetorical rules figured out, a maverick speaker or tangled rhetorical situation comes along that upends our settled principles. No two speakers and no two rhetorical situations are ever exactly alike. It is this potential for creativity and variety that has kept rhetoric at the heart of humanistic studies for millennia. Also, connected to rhetoric's longevity are constructs from classical rhetoric that continue to inform rhetorical studies. The Classical Concepts are intended to introduce students to these constructs in small increments. For the most part, the concepts are related to the chapter commentary, but sometimes the relationship is elastic. The concepts can be omitted from your course altogether or can create a starting point for more in-depth discussion of classical rhetoric, or anything in between, depending on your own and the class's interests.

A final notable feature of *Advanced Public Speaking* is its flexibility. We assume that it will be impossible for all the students in any one class to complete all the assignments in this book. Selecting from among the various assignments is mandatory. There are many ways to go about this. For example, one or two assignments can be given to the entire class, with students choosing other assignments based on their own interests. Or perhaps students could choose three speeches from Unit I and two from Unit II. As the instructor, you might also construct your own assignments to supplement those in the text. Flexibility is also possible in the example speech readings. Most rhetoric professors will have their own lists of preferred examples that can easily be substituted for the speeches provided here. Feel free to pick and choose, and substitute and replace. *Advanced Public Speaking* is a book that offers both a solid platform for classroom work and a launching pad for a variety of pedagogical options.

INSTRUCTOR SUPPORT

This text has an accompanying Instructor's Manual and Test Bank prepared by the authors. This instructor resource provides suggestions for additional class activities, assignments, and discussion questions. The Test Bank portion offers a variety of question types: multiple-choice, true/false, and essay format. Each question is referenced by page. This resource can be downloaded at www.pearsonhighered.com/irc (access code required).

ACKNOWLEDGMENTS

We would like to thank the following reviewers for their expertise, insight, and suggestions for the development of this text:

Amber Erikson, University of Cincinnati; Gary K. Hughes, Western Kentucky University; Christina Knopf, SUNY Potsdam; Jace Lux, Western Kentucky University; Michele Mega, California State Northridge; David Payne, University of South Florida; Chris R. Sawyer, Texas Christian University; Sydney Scott, Pace University; Robert E. Terrill, Indiana University.

Speaking Situations

The Speech of Introduction

ASSIGNMENT

Interview and introduce to the class one of your professors or an official of your college or university.

COMMENTARY

It is not unusual in leadership situations for a public speaker to be introduced to the audience by another speaker. This common speaking situation may be lightly regarded as a routine presentation, but a little reflection on the speech of introduction reveals that there is more to it than first appears. The starting point for preparing a speech of introduction is to consider how the introducer situates himself or herself in the overall rhetorical transaction. In other words, where does the introducer stand in relationship to the participants in the event? Do you see yourself as speaking on behalf of the audience in welcoming the speaker? If so, some of your remarks will be directed to the speaker. Or do you see yourself speaking *on behalf of the event's sponsor* in welcoming both the speaker and the audience? In these cases, it may be necessary to introduce the topic as well as the speaker. Perhaps the most common approach is to see the introducer as speaking *on behalf of the speaker* to the audience. Regardless of how you see your role in the overall event, it is important to keep in mind that when you give a speech of introduction, it is not about you, it's about others. Your job is to draw attention to the speaker, the topic, or the audience in such a way that the speaking event is satisfying to the greatest possible extent to all those involved. The speech of introduction is a service to others.

One important purpose of the speech of introduction focuses on the main speaker by building up his or her ethos or credibility. There are several ways to go about this. The most common method, citing the speaker's accomplishments or awards, is a starting point. Most audiences, however, do not appreciate the recitation of a laundry list of academic degrees, publication titles, or awards. Choose to magnify two or three accomplishments of the speaker that are clearly relevant to the topic and audience at hand. For example, when introducing an environmental activist to an audience of like-minded activists, it would be appropriate to mention the speaker's past involvement in the movement and current projects. When introducing the same speaker at an academic conference, it might be better to emphasize his or her academic degrees and publications.

Another way to enhance a speaker's credibility is to tell an anecdote that puts the speaker in a favorable light. Make sure the speaker is comfortable with you telling the anecdote and is not planning to use the same story in the speech. Sometimes a speaker's standing in the eyes of an audience might be enhanced by seeing the speaker in an unexpected light. For example, if the speaker is a research scientist or an academic philosopher, a story about his or her interpersonal qualities or avocation might be telling. Yet another way to build up a speaker's credibility is to share some of your own. In situations where you are introducing a protégé or someone who is subordinate to you in an organizational hierarchy, your own endorsement and positive comments will carry weight with the audience.

A second purpose of the speech of introduction focuses on the audience by preparing or conditioning it for what the speaker has to say. Columbia University President Lee Bollinger's introduction of Iranian President Ahmadinejad, cited later, is a highly unusual example of preparing an audience by attacking the credibility of the speaker. A more typical example of audience preparation was evident in Archie Epps' introduction of Malcolm X to an audience at Harvard University in 1964.[1] Epps began by using a medical metaphor to describe how many in the audience probably viewed radicalism within the Civil Rights Movement. He then challenged those in the audience who "have come for the reason one would attend a circus—to watch the dancing bear." The purpose of Epps' pointed audience analysis was to challenge it to sober reflection, to see social movements "and all social history in light of discovering the social reality which is contained in them." In other words, he wanted the audience to take Malcolm X seriously. That said, he introduced X: "The speaker this evening is Mr. Malcolm X, who lives in New York State and is at this time Minister of Moslem Mosque, Incorporated."

Here are a few practical points regarding the speech of introduction:

- There is nothing wrong with going over your introduction with the main speaker ahead of time. You don't want to be surprised that something in your introduction is factually erroneous (e.g., the speaker went to USC, not UCLA), and the speaker will probably not be comfortable correcting your gaff in front of the audience. Best to deal with these sorts of things ahead of time.

---

[1] For the introduction and speech, see *Malcolm X Speeches at Harvard*, Archie Epps, Ed. New York: Paragon House, 1991, pp. 131–160.

- Keep it short. The audience is there to hear the speaker, not you. You need a really strong reason to speak longer than three to five minutes.
- Be certain of the pronunciation of the name of the person you introduce. In our multicultural world, the pronunciation of names can be a tricky business. Ask for the correct pronunciation, and practice until you get it right. The surest way to look like a fool is to muff the pronunciation.
- Unless you have specifically set out to introduce the topic to the audience, steer clear of it. Anything you say about the topic should be stated in such a way as to defer to the speaker.
- Conclude the introduction by repeating the speaker's name and perhaps the title of the speech. For example, "Ladies and gentlemen, please welcome Candace Jones on the topic, 'The Roots of American Democracy.' "
- Reinforce words with nonverbal behavior. When the speaker comes to the podium, will you shake hands? Hug? A little advanced planning can help avoid an awkward moment.

Finally, keep in mind that some speaking situations may call for extra care by an introducer. In a tense or antagonistic forum, the introducer may need to defuse tension, perhaps by using humor. In such situations, it may fall to the introducer to make a statement about civility, emphasizing the right to dissent and the duty to listen. By speaking first at an event, the introducer has the opportunity to exercise leadership and set a tone for the whole event.

CLASSICAL CONCEPT: PRAISE AND BLAME

In classical times, juries relied less on physical evidence and testimony than on the probability that a person did or did not commit some offense. If a person's good character could be established, then it was unlikely he committed the crime and vice versa. As a result, the process of "praise and blame" became an important part of forensic rhetoric. Aristotle lists nine forms of virtue for which a person could be praised: justice, courage, temperance, magnificence, magnanimity, liberality, gentleness, prudence, and wisdom. Some virtues, like courage, seem to transcend culture, but many others vary with time and culture. Aristotle reminds us that it is important to recognize what our audience believes to be virtuous. "If the audience esteems a given quality, we must say that our hero has that quality, no matter whether we are addressing Scythians or Spartans or philosophers." Cicero reminds us that natural advantages are not praiseworthy. In other words, being born into a wealthy family or with natural good looks are not qualities for which someone deserves praise. Once a virtue is identified, it needs to be magnified or built up. For example, Aristotle writes, we could "point out that a man is the only one, or the first, or almost the only one who has done something, or that he has done it better than anyone else. . . ." These and other classical ideas of praise and blame are useful today for speeches of introduction, nominating speeches, award speeches, eulogies, sentencing hearings, and other occasions when a person's character or actions are discussed.

Sources: Aristotle *Rhetoric* 1, 9; Cicero *De Oratore* 2, 341–350.

EXAMPLES

INTRODUCTORY REMARKS AT SIPA-WORLD LEADERS FORUM
with Mahmoud Ahmadinejad, President of Iran
LEE C. BOLLINGER, PRESIDENT
COLUMBIA UNIVERSITY, NEW YORK
SEPTEMBER 24, 2007

Seldom has a speech of introduction drawn more attention and controversy than that delivered by Lee C. Bollinger when Iranian President Ahmadinejad spoke at Columbia University.

I would like to begin by thanking Dean John Coatsworth and Professor Richard Bulliet for their work in organizing this event and for their commitment to the role of the School of International and Public Affairs and its role in training future leaders in world affairs. If today proves anything it will be that there is an enormous amount of
5   work ahead for all of us. This is just one of many events on Iran that will run throughout this academic year, all to help us better understand this critical and complex nation in today's geopolitics.

Before speaking directly to the current President of Iran, I have a few critically important points to emphasize. First, since 2003, the World Leaders Forum has advanced
10   Columbia's longstanding tradition of serving as a major forum for robust debate, especially on global issues. It should never be thought that merely to listen to ideas we deplore in any way implies our endorsement of those ideas, or the weakness of our resolve to resist those ideas or our naïveté about the very real dangers inherent in such ideas. It is a critical premise of freedom of speech that we do not honor the dishonorable when we open the
15   public forum to their voices. To hold otherwise would make vigorous debate impossible. Second, to those who believe that this event never should have happened, that it is inappropriate for the University to conduct such an event, I want to say that I understand your perspective and respect it as reasonable. The scope of free speech and academic freedom should itself always be open to further debate. As one of the more famous quo-
20   tations about free speech goes, it is "an experiment, as all life is an experiment." I want to say, however, as forcefully as I can, that this is the right thing to do and, indeed, it is required by existing norms of free speech, the American university, and Columbia itself. Third, to those among us who experience hurt and pain as a result of this day, I say on behalf of all of us we are sorry and wish to do what we can to alleviate it. Fourth, to be
25   clear on another matter—this event has nothing whatsoever to do with any "rights" of the speaker but only with our rights to listen and speak. We do it for ourselves. We do it in the great tradition of openness that has defined this nation for many decades now. We need to understand the world we live in, neither neglecting its glories nor shrinking from its threats and dangers. It is consistent with the idea that one should know thine enemies,

to have the intellectual and emotional courage to confront the mind of evil and to pre-   30
pare ourselves to act with the right temperament. In the moment, the arguments for free
speech will never seem to match the power of the arguments against, but what we must
remember is that this is precisely because free speech asks us to exercise extraordinary
self-restraint against the very natural but often counter-productive impulses that lead us
to retreat from engagement with ideas we dislike and fear. In this lies the genius of the   35
American idea of free speech. Lastly, in universities, we have a deep and almost single-
minded commitment to pursue the truth. We do not have access to the levers of power.
We cannot make war or peace. We can only make minds. And to do this we must have
the most full freedom of inquiry. Let me now turn to Mr. Ahmadinejad.

Over the last two weeks, your government has released Dr. Haleh Esfandiari and   40
Parnaz Axima; and just two days ago Kian Tajbakhsh, a graduate of Columbia with a
PhD in urban planning. While our community is relieved to learn of his release on
bail, Dr. Tajbakhsh remains in Tehran, under house arrest, and he still does not know
whether he will be charged with a crime or allowed to leave the country. Let me say this
for the record, I call on the President today to ensure that Kian Tajbakhsh will be free   45
to travel out of Iran as he wishes. Let me also report today that we are extending an
offer to Dr. Tajbakhsh to join our faculty as a visiting professor in urban planning here
at his Alma Mater, in our Graduate School of Architecture, Planning and Preservation.
And we hope he will be able to join us next semester. The arrest and imprisonment of
these Iranian Americans for no good reason is not only unjustified, it runs completely   50
counter to the very values that allow today's speaker to even appear on this campus.
But at least they are alive. According to Amnesty International, 210 people have been
executed in Iran so far this year—21 of them on the morning of September 5th alone.
This annual total includes at least two children—further proof, as Human Rights Watch
puts it, that Iran leads the world in executing minors. There is more. Iran hanged up to   55
30 people this past July and August during a widely reported suppression of efforts
to establish a more open, democratic society in Iran. Many of these executions were
carried out in public view, a violation of the International Covenant on Civil and Political
Rights, to which Iran is a party. These executions and others have coincided with
a wider crackdown on student activists and academics accused of trying to foment a   60
so-called "soft revolution." This has included jailing and forced retirements of scholars. As
Dr. Esfandiari said in a broadcast interview since her release, she was held in solitary
confinement for 105 days because the government "believes that the United States . . . is
planning a Velvet Revolution" in Iran. In this very room last year we learned something
about Velvet Revolutions from Vaclav Havel. And we will likely hear the same from our   65
World Leaders Forum speaker this evening—President Michelle Bachelet Jeria of Chile.
Both of their extraordinary stories remind us that there are not enough prisons to prevent
an entire society that wants its freedom from achieving it. We at this university have not
been shy to protest and challenge the failures of our own government to live by these
values; and we won't be shy in criticizing yours. Let's, then, be clear at the beginning,   70
Mr. President you exhibit all the signs of a petty and cruel dictator. And so I ask you: Why
have women, members of the Baha'i faith, homosexuals, and so many of our academic

colleagues become targets of persecution in your country? Why in a letter last week to the Secretary General of the UN did Akbar Gangi, Iran's leading political dissident,
75 and over 300 public intellectuals, writers and Nobel Laureates express such grave concern that your inflamed dispute with the West is distracting the world's attention from the intolerable conditions your regime has created within Iran? In particular, the use of the Press Law to ban writers for criticizing the ruling system. Why are you so afraid of Iranian citizens expressing their opinions for change? In our country, you are interviewed
80 by our press and asked that you speak here today. And while my colleague at the Law School Michael Dorf spoke to Radio Free Europe [sic, Voice of America] viewers in Iran a short while ago on the tenets of freedom of speech in this country, I propose going further than that. Let me lead a delegation of students and faculty from Columbia to address your university about free speech, with the same freedom we afford you today? Will you
85 do that?

In a December 2005 state television broadcast, you described the Holocaust as a fabricated "legend." One year later, you held a two-day conference of Holocaust deniers. For the illiterate and ignorant, this is dangerous propaganda. When you come to a place like this, this makes you, quite simply, ridiculous. You are either brazenly pro-
90 vocative or astonishingly uneducated. You should know that Columbia is a world center of Jewish studies and now, in partnership with the YIVO Institute, of Holocaust studies. Since the 1930s, we've provided an intellectual home for countless Holocaust refugees and survivors and their children and grandchildren. The truth is that the Holocaust is the most documented event in human history. Because of this, and for many other reasons,
95 your absurd comments about the "debate" over the Holocaust both defy historical truth and make all of us who continue to fear humanity's capacity for evil shudder at this closure of memory, which is always virtue's first line of defense. Will you cease this outrage?

Twelve days ago, you said that the state of Israel "cannot continue its life." This echoed
100 a number of inflammatory statements you have delivered in the last two years, including in October 2005 when you said that Israel should be "wiped off the map." Columbia has over 800 alumni currently living in Israel. As an institution we have deep ties with our colleagues there. I personally have spoken out in the most forceful terms against proposals to boycott Israeli scholars and universities, saying that such boycotts might as well include Columbia.
105 More than 400 college and university presidents in this country have joined in that statement. My question, then, is: Do you plan on wiping us off the map, too?

According to reports by the Council on Foreign Relations, it's well documented that Iran is a state sponsor of terror that funds such violent group as the Lebanese Hezbollah, which Iran helped organize in the 1980s, the Palestinian Hamas, and Palestinian Islamic
110 Jihad. While your predecessor government was instrumental in providing the US with intelligence and base support in its 2001 campaign against the Taliban in Afghanistan, your government is now undermining American troops in Iraq by funding, arming, and providing safe transit to insurgent leaders like Muqtada al-Sadr and his forces. There are a number of reports that also link your government with Syria's efforts to desta-
115 bilize the fledgling Lebanese government through violence and political assassination.

My question is this: Why do you support well-documented terrorist organizations that continue to strike at peace and democracy in the Middle East, destroying lives and civil society in the region?

In a briefing before the National Press Club earlier this month, General David Petraeus reported that arms supplies from Iran, including 240 mm rockets and explosively formed projectiles, are contributing to "a sophistication of attacks that would by no means be possible without Iranian support." A number of Columbia graduates and current students are among the brave members of our military who are serving or have served in Iraq and Afghanistan. They, like other Americans with sons, daughters, fathers, husbands and wives serving in combat, rightly see your government as the enemy. Can you tell them and us why Iran is fighting a proxy war in Iraq by arming Shi'a militia targeting and killing U.S. troops?

This week the United Nations Security Council is contemplating expanding sanctions for a third time because of your government's refusal to suspend its uranium-enrichment program. You continue to defy this world body by claiming a right to develop peaceful nuclear power, but this hardly withstands scrutiny when you continue to issue military threats to neighbors. Last week, French President Sarkozy made clear his lost patience with your stall tactics; and even Russia and China have shown concern. Why does your country continue to refuse to adhere to international standards for nuclear weapons verification in defiance of agreements that you have made with the UN nuclear agency? And why have you chosen to make the people of your country vulnerable to the effects of international economic sanctions and threaten to engulf the world with nuclear annihilation? Let me close with this comment. Frankly, and in all candor, Mr. President, I doubt that you will have the intellectual courage to answer these questions. But your avoiding them will in itself be meaningful to us. I do expect you to exhibit the fanatical mindset that characterizes so much of what you say and do. Fortunately, I am told by experts on your country, that this only further undermines your position in Iran with all the many good-hearted, intelligent citizens there. A year ago, I am reliably told, your preposterous and belligerent statements in this country (as in your meeting at the Council on Foreign Relations) so embarrassed sensible Iranian citizens that this led to your party's defeat in the December mayoral elections. May this do that and more. I am only a professor, who is also a university president, and today I feel all the weight of the modern civilized world yearning to express the revulsion at what you stand for. I only wish I could do better.

Source: © Columbia University

DISCUSSION STARTERS

Bollinger's speech does not follow some of the guidelines given in this chapter. Why not? What orientation in regards to speaker, audience, and sponsor did Bollinger adopt? If a speech of introduction is a service to others, on whose behalf does it seem Bollinger was speaking? Do you think Bollinger's hostile and aggressive approach was justified or ill-advised?

INTRODUCTION OF PRESIDENT CLINTON
Gen. Colin L. Powell
VIETNAM VETERAN'S MEMORIAL, WASHINGTON, D.C.
MEMORIAL DAY, 1993

Early in his first term, President Bill Clinton's relationship to the American military was strained. Not only had Clinton not served in and had actively opposed the Vietnam War, he had also proposed a liberalization of military policy toward gays and lesbians that was rejected by senior officers. Clinton's decision to speak at the Vietnam Memorial was sure to stir up controversy. General Colin Powell, chairman of the Joint Chiefs of Staff, faced a challenging rhetorical situation when he introduced the president on Memorial Day, 1993.

Thank you very much, Jan. Mr. President, distinguished guests, fellow veterans, ladies and gentlemen, it is a great pleasure to be with you again at this sacred memorial to our fallen Vietnam buddies. For over ten years, the Wall has stood as a poignant and silent symbol of sacrifice, yet in its silence, it still speaks to us of valor, of honor, of

5   devotion to duty. It speaks to us of the horror of war and reminds us of who pays the ultimate price. It inspires us to use our strength to preserve the peace and to prevent war at all costs.

I never come here, never, never come here without being touched to the depth of my soul as I run my hand over the name of a friend long departed, but never forgotten.

10   I always leave here comforted by a final glance at the statue of the three GIs behind you who approach the Wall to stand guard, to search for the name of a friend, or perhaps to search for their own name. They symbolize the eternal vigilance of American warriors, of America's armed forces.

I have brought many foreign visitors here to visit this wall, but I don't bring them

15   directly here. First, I take them to visit the Jefferson Monument to see the words inscribed there, which capture the essence of the American spirit and dream. Next, we go to the Lincoln Memorial, and I draw their attention to the words that President Lincoln spoke as the Civil War was coming to a close and Lincoln knew that his next task in life was to heal and reunite a nation. Your remember those words, "With malice toward

20   none, with charity for all, with firmness in the right as God gives us to see the right, let us strive on to finish the work we are in, to bind up the nation's wounds, to care for him who shall have borne the battle and for his widow and his orphan."

To bind up the nation's wounds. In the sad aftermath of the Vietnam War, no single act by a grateful people has done more to bind up our nation's wounds than

25   this Memorial Wall. Two years ago, celebrations following Desert Storm furthered the national healing process as those parades and celebrations gave us the opportunity to pay tribute to our Korean and Vietnam veterans, as well as the veterans of the Gulf War, to give those Vietnam veterans the parades that they never had. The healing process, as we know, will never be complete until we have accounted for all those who did not come

30   home from Vietnam.

We all here know that the Vietnam War caused deep wounds within American society, but now the passage of time, a growing spirit of understanding of different views, a pressing need to move forward together as a nation, allow us now to complete our reconciliation and to heal those wounds. And therefore, my dear friends, at this Wall of honor, as the senior Vietnam veteran on active duty and as chairman of the Joint Chiefs of Staff, I want to welcome, I want to welcome and introduce you to the commander-in-chief of the armed forces of the United States, our President, President Bill Clinton.

35

Source: "Contemporary Speeches: The Contentious Society," Videorecording, Houghton Mifflin Co., 1994.

DISCUSSION STARTERS

How does Gen. Powell share some of his own military ethos with the president? In hierarchical organizational settings, what is the difference between introducing a peer and introducing someone who ranks over or below you in the organization?

BIBLIOGRAPHY

Nearly all public speaking books briefly discuss introduction speeches. To better understand the controversial contexts for the Bollinger and Powell speeches, see the following.

Grossberger, Lewis. "You No-Good, Dirty Rascal You." *MediaWeek* 17, no. 35 (Oct. 2007):10.

> Grossberger reviews the name-calling that President Ahmadinejad's visit provoked in the New York City media. By comparison, Lee Bollinger's introductory speech was civil.

Snee, Brian J. "Clinton and Vietnam: A Case for Amnestic Rhetoric." *Communication Quarterly* 49, no. 2 (Spring 2001):189–202.

> Prof. Snee's discussion of President Clinton's speech helps put in context the challenge faced by General Powell in his introduction.

Opinion Give and Take

ASSIGNMENT

Divide your class into groups for what is called a "long table debate."[1] Here's how it works. One group will take the affirmative side of a controversial proposition, and the other group will take the negative. Each person will give a three to five minute speech for his or her side, alternating sides until everyone has spoken. Listen carefully to the opposing speaker who goes just before you, and respond to what he or she says.

COMMENTARY

The *Oxford English Dictionary* describes the common usage of the term "argument" as a reasoning process in which a connected series of statements or reasons are set forth to establish a position. As it refers to a discussion of a question or debate of an issue, "argument" implies a dialogue between communicators. Argument is critical in a host of contexts, especially in public decision making and politics. Democratic government and its benefits depend on what philosopher Amanda Anderson describes as "argument conducted within conditions of fairness and reciprocity, and animated by a moral point of view committed to the enlargement of perspective that argument itself promotes and demands."[2]

Unfortunately, argument has developed a bad reputation with many people. "Fairness," "reciprocity," and "enlargement of perspective" are often not the qualities people think of when they think of an argument. Cable television news seems to promote argument as an entertainment spectacle in which loquacious personalities yell, interrupt, and smirk through interminable pseudodiscussions of everything from nuclear deterrence to celebrity pregnancies. As a result, argument is often associated with verbal aggression, humiliation, and broken relationships. Wanting

---

[1]Your instructor may opt to choose from a number of other possible debate formats.

[2]Amanda Anderson. *The Way We Argue Now*. Princeton: Princeton University Press, 2006, p. 161.

to avoid these perceived negative consequences of argument, many people opt for disengagement from others and apathy toward the issues of the day. The decision to opt out in this way, however, is not as harmless and inconsequential as you might think. As critic Michiko Katutani puts it, the reluctance to embrace civil, informed debate about matters that are important to us "represents a failure to fully engage with the world, a failure to test one's convictions against the logic and passions of others. It suggests a closing off of the possibilities of growth and transformation and a repudiation of the process of consensus building."[3] While some people may be able to retreat into a private world of serenity where interactions occur only with people who already agree with them, leaders enjoy no such luxury. Leaders must learn the difference between "having" an argument and "making" one. Even more important, leaders must learn to make arguments that, in Katutani's words, engage others and promote growth, transformation, and consensus building. To do this, the more a speaker knows about argumentation principles and practices the better.

Much has been written about the theory and criticism of argumentation. One well-known approach was suggested by the British philosopher Stephen Toulmin in his 1958 book, *The Uses of Argument*.[4] Toulmin's model constructed claims—statements offered for the consideration of others—as central to argument. Claims grow out of data, what we know or think we know about a given issue. The rational connection that allows us to connect data to the claims we want to make is what Toulmin labeled a "warrant." Warrants might rest on comparison, generalization, definition, authority, causation, or circumstance. For example, a dispute developed over where the federal government should display original copies of Lincoln's Gettysburg Address. In an editorial,[5] *the New York Times* pointed out the relevant *data*: five copies of the speech exist, two of which are owned by the Library of Congress. The *Times* argued the *claim* that one copy should be on display in Gettysburg, Pennsylvania. The *warrant* for this claim was causal: seeing the speech on site causes a greater impact on viewers. Some theorists have pointed out that appropriate claims and data are often conditioned by the context of an argument. In other words, standards of argumentation vary depending on the sphere of human activity in which the argument occurs. Standards may be different for arguments in the areas of business, science, politics, or religion.

Along with argumentation structure and analysis, bad argumentation, the "fallacies," also receive much attention in communication literature. Some of the fallacies have colorful names like slippery slope, red herring, and straw man. You should be familiar with these terms.[6] Keep in mind, however, that merely knowing the terminology of either argument analysis or fallacies may not help you in the heat of argument. A clear model like the one developed by Toulmin is harder

---

[3]Michiko Kakutani. "Debate? Dissent? Discussion? Oh, Don't Go There!" *New York Times*, March 23, 2002. Kakutani also points out that philosophical relativism and diversity sensitivity, often resulting in overtactfulness about differences, also contribute to verbal reticence.

[4]Stephen Toulmin. *The Uses of Argument*. London: Cambridge University Press, 1958.

[5]"The Right Address Is Gettysburg, PA." *New York Times*, February 21, 1994, p. A19.

[6]For a list of some common fallacies and their definitions, see the basic course review in the appendix.

to apply than first appears. Claims are sometimes unclear, multiple claims can be contradictory, and warrants are usually unstated. Fallacies are also often hard to pin down. A famous example is a speech given by Richard Nixon in 1952. Using the new medium of television, Nixon defended his vice-presidential candidacy against charges of corruption. Nixon revealed what at the time was considered embarrassing personal information about his finances and told of a dog named Checkers, which was given to his daughters by a supporter. The speech was wildly successful and saved his candidacy. Only later, when the applause died down, did thoughtful listeners realize that the speech may have been one of the greatest examples of the red herring fallacy in American political history.

In addition to knowing something about argumentation theory, there are several other practical guidelines that, if followed, would help leaders become good arguers.

First, leaders should promote good arguments by example. It is easy, and usually wrong, to substitute the exercise of power for reasoned discussion. Sometimes leaders must issue orders, but in most common civic and business situations in American culture, autocratic decrees are unwelcome and counterproductive. Good leaders recognize that the same standards that apply to all arguers apply to them. Argument must be built on thorough knowledge of issues and alternatives, compelling evidence, and careful thought. All of this takes time. Issuing orders is a fast way to respond to emergencies, but engaging in reasoned argument to achieve consensus will take a while. In planning processes, leaders must make time for discussion.

Second, leaders must plan for life after an argument. Even with the most sensitive effort to achieve consensus, at the end of the day and the argument, one set of priorities or ideas will probably win favor over other options. But if winning an argument means proving your point at all costs and humiliating others in the process, what really has been won? Leaders recognize that very frequently the same people who lost today's argument will be the very people needed next week for support and advice. The U.S. Congress provides a good example of this principle. If you have ever listened to debates in the House or Senate, you will surely notice the effort made to speak politely and courteously—"The Chair recognizes the distinguished gentlewoman from Kansas." In legislatures, bruising political battles result in votes that create winners and losers almost on a daily basis. Representatives have long realized, however, that tomorrow they must convene again to do the people's business. Today's foe may be tomorrow's ally. Therefore, a courteous decorum has been developed and maintained (although there are lapses), which has helped create a space for passionate argument for over 200 years.

Finally, leaders need to cultivate a mature self-awareness of their own limitations and capacity to be wrong and make mistakes. What do you do when the facts you are relying on are clearly refuted by others? How do you respond when you are confronted by compelling evidence contrary to your stated views? In almost no other area is it more important to lead by example. Admitting your errors and changing your mind when you need to should be regarded among a leader's greatest strengths. Unfortunately, they are often derisively dismissed as flip-flopping. Granted, casually changing your opinion in response to transitory circumstances or for your own selfish gain is no virtue. A principled change in direction, however, based on solid evidence, is always a virtue. In short, leaders must not only be adept at making arguments; they must also be open to being changed by arguments.

CLASSICAL CONCEPT: LOGOS

Aristotle divided persuasive appeals into three types called proofs. "There are, then, these three means of effecting persuasion. The man who is to be in command of them must, it is clear, be able (1) to reason logically, (2) to understand human character and goodness in their various forms, and (3) to understand the emotions" (*Rhetoric* I, 2). Reasoning logically, or logos, has to do with rational or logical arguments.

Rhetorical logic is not quite the same as the logic pursued by philosophers and mathematicians. The best way to think about rhetorical logic is more in terms of the probability of human behavior than in empirical certainty. While philosophers seek to reason out the nature of ultimate reality, rhetoricians are more likely trying to reason out what to do next. As Aristotle put it, "The duty of rhetoric is to deal with such matters as we deliberate upon without arts or systems to guide us . . . the subjects of our deliberation are such as seem to present us with alternative possibilities" (*Rhetoric* I, 2). Lacking certainty and working under the time constraints of specific rhetorical situations, rhetors must make decisions based on probabilities. Rhetorical logic, therefore, is not the same as the super-rationalism of Commander Spock of Star Trek fame.

An example of rhetorical logic can be seen in one of the most famous American political speeches of the twentieth century. During the 1960 presidential campaign, John Kennedy sought to allay Protestant fears that his Catholic faith would automatically determine his position on some hot-button church–state issues. In his speech to the Houston Ministerial Association, he said, "judge me on the basis of fourteen years in the Congress—on my declared stands against an ambassador to the Vatican, against unconstitutional aid to parochial schools, and against any boycott of the public schools. . . ." Kennedy's rhetorical argument works like this. If you know how someone has behaved in the past, can you pretty much tell what he or she will do in the future? Of course. Therefore, if Kennedy's positions on some church–state issues were unobjectionable to his audience in the past, then, chances are, his future positions will be equally unobjectionable.

While rhetorical appeals may certainly include more formal types of logical proofs, the most common kind of rhetorical logic is common-sense reasoning, the kind on which most people base their everyday decisions. That's why Aristotle says that "ordinary people" engage in rhetoric all the time (I, 1) and that rhetorical appeals should be accessible for "persons who cannot take in at a glance a complicated argument, or follow a long chain of reasoning" (I, 2).

EXAMPLES

The U.S. telecommunications industry was scheduled by law to switch from analog to digital over-the-air transmission on February 17, 2009. Older television sets would need to be outfitted with converter boxes so they could receive the new digital signals. The federal government issued coupons to people to help them pay for the converter boxes. Toward the end of 2008, however, it appeared that too few people were aware of the impending change, and there were not enough converter box coupons to go around. As a result, some federal legislators proposed a new law that would delay the switch to digital by a few months. The Senate bill (S. 328, the DTV Delay Act) was passed and was sent to the House of Representatives where it was debated on January 27 and 28, 2009. What follows are statements by House members both for and against S. 328. The House voted against the bill, 258–168. After the vote, supporters of the delay regrouped, and on February 11, both houses agreed to delay the switch to digital until June.

REP. CLIFF STEARNS (R—FL) IN OPPOSITION

I rise in strong opposition to this bill. And I want to tell my colleagues that I had the opportunity to ask President Barack Obama a question 3 hours ago on this very debate. And I asked him, I said, Mr. President, in light of the fact that you have a stimulus package that you're pushing and you want to create more jobs, then certainly broadband and digital television and third and fourth generation wireless will do just that. And he agreed.

5

And I said, Then why would you want to delay the transition when we have spent all this money, billions of dollars, to publicize the date? We're going to waste all this time and money, and it's going to create a hardship for broadcasters and so many other people. We should go ahead with the transition.

10

He said, Well, well.

I said, Now, if it's a question of money, Secretary Gutierrez sent a letter last year indicating $250 million would take care of anything; so it's not a question of money.

So the President said, Well, I agree with you, it's not a question of money, but it appears to be some kind of administrative or accounting problem that we need to fix.

15

Well, I said to the President, I said, Mr. President, we had a demonstration project in Wilmington, North Carolina, in which we had a transition, and it turns out almost 99 percent of the people were satisfied. So the demonstration project in Wilmington, North Carolina, showed that we could transition back in September in Wilmington. Surely, we can transition February 17 in the United States.

20

I liken this to a football stadium. Just bear with me for this metaphor, this example. Let's say you have a large stadium with 90,000 people in it, and it actually takes 92,000 people. Well, it turns out at the front door, the door is locked. By chance a nail is caught in the door, and there are 2,000 people, just 2,000 people out there that can't get into this championship game. And the coin is tossed, they're ready to go, the lights are

25

there, the televisions are going, everybody's roaring, they're waiting for the kickoff; and suddenly they say we've got to stop the game because these very few people, maybe 1 percent, maybe ½ percent, can't get in the stadium; so we're going to stop the whole game because of those people. And that's what we have here. That is the analogy. We're delaying legislation on a very, very small amount. And, frankly, the demonstration

30

in Wilmington, North Carolina, showed that we are ready to go.

Mr. Obama has made it a priority to make the government work for the people. So now in his first decision in his administration and this Congress, we're saying delay, delay, delay. We're going to delay and put a placeholder on this, and then the consumer is going to have to hold off. And by delaying 115 days, we are sending, I think, the wrong message to the people who are trying to put this in place.   35

So if you look at the players on the field, they're ready to go. All the stakeholders are ready to go. I urge you to defeat this.

REP. JIM MATHESON (D—UT) IN SUPPORT

Mr. Speaker, I'd like to thank Chairman Waxman for addressing problems with the transition to digital television which was due to happen next month.

The simple fact is that millions of Americans are not prepared for the digital switch. In Salt Lake City, Nielson Media Research reports that nearly 9 percent of households are completely unprepared. Salt Lake ranks as the sixth least-ready out of 56 surveyed.   5

The coupons authorized by Congress 4 years ago—to help families acquire the hardware they need to view programs once the digital change is made—aren't getting to the customers. Millions of Americans are currently waiting to receive the coupons. The agency charged with distributing them has fallen behind. My office has been attempting to assist constituents with the program for several months. I know of cases where coupons have   10 expired before they even reach consumer mail boxes. That's ridiculous.

I'd like to thank Chairman Waxman for working with the Senate to address concerns I raised about the coupon program. This is a Senate bill, but it is important to acknowledge the work of the Energy and Commerce Committee in trying to fix the DTV problems.

The last thing families need right now is the prospect of additional monthly bills in   15 order to watch television.

Finally, I am pleased to see that this bill allows for emergency services to begin using some analog space. It also provides flexibility by allowing broadcasters who are ready-to-go to switch to digital service earlier than June, which is a good idea.

REP. MICHAEL N. CASTLE (R—DE) IN OPPOSITION

Mr. Speaker, I rise in opposition to S. 328, DTV Delay Act.

Since 1966, our nation's first-responders have been calling for more broadcast spectrum to be made available for better and more effective communication among emergency services. Tragically, the lack of such spectrum was cited by experts as partially leading to many unnecessary deaths among those responding to the 2001 ter-   5 rorist attacks in New York City. In fact, completing the digital television transition so that this spectrum may be used by police, firefighters, and emergency personnel was the main communications-related recommendation of the 9/11 Commission.

In 2005, after years of delay, Congress finally established February 17, 2009, as the date when the country will switch to all-digital broadcasting and eliminate the disruptions   10 to public safety communications. Unfortunately, after more than a decade of preparing for the transition, the bill before us today would delay the digital transition for another three months.

15   Like many, Delawareans, I am concerned about the management of the digital transition process and the shortfall in the number of converter box coupons available. It is critical that we act quickly to provide additional resources to address these complications and ensure our constituents are prepared for the transition date. Still, public safety services and broadcasters have spent millions of dollars preparing for the February 17th transition date and postponing the deadline again will only create more confusion and delay the im-
20   plementation of this vital 9/11 Commission recommendation.

REP. SHEILA JACKSON-LEE (D—TX) IN SUPPORT

Mr. Speaker, today I speak in strong support of S. 328, and I also want to thank my colleague Senator Jay Rockefeller for authoring this insightful resolution.

The digital television transition is an unnecessary burden to be passed onto the American people at a time when the pressures of day to day life are heavy and growing.

5   To assist consumers through the conversion, the Department of Commerce through its National Telecommunications and Information Administration, NTIA, division handled requests from households for up to two $40 coupons for digital-to-analog converter boxes beginning January 1, 2008, via a toll free number or website.

However, the Commerce Department has run out of funds to cover the cost of coupons
10   and there are millions of Americans who have yet to receive the boxes. These Americans should not be expected to purchase the converter box without the aid of the government, seeing as the entire Nation is under extraordinary pressure caused by the recession.

Last week, President Obama's team joined a chorus of concerned voices requesting a delay because the National Telecommunications and Information Administration,
15   NTIA, which is to provide education and $40 vouchers for people to buy digital TV converter boxes, ran out of money on January 4. There is also concern that many people, especially poorer and more rural areas, have not yet heard that they will need a converter and a larger antenna.

Older homes cannot be easily wired for cable. The house walls might be made of
20   concrete, brick, or stone that is difficult to wire through. This has caused some local residents to opt for analog over-the-air TV instead of cable or FIOS. Other people have decided to only wire their living room, and still use analog over-the-air in other rooms. The old construction can also cause problems running an antenna to a window, roof, or attic. These older homes are generally owned by lower income families that are being hit
25   particularly hard by the current economic recession.

On January 22, the Nielsen Company said 6.5 million Americans had not prepared for the switch, a startling number considering the Commerce Department's inability to assist these Americans in the purchase of the converter boxes. TV stations would face extra expenses, which is a burden that they also cannot be expected to take on in times like these.   30

Mr. Speaker, I understand that the long-term effects of this transition will benefit the American people and support the eventual transition. Mr. Speaker, we are in a recession at best. Our seniors can barely afford their prescriptions and we are asking them to pay another 45 dollars for a converter box? To some of us that may not seem like much, but for many it is a small fortune. Especially for our senior population who may have only the   35
television as company.

I ask that my colleagues support this legislation and give Americans more time to properly prepare for the conversion.

Source: GPO, public domain.

DISCUSSION STARTERS

Make a list of all the arguments in these speeches, both pro and con. Rank the arguments from what you think are the strongest to the weakest, and discuss your results.

BIBLIOGRAPHY

Meany, John, & Kate Schuster. *Art, Argument, and Advocacy: Mastering Parliamentary Debate* (New York: International Debate Education Association, 2002).

This book is geared to competitive debating but offers an array of interesting, useful information even if you are not on the debate team.

Proposals

ASSIGNMENT

Compose a ten minute oral proposal for either (1) a change in an organization of which you are currently a member or (2) a new course to be offered by the department of your major.

COMMENTARY

When you present an oral proposal, you are formally recommending and defending a specific and carefully developed plan or course of action. Often the impetus for presenting a proposal may be your own—you have a good idea which you would like to have adopted. Other times, however, you may be called upon to develop a proposal at the request of your boss. Just as the reasons for making proposals vary, so do the possible audiences for these presentations. The audience may be a small group of your peers, or it may be a group of higher-level decision makers. In either case, you can usually count on the fact that your auditors have some amount of status and that they possess the authority to accept or reject your ideas. Because your audience will often be composed of leaders who manage their schedules carefully, you may find that you must make the case for your proposal within a particular time limit.

Proposal presentations should be constructed to organize and articulate a large amount of information in a relatively short length of time, often a period of no more than ten or fifteen minutes. In practical terms, your primary objectives will be to explain an idea and to report on as many ramifications of that idea as possible. Your ultimate goal is to persuade your listeners to adopt your proposal. In this regard, you are functioning as a persuasive speaker who pitches your idea in a comprehensive—yet compact—package to a small group of decision makers. Almost all of the principles of persuasive speaking with which you are familiar may be used profitably in designing proposals. Here we discuss some of these considerations.

Understand Your Audience

Prepare your proposal with the characteristics of your audience in mind. Learn whatever you can about your auditors before you begin to compose your presentation, including an estimation of their existing beliefs, values, and attitudes regarding your topic. Learn the knowledge specializations of your listeners, understand how members of this decision-making group function as a team, and determine who usually performs leadership functions within the unit.[1] If your proposal is made in an organizational setting, find out about the structure of the company and about any problems it may be encountering, especially if these things may have a bearing on the acceptance of your ideas. Being audience centered will increase your chances of gaining a positive hearing for your proposal because you will be speaking directly and realistically to the needs of your auditors or the organization.

Focus on Solving Problems

As you compose your proposal, focus clearly on the problem or need that your idea addresses. You will most likely want to spend a few minutes demonstrating your understanding of the problem's significance and its effect on the current situation. You may want to speak briefly about other attempts to solve the problem, if any, and about the positive outcomes you envision resulting from your plan. Fairly early in your presentation you will want to offer a concise statement of your major idea. Don't keep your audience guessing about what you are proposing: using suspense in these situations is not to your advantage. Your speech is a proposal, not a riddle. Early articulation of your idea functions as a thesis statement, allowing your listeners to begin processing your proposal more quickly and thoroughly.[2]

Organize the Oral Proposal Carefully

Because you are imparting a substantial amount of information in a relatively short period of time, you will want to make sure that your presentation is well organized. Certainly your speech should have an introduction, a body, and a conclusion. Beyond this, there are specific patterns of organization that are especially well suited to persuasive speaking and so are easily adapted to making proposal presentations. Three patterns that work well for proposals are (1) the deductive approach, often called "state the case and prove it pattern" that focuses on solutions; (2) the inductive approach, often called the "problem-solving pattern" that grows from John Dewey's Reflective Thinking Agenda,[3] and (3) the

---

[1]Patricia Hayes Andrews and John E. Baird, Jr., *Communication for Business and the Professions*, 7th edition, Boston: McGraw Hill, 2000, pp. 203–204.

[2]Jo Sprague and Douglas Stuart, *The Speaker's Handbook*, 8th edition, Belmont, CA: Thomson Wadsworth, 2008, p. 410.

[3]John Dewey, *How We Think*, Boston: Heath, 1910.

motivated sequence, based on the work of pioneering communication scholar Alan Monroe.[4] Regardless of which organizational pattern you adopt for your proposal, you should make sure that your speech is unified by a central theme, demonstrates logical coherence between points, emphasizes your most important arguments, and is as comprehensive as time allows.

Address Decision-Making Criteria

You should also determine if there are any criteria by which your proposal will be judged and make sure to address these factors directly in your presentation. If you maintain your focus on solving a problem or need, it will be easy for you to incorporate decision-making rules into your presentation: simply tell your auditors how your plan measures up to any criteria they must follow. If your audience is not using any predetermined criteria, feel free to mention some guidelines of your own and employ them to highlight the merits of your proposal. For example, you might state that any worthy proposal must create revenue for the organization followed by some projections about how much money your plan will generate.

Answer Potential Objections

Skilled persuaders often anticipate audience objections and answer them in the course of their speeches before listeners have a chance to ask questions. If time allows, you may choose to do this in your proposal presentation. Your understanding of audience attitudes, leadership dynamics, or decision-making criteria may allow you to foresee potential objections and address them directly. You may want to use some two-sided arguments in your proposal, developing claims in which you assert your positive position, articulate a fair version of anticipated objections, and then refute those objections forcefully.

Plan for a Polished Delivery

If at all possible, determine how to conduct yourself during your proposal presentation by learning about your audience's past practices and preferences. Do most presenters sit or stand? Are there institutional expectations for the use of PowerPoint or Smart Boards? Do decision makers prefer low-tech handouts or high-tech CD-ROMs? Adjust your use of presentational aids and your general demeanor to the culture of the group or the organization. Also, be sure to familiarize yourself with all the facts of your talk so that you can speak extemporaneously. Make eye contact with your listeners frequently. This is especially helpful in achieving persuasive goals in a small group setting.

Finally, consider the matter of time. Adhere to any time limits that have been imposed or suggested for your talk, being careful to leave sufficient time for

---

[4]Alan H. Monroe, *Principles and Types of Speech*, New York: Scott, Foresman, 1935. The Motivated Sequence has undergone subsequent revisions.

questions and answers. Be prepared with answers to likely questions. If you call for questions and none are posed, you can then use these prepared questions and answers to extend your remarks, if necessary. On the other hand, if the question and answer period threatens to exceed your allotted time limit, ask the individual who is running the meeting if the discussion can be extended briefly. As you prepare your proposal presentation, consider the use of time in one additional context—that of timeliness. Make sure that you choose a propitious time to pitch your proposal: a strategic understanding of the "right time" is often a key component in successful persuasion.

CLASSICAL CONCEPT: KAIROS

You may have heard the saying, "Strike while the iron is hot." It comes from metal-working and refers to the fact that metal must be superheated before it can be molded by hammering. Once taken out of the fire, the metal cools quickly, so the metal worker must be quick and decisive.

Classical rhetoricians would advise speakers to strike while the iron is hot. They realized that successful communication must be carefully timed to advantageous, but often fleeting, opportunities. The Greek term for this "best moment" is *kairos*.[5] It is a kind of temporality that emphasizes the quality of time as opposed to its quantity. Cicero expressed this difference in his early work *De Inventione*, drawing a distinction between "time" and "occasion." "An occasion is a period of time offering a convenient opportunity for doing or not doing something." It is "opportunity" that distinguishes time from occasion. "Under the category of time," Cicero says, "a space is fixed and limited . . . but under the category of occasion it is understood that to the space of time there is added the concept of an opportunity for performing the action" (I, 40).

Early Christian rhetoric operated under the influence of Ciceronian ideas. One early text, traditionally attributed to St. Paul, engages the concept of *kairos*. Christian preachers are encouraged to "proclaim the message; be persistent whether the time is favorable [*eukairos*] or unfavorable [*akairos*]" (2 Tim. 4:2).[6] Apparently the Christians believed that their message was so urgent and important that it transcended the need for moderation implied in the classical idea of *kairos*.

The need to speak at the right time is easily illustrated. If you take a public speaking class during the fall semester of an election year, you could have a persuasive speech assignment connected to the election. To be effective and interesting, your speech has to be given before election day. If for some reason the assignment is postponed until after the election, your campaign speech will be awkward to say the least. This same need for strategic timing applies to virtually every rhetorical situation.

---

[5]For an extended and excellent discussion, see *Ancient Rhetorics for Contemporary Students, 4th edition*, by Sharon Crowley and Debra Hawhee, New York: Pearson Longman, 2009, pp. 44–62.

[6]For more on how Christians adapted and modified the classical concepts of rhetoric, see St. Augustine's *On Christian Doctrine*.

EXAMPLE

Joan Lawrence-Bauer, an employee of the Rural Ulster Preservation Company, gave this proposal to the Saugerties, New York, Chamber of Commerce in May 2010. Ulster County is one of New York's poorest counties.

GIVE HOUSING A VOICE: ADDRESSING THE HOUSING CRISIS IN ULSTER COUNTY

RUPCO Proposal

JOAN LAWRENCE-BAUER

SAUGERTIES CHAMBER OF COMMERCE

MAY 2010

In a housing survey done for Ulster County in the summer of 2008, 90% of the 900 people responding said that Ulster County has a housing affordability problem. Further, 60% of the respondents were, themselves, having trouble paying for their housing. That was a remarkable result because the survey was done on-line, and promoted by the

5   Ulster County Chamber of Commerce and the Ulster County Development Corporation. So it's fair to assume that most of the respondents were employed and had easy access to the Internet. Many who have housing problems have no such access.

Two years later, the situation is worse. Ulster County leads the state of New York in the number of foreclosure notices as a percentage of the mortgages written. And

10 thousands of residents have lined up for free counseling on how to avoid foreclosure. Waiting lists for rental assistance have been closed for years. A Homeless Prevention and Rapid Re-housing Program (HPRP) grant that was expected to serve 500 people in 18 months was exhausted after serving more than 1,000 people in just nine months. Like most people in Ulster County, you've undoubtedly felt this. You, or a family member, or

15 an employee of yours is probably worrying right now about the cost of housing and the related taxes.

My name is Joan Lawrence-Bauer and I appreciate this opportunity to be with you today and speak on behalf of the Ulster County Housing Consortium. I've seen the housing crisis evolve over decades of work in the region; work in the private for profit sector;

20 in the not-for-profit sector and in the government sector. I've worked directly in the field of housing for more than a decade now and I can tell you we haven't made a dent in the need for affordable housing in our region. So in our few minutes together, I will outline in some detail, the problem; the need for affordable housing in Ulster County and I will offer a number of things you can do to help solve that problem.

25 Please keep in mind that this is not just a low-income problem. Difficulty in covering housing costs is an issue for all income groups and impacts not only residents but the businesses and organizations that employ them. The area median income in Ulster County now is $70,100 and yet even people earning that and more struggle to find affordable housing in this county.

Example **25**

The survey I referenced in my opening remarks was conducted on behalf of the   30
Ulster County Housing Consortium. A collaborative of private sector business owners,
non-profit human service organizations and government agencies, the Consortium
was established by the Ulster County Legislature in 2001. The group came together
in response to federal requirements that housing growth trends be studied. Its mission is to provide a cooperative and collaborative environment in which people can   35
work together to ensure access to safe, decent, affordable housing for all Ulster County
residents.

But even a group of practitioners in the field of human services were challenged
when they tried to understand the status of the housing market in Ulster County. Even
they had difficulty agreeing on what "affordable housing" meant. After all, every house and   40
every apartment is affordable to someone. Did we need "senior housing," or "workforce
housing," or "low income housing," or "housing for homeless"?

Today, those questions have been answered. Affordable housing is simply and clearly
defined: affordable housing is housing that costs no more than 30% of the gross household income. Owner occupied housing is affordable if not more than 30% of a household's   45
gross income is spent on a mortgage payment, utilities, taxes, and insurance. For renter
units, the HUD standard is that no more than 30% of a renter household's income should
be spent on rent and utilities (including fuel for heat, hot water and cooking, electricity for
lights, water and waste water charges, and trash removal).

With that as a definition and in response to the growing challenge of housing supply   50
and costs, three area counties (Dutchess, Orange, and Ulster counties) commissioned
a Regional Housing Needs Assessment (RHNA). The RHNA utilizes a base year of
2006, and forecasts housing needs out to 2020. The effort was funded by the Dyson
Foundation. Technical assistance for the project was provided by consulting economists,
Economic & Policy Resources, Inc.   55

The RHNA estimates the need for housing to accommodate anticipated growth in
the three counties. Estimates are provided at the regional, county, and municipal level.
The RHNA also includes an assessment of the need for affordable housing. The affordability needs estimate takes into account the current downturn in the housing market
and the overall economy, and its impact on the Three-County region.   60

So where do we stand? The affordability analysis for Ulster County yielded the
following results. The affordable mortgage payment for a household earning 120% of
median household income was $1,022. The household was still short of the county
median house price by about $73,000 and only 21.3% of the total house sales were at or
below the affordable price. On the renter side in Ulster County, only the lowest income   65
group had an affordable rent that was less than the median rent, similar to the other two
counties, however in Ulster the dollar gap was greater by more than $60.

In terms of housing units, that meant that in 2006 Ulster County had an affordability gap of 15,953 units (10,696 owner and 5,257 renter) in 2006, which is expected to
increase by 6,079 units by 2020. Ulster County could construct 6,624 units by calendar   70
year 2020 in order to begin to address the affordability gap faced by its residents. This
portion was derived based on the demographic trend of a declining average household

size, and the additional pressure that is placed on the housing stock as a result of this trend in all three counties.

75   The housing picture has only gotten bleaker since this study was done. Incomes have been reduced due to the economic downturn, so a higher percentage of a household's income is now required to cover housing costs. Foreclosures are forcing people who once owned to rent. And rental prices are increasing significantly.

     We must act. And the people answering the survey I referenced in my opening re-
80 marks expressed a passion for dealing with what has become an affordable housing crisis. As you well know, New York is a "home rule" state, meaning that solutions must come from within each community. Each municipality must actually solve its affordable housing problems internally. Sadly, in most communities in Ulster County, zoning, planning and building regulations act to stop, not to encourage, the construction of afford-
85 able housing. And the reality—as clearly demonstrated in our needs assessment, is that elected officials have not taken the lead on this issue.

     So we at the Ulster County Housing Consortium urge you to take the lead. We have developed information you need and tools you can use. We urge you to understand this problem and help develop solutions. What can you do?

90   – Sign a petition supporting the development of affordable housing.

     – Start an affordable housing committee in your community.

     – If your municipality does not have an updated Comprehensive Plan, push for one.

     – Study your zoning, planning and building laws and codes. If they prevent or discourage the construction of affordable housing, get them changed.

95   These are just the beginning steps but as has often been said, the journey of a thousand miles begins with a single step.

     If you are a business owner or a decision maker within your professional organization, be it for profit, not-for-profit, or government agency, you can do more. Raise the awareness of others by supporting Consortium sponsorship opportunities. Consider
100 co-op advertising and display our posters in your workplace. Place Public Service announcements in your newsletter or on your website and do email blasts to friends and colleagues.

     As anthropologist Margaret Mead said, "Never doubt that a small group of thoughtful citizens can change the world. Indeed, it is the only thing that ever has." Change your
105 world. Give Housing a Voice!

     I'll be happy to answer any questions that you may have.

Source: "Give Housing a Voice: Addressing the Housing Crisis in Ulster County; RUPCO Proposal" by Joan Lawrence-Bauer, Saugerties Chamber of Commerce, May 2010. (c) 2010. Reprinted with permission.

DISCUSSION STARTERS

Where in this presentation would you include one or two PowerPoint slides as aids to understanding? Can you identify points in the proposal to which anecdotes or examples could be added to facilitate identification and persuasion? Could the list

Example | **27**

of suggested actions be more specifically targeted to the Chamber of Commerce audience? How?

BIBLIOGRAPHY

James Jasinski, *Sourcebook on Rhetoric: Key Concepts in Contemporary Rhetorical Studies*, Thousand Oaks, CA: Sage, 2001.

For an interesting discussion of *kairos* and its relationship to the rhetorical concepts of *appropriateness* and *propriety*, see Jasinski's entry on "Decorum," pp. 146–151.

Jasinski asserts that contemporary scholarship on the topic of timing (*kairos*) frequently focuses on the evolution of the rhetorical situation, on meeting audience expectations, and on shifting persuasive strategies at opportune moments.

Civic Persuasive Appeals

ASSIGNMENT

Present a four to six minute persuasive speech about a grassroots local issue affecting your campus or community. Alternate: speak about a national issue that has a direct bearing on you and your audience.

COMMENTARY

When he toured the United States in the 1830s, the French philosopher Alexis de Tocqueville was impressed to the degree that Americans participated in all manner of civic groups and organizations. He wrote, "Americans of all ages, all conditions, all minds constantly unite. Not only do they have commercial and industrial associations in which all take part, but they also have a thousand other kinds: religious, moral, grave, futile, very general and very particular, immense and very small. . . ."[1] Sociologists have recently debated whether Americans are currently as prone to join organizations as they were in the past.[2] Whatever the outcome of that debate, civil society in America continues to consist of a plethora of groups of all kinds. There are tens of thousands of elected officials at all levels of government. In New York State alone there are 62 counties, 3,000 villages, and 1,000 cities or towns (called townships or parishes in other states). Elected citizens serve them all. Thousands of people serve as elected leaders of nonprofit organizations, educational institutions, and arts organizations. Volunteers serve in many ways: homeowners' associations, PTAs, athletic leagues, volunteer fire companies and ambulance corps, boards and committees connected to religious organizations, long-standing groups like Rotary, not to mention various political entities like school boards, zoning committees, and

---

[1]Alexis de Tocqueville, *Democracy in America*, Harvey C. Mansfield and Delba Winthrop, eds. Chicago: University of Chicago Press, 2000, p. 489.

[2]See "Civic Associations" by David Davenport and Hanna Skandera in *Never a Matter of Indifference: Sustaining Virtue in a Free Society*, Peter Berkowitz, ed. Stanford: Hoover Institution Press, 2003, pp. 59–83.

library boards. The lists could go on. The task of leadership in all of these varied contexts often falls to college-educated people.

Participating in civic venues is no idle avocation. Civic participation is critical to the health of democratic political culture. The civic involvement necessary to democracy takes many forms. At the least, citizens should inform themselves of important issues and vote in elections. Beyond following events and voting, however, involvement occurs in ways that require skill in public communication, especially public speaking. Sometimes civic meetings are held to allow people to express their opinions, while at other times formal meetings are held to discuss and decide policies or courses of action. For example, public hearings are often conducted by governmental agencies to solicit input from citizens. At meetings of school or homeowner association boards elected members speak to one another or to constituents. In these and countless other situations, communities benefit from people who can speak up—clearly, wisely, and considerately. Don't be surprised if, as a college-educated person, you find yourself involved in civic activities where such speaking is expected of you.

Civic groups vary widely in how meetings are conducted and decisions are reached. Many of the persuasive principles discussed in Chapter 3 in regard to making proposals also apply in civic organizational settings. In addition, here are some guidelines that may prove helpful to you when speaking in civic organizations.

- Be ready to speak. Many meetings are governed by a set agenda where you will be assigned an opportunity to speak. Other meetings might be more loosely organized, and you will need to determine when in the course of the meeting is the best time for you to say what's on your mind. It is almost always ill-advised to wait until the end of a long meeting, when the audience longs for adjournment, to bring up some new or difficult topic. If you are not a designated leader of the group, it is best not to surprise the leadership by bringing up some sensitive or difficult issue at an inopportune time. That might be a way to "get your say" or vent your emotions, but it is seldom useful in actually accomplishing anything. Be ready for the right opportunity, and, when it arrives, make the most of it.
- Communicate, don't antagonize. At their best, the groups we belong to should enhance civic virtues such as "respect for others, self-restraint, public spiritedness, and the willingness and ability to participate in the give and take of self-government."[3] Achieving these lofty goals depends on the web of relationships among group participants. Our discourse is what builds and nurtures these relationships. Although often featured prominently in the arts and mass media, the roles of radical gadfly or denouncing prophet are rare in real life. Create discourse that avoids sarcasm and invective. Focus on the interests of the group by using the pronoun "we" instead of "I." Convince your hearers that "It's not about me—it's about us."
- Focus on today, not yesterday or someday. As it is in so many speaking situations, brevity remains the soul of wit in civic organization speaking. Long-term

---

[3]Davenport and Skandera, p. 62.

members of groups often get long-winded by reminiscing about the past even when the past has little or nothing to do with the issue at hand. The opposite long-winded mistake is going on excessively about the future—"wouldn't it be great if . . . ?" Stay focused on the business under discussion. When speaking for or against a proposal, do not repeat arguments already advanced by other speakers. Cite those arguments, amend them if you like, and then introduce new evidence or considerations without repeating what others have said.

- Finally, in many organizations, familiarity with agreed-upon rules of debate is important. Many organizations in the United States follow standard parliamentary procedure known as "Robert's Rules of Order."[4] These rules were devised by a U.S. Army officer named Henry M. Robert, who published them in 1876 under the title *Pocket Manual of Rules of Order for Deliberative Assemblies*. Parliamentary procedure is designed to facilitate orderly discussion, especially when there are differences of opinion. While the rules may seem like annoying rigmarole when disagreements are few, they are invaluable in controversy. The idea is to assure both that the will of the majority is carried out and that the minority is fairly heard. Granted, the minority can try to use the rules to thwart the majority and the majority can attempt to use them to silence the minority. Nevertheless, over the decades, the rules have been tested and found to be useful. Circumventing the rules in organizations that have adopted them is almost always a bad idea. Depending on an organization's legal standing, actions taken outside the parameters of the rules may lead to lawsuits. People who aspire to leadership in most civic settings should be familiar with parliamentary procedure and their obligations to follow it.

CLASSICAL CONCEPT: ARTISTIC PROOF

In addition to "inartistic proof" (discussed under Classical Concept: Praise and Blame in Chapter 1), Aristotle identified "artistic proof" as crucial to persuasion (*Rhetoric* I, 2, 1355b). By artistic proof, he meant the resources of thought and language that come together in the mind of the speaker. They are intrinsic, that is, part and parcel, to the rhetorical art. Speakers find extrinsic evidence but must invent intrinsic materials. Cicero put it this way, "For purposes of proof, however, the material at the orator's disposal is twofold, one kind made up of the things which are not thought out by himself . . . the other kind is founded entirely on the orator's reasoned argument" (*De Oratore* II, 116). Much of the classical rhetorical literature is given to discussions of how to find and develop such "reasoned argument."

Artistic or purely rhetorical arguments can be based on common sense, probability, or the collective wisdom of a community. Such arguments may be expressed as proverbs; maxims; general principles; or what were called commonplaces, lines of argument that most people would follow. Lines of argument tend to lead audiences away from the particulars of an issue to widely agreed-upon abstract principles. Cicero says, "all the possible subjects of debate are not founded on a countless host of human beings or an endless diversity of occasions, but on typical

---

[4]See the website www.robertsrules.com

Example | **31**

cases and characters," which are few in number (II, 145). Furthermore, lines of argument are often connected to specific disciplines. So there would be certain lines of argument appropriate for philosophers and others for lawyers or scientists.

Consider this example. Suppose Marcus and Cato were known to be bitter enemies. Cato is murdered. Did Marcus do it? Apart from any crime scene evidence (the kind of thing modern people would look for), arguments could be made regarding Marcus' guilt or innocence. Marcus did it. Your archenemy will kill you if given the chance. Marcus did not do it. Realizing everyone knew they were enemies, Marcus knew that if anything happened to Cato, he would be the prime suspect. People do not generally put themselves in a compromised position where they could lose everything. Clearly, this defense of Marcus is something that a speaker would have to "think up." Thinking up arguments (minus the implication of lying or making up) is pretty much what artistic proof is about.

EXAMPLE

The Food Bank for New York City describes itself "as the city's major hunger-relief organization working to end food poverty throughout the five boroughs" (www.foodbanknyc.org). New York City Council Speaker Christine Quinn addressed the organization and the issue of nutrition in the following speech.

ADDRESS TO THE FOOD BANK FOR NEW YORK CITY
CHRISTINE C. QUINN, SPEAKER, NEW YORK CITY COUNCIL
SEPTEMBER 5, 2006

Thank you. Thank you. Thank you, Lucy and all of the members of the Food Bank for inviting me. I am happy to be here with you today.

One of the rewarding things about being the speaker of the City Council is that you get to visit with New Yorkers from across the City and talk with them about the problems they face.   5

A couple of months ago, Council Member Eric Gioia and I visited a food pantry in Sunnyside, Queens where we helped distribute meals. There were 25 or 30 men and women, most of them senior citizens, waiting in line for food.

After the event, as we were coming back to City Hall, I noticed another group of people waiting in line. But this group wasn't outside a food pantry. They were teenagers   10
outside a McDonalds.

When you see hungry seniors not far from teenagers about to eat unhealthy food, you come to a simple realization: hunger and obesity are two sides of the same problem—a lack of access to nutritious food. And if we are going to take on—and solve—the problems of hunger and obesity in our City, we need to start by increasing New Yorkers' food   15
options.

Hunger and obesity are, without a doubt, major citywide issues. Indeed, an estimated 1.2 million New Yorkers—including more than 400,000 children—live in households where having food is in question. And one in four New York Public School children are obese.

20   For all of us on the frontlines of the fight to end this crisis, these frustrating facts are not new. We, the richest City in the world, must be able to feed our people. More than that, we must be able to give our people food that keeps them healthy. The City Council is committed to working with each one of you to reach this goal.

Our task is threefold: first, increase New Yorker's access to nutritious food; second,
25   make sure government is helping—not hindering—New Yorkers to obtain food assistance; and, finally, find out which services are and are not working, so we can improve our food system.

You know, six months ago the Council launched a campaign to reduce hunger and improve nutrition in New York City. I am here today to let you know we have made great
30   progress.

First, we realized that too many kids in this City needlessly go to school hungry. And, when children go to school hungry, they have trouble paying attention in class and focusing on their work.

To his credit, a few years ago, Mayor Bloomberg made it possible for every public
35   school student in New York City to have breakfast at school for free. The problem is that only two students in ten participate in the program.

We can—and must—do better.

That's why we are working to increase participation by reaching out to parents, teachers, and most importantly, kids to tell them about eating breakfast at school.
40   It's simple: when kids eat breakfast in the morning, they can do better in school all day long.

That's why, on National Hunger Awareness Day, a majority of Council Members ate breakfast with students in their local districts to promote the school breakfast program.

45   And just last month, we held a citywide competition where public school students submitted posters to promote the school breakfast program. We had over twenty submissions, and the Bloomberg Administration has agreed to use the winning poster to promote the school breakfast program in public schools throughout the City.

Second, people who receive food stamps have been unable to access fresh, local
50   produce at farmers' markets.

In response, the Council has invested in a citywide pilot project to give farmers the technology to accept food stamps. Earlier this month, I visited a new greenmarket at Harlem Hospital with this technology. People were excited that they could use their electronic food cards to buy healthy fruits and vegetables. And farmers were of course
55   pleased with the additional business.

Finally, many food assistance services, such as Citymeals on Wheels and soup kitchens, haven't had the resources they needed to provide the highest quality meals.

That's why the Council has invested more than $7 million in this year's budget to help these essential community organizations provide healthier, more substantial meals. In
60   particular, part of this money will help seniors access more nutritious meals at senior centers across the City. Specifically, the Council has increased funding for senior congregate

Example | **33**

meals by 35 cents per meal, to ensure that senior centers are able to pay for the more nutritious meals they provide.

Together, these steps are going to help more New Yorkers, especially senior citizens and low-income families, access the food they need to stay healthy.   65

Now, while we've made some progress, we're not satisfied. If we're going to help more New Yorkers, we're going to have to change the way government operates.

Today, 60,000 New Yorkers who qualify for food stamps don't get them. The Administration worked to enroll more families, but we are still leaving nearly $1 billion in federal aid in Washington. The tragedy of this situation is that many New Yorkers don't   70 sign up because they do not know they are eligible.

Government has to be a partner, and help New Yorkers learn about food stamps. For example, as many of you know, families eligible for free school meals are also likely eligible for food stamps.

Well, what if, when parents sign their kids up for free school meals, we gave them   75 information about food stamps? That would make sense, right?

And what if, when New Yorkers who are eligible for public health insurance visit public hospitals, we let them know they may be eligible for food stamps? That would make sense, right?

Well, we are currently working with the Administration to make these things happen.   80

To do our part in promoting the food stamp program, I am happy to announce that the City Council is launching the "Food Today, Healthy Tomorrow" campaign.

As part of the campaign, my fellow Council Members and I will hit the streets and talk to key communities, such as seniors and the working poor, about food stamps and their possible eligibility. Through these efforts, the Council has set a goal of reducing the   85 number of hungry New Yorkers by more than half over the next three and half years—over this time we'll work with all of you to enroll 350,000 more people into the food stamp program.

Outreach isn't going to be enough, though. We also need to cut through governmental red tape and improve coordination across agencies.   90

Right now, over 20 City agencies have a role in procuring or serving food or administering food programs. Yet many of these agencies don't coordinate with each other.

A perfect example: a few weeks ago my office received a City guide of summer activities for kids. This 187-page resource was put in the hands of countless New York parents. Yet there is not one mention of the summer meals program, an historically under-enrolled   95 nutrition program available to all of our city's youth.

What a missed opportunity.

That's why the Council has called for one body to have the sole responsibility of coordinating the City's food system. Our plan will make sure the right and left hands of the City's food system work together. Only then will New Yorkers have the information they need to   100 access food assistance. Luke tells us that "to whom much is given, much is required."

Indeed, eliminating hunger and obesity across our City is not going to be easy—life-changing work rarely is. But with everyone—government agencies, community leaders,

and most importantly, all of you—who dedicate yourselves to serving meals to those
105   most in need—by working closely together, I have no doubt that we can:

- Inform all New Yorkers about the food assistance available to them;
- Ensure that government helps New Yorkers obtain high-quality meals; and
- Create a City where every New Yorker has access to healthy, nutritious food, three
  meals a day, seven days a week.

110   Every New Yorker should start the day with a nutritious breakfast.
Every New Yorker should go to sleep with a full stomach.
Every New Yorker should have access to healthy and affordable food.
When all New Yorkers are able to feed themselves and their families, we will have truly
made the City better for every single New Yorker. Together, we will make it so.
115   Thank you.

Source: Address to the Food Bank for New York City by Christine C. Quinn, New York City Council
Speaker, September 5, 2006. Reprinted by permission.

DISCUSSION STARTERS

How does Speaker Quinn turn hunger and obesity, issues usually seen in national
and global terms, into local concerns? How persuasive do you find Quinn's claim
that as social problems hunger and obesity are closely related?

BIBLIOGRAPHY

Sproule, J. Michael. "Oratory, Democracy, and the Culture of Participation." *Rhetoric and
    Public Affairs* 5, 2 (2002):301–310.

    Prof. Sproule discusses the importance of public speaking to a renewal of civic
    participation.

Eulogies

ASSIGNMENT

Present a five minute eulogy for someone who has died within the last week. Since it is unlikely this will be someone known to you, check current obituaries for an appropriate subject. Keep in mind that eulogies are time sensitive, which means that you may often not have as much as one week to prepare one.

COMMENTARY

In spite of the fact that American culture goes to great lengths to hide, deny, and postpone it, death is common to us all. When someone dies, the leaders of families, businesses, and civic associations are the people often called upon to show the way in coming to terms with grief and loss. The eulogy is an ancient and recurring type of speech used to help human beings deal with death. By etymology, "eulogy" means something like "good word." The eulogist says something good about the deceased to give something good to the mourning community—perspective, comfort, and hope. According to Campbell and Jamieson, ". . . the eulogy affirms that the community will survive the death." The eulogist employs "rhetorical devices which appeal to the audience to carry on the works, to embody the virtues, or to live as the deceased would have wished."[1]

Throughout the history of European culture, the eulogy has been an important part of public civic discourse, serving as "a powerful ideological instrument in the construction of social identity."[2] Drawing on a comparison of Pericles' Funeral Oration to the speech of Mayor Rudolph Giuliani at the "Citywide Prayer Service" held at Yankee Stadium after the 9/11 attacks, Christina Pepe argues that

---

[1]Karlyn Kohrs Campbell and Kathleen Hall Jamieson, "Form and Genre in Rhetorical Criticism: An Introduction," in *Form and Genre: Shaping Rhetorical Action*, Campbell and Jamieson, eds. Annandale, VA: Speech Communication Association, 1978.

[2]Christina Pepe, "Civic Eulogy in the *Epitaphios* of Pericles and the Citywide Prayer Service of Rudolph Giuliani." *Advances in the History of Rhetoric* 10 (2007):132.

the essential features of the civic eulogy are consistent across the centuries.[3] Those features include the centrality of praise for the deceased; the close identity of speaker with audience (often evident in the use of personal pronouns); reference to the ancestors; emphasis on shared civic values with praise for the civic entity (the city, for example, or the nation); and, finally, the consolation of the audience.[4]

The civic eulogy has certainly been a prominent part of American public address. For example, in the three months following the death of George Washington in late 1799, hundreds of eulogies honoring him were given throughout the country, with more than 400 of them subsequently published.[5] Arguably the most famous speech in American history, Lincoln's Gettysburg Address, was a eulogy given at a cemetery dedication.[6] Perhaps the most memorable speeches given by several American presidents have been eulogies: Ronald Reagan, *Address to the Nation on the "Challenger" Disaster* (1986); Bill Clinton, *Oklahoma City Bombing Memorial Prayer Service Address* (1995); George W. Bush, *Remarks at the National Day of Prayer and Remembrance* (2001).

You will probably never be asked to eulogize a national catastrophe, but when you are asked to give a eulogy in your own community, keep in mind that there are many ways to say good words about the deceased. In the first place, don't be hesitant to recount some specific details about the person's life. His or her date and place of birth, graduations, jobs held, professional accomplishments, and organizational memberships may be specifically stated. Somehow, the speaking of these details, even if there are not many, communicates something definite about the person and something concrete that can be remembered, facts that suggest significance. Because relationships as well as deeds constitute a legacy, it is also common to mention the deceased's family, by name, including both those who have already died and survivors.

In addition to the factual details about a person's life that might appear in a newspaper obituary, eulogies almost always include an emphasis on personal virtues and the recounting of telling anecdotes. Eulogists often speak of a person's positive influence or other admirable personality traits such as hard work, loyalty, compassion, or generosity, to name but a few. Anecdotes are often the best way to illustrate these qualities. Eulogists also often incorporate poetry, song lyrics, and religious texts into the speech. The more personal the connection between these resources and the deceased, the better.

Eulogists must face the fact that most funerals are conducted in religious venues. Even if the funeral is not held in a house of worship, it may still be conducted as

---

[3]For an alternative view that eulogies are more situated to specific rhetorical situations reflecting the power relationships within society, see Takis Poulakis, "Historiographies of the Tradition of Rhetoric: A Brief History of Classical Funeral Orations." *Western Journal of Speech Communication* 54 (1990):172–188.

[4]Pepe, 140–141.

[5]Margaret B. Stillwell, "Checklist of Eulogies and Funeral Orations on the Death of George Washington, December 1799–February 1800." *Bulletin of the New York Public Library* 20 (1918):403–441.

[6]For a discussion of the Gettysburg Address in relationship to classical funeral orations, particularly that of Pericles, see Garry Wills, *Lincoln at Gettysburg: The Words That Remade America*. New York: Simon & Schuster, 1992.

a religious service and be presided over by a member of the clergy. The religious dimension of the proceedings is not your primary concern as a eulogist. However, it is always inappropriate to communicate any indifference or disrespect to the religious sensibilities of mourners. If you share the religious beliefs of the family and other mourners, acknowledge this without excluding mourners of differing beliefs. If not, and this is often the case when eulogizing colleagues, you should convey sincere respect for the beliefs of others without condescension. If you cannot do this, you should decline the role of eulogist.

Eulogies are also frequently delivered at memorial services, rather than at funerals. Memorial services may be held some weeks or even months after a person has died. Most memorial services do not have the deeply religious connotations of a funeral and may often take place in secular settings such as a community center or a school auditorium. Eulogies given in these circumstances usually acknowledge religion less overtly and should typically reference the length of time between the deceased's passing and the present. In these situations the eulogist may want to incorporate additional comments that discuss specifically how the influence of the deceased has been carried forward in the life and work of surviving family, friends, and colleagues.

The eulogy is perhaps the most personal form of public speaking. This undoubtedly raises the anxiety factor for the eulogist. Consider ahead of time if you will be able to handle the emotional stress of the occasion. But don't decline the opportunity to give a eulogy out of fear of your emotions. The discipline of writing and rehearsing a eulogy will usually help you to cope with your own grief. In turn, your eulogy, competently written and sincerely delivered, will have the same effect on others. In the end, you will have said and done something good.

CLASSICAL CONCEPT: DECORUM

Classical rhetoricians were concerned with communication that was considered appropriate to its subject and circumstances. This concern is often expressed by the term "decorum." According to Gideon Burton, "decorum" is a central and overarching principle of rhetoric "requiring one's words and subject matter be aptly fit to each other, to the circumstances and occasion, the audience and the speaker. . . . Decorum invokes a range of social, linguistic, aesthetic, and ethical proprieties for both the creators and critics of speech or writing. Each of these must be balanced against each other strategically in order to be successful in understanding or creating discourse" (*Silva Rhetoricae*, http://rhetoric.byu.edu/).

Cicero was particularly interested in the connection of style and decorum and believed that both common sense and training help a speaker determine what is appropriate. He wrote, ". . . in every case while the ability to do what is appropriate is a matter of trained skill and natural talent, the knowledge of what is appropriate to a particular occasion is a matter of practical sagacity" (*De Oratore*, III, 212).

Although they are sometimes seen to be fixed in a "hierarchical model of culture,"[7] standards of decorum vary according to time and place and may be

---

[7]Baldick, Chris, *The Concise Oxford Dictionary of Literary Terms*, New York: Oxford University Press, 1990, p. 53.

contested. In 2003, the Archdiocese of the Roman Catholic Church in New Jersey banned eulogies by laypeople in church funerals. The reason for this decision was the repeated and egregious violation of decorum by many eulogists. For example, one man told the story of how his uncle had taken him on his first trip to a brothel.[8] Apparently, not all eulogists possess the "practical sagacity" Cicero believed necessary to craft decorous communication.

EXAMPLES

It is hard for us to comprehend the high regard and deep affection Americans held for George Washington at the time of his sudden passing at the end of 1799. Virginia Congressman Henry "Light Horse Harry" Lee, father of Robert E. Lee, one of Washington's comrades and a hero in his own right, was asked to eulogize the fallen leader before a joint session of the U.S. Congress. Although the speech contains one of American rhetoric's most famous aphorisms, "First in war, first in peace, first in the hearts of his countrymen," and was widely acclaimed in its time, it has not often been anthologized recently.[9]

A FUNERAL ORATION OF THE DEATH OF GEORGE WASHINGTON

HENRY LEE

JOINT SESSION OF CONGRESS

DECEMBER 26, 1799

In obedience to your will,[10] I rise your humble organ, with the hope of executing a part of the system of public mourning which you have been pleased to adopt, commemorative of the death of the most illustrious and most beloved personage this country has ever produced; and which, while it transmits to posterity your sense of the awful
5   event, faintly represents your knowledge of the consummate excellence you so cordially honor.

Desperate indeed is any attempt on earth to meet correspondently this dispensation of heaven: for, while with pious resignation we submit to the will of an all-gracious Providence, we can never cease lamenting in our finite view of Omnipotent wisdom, the
10   heart-rending privation for which our nation weeps. When the civilized world shakes to its centre; when every moment gives birth to strange and momentous changes; when

---

[8]Ramirez, Anthony, "She Loved Life. (And Bourbon. And Bawdy Jokes)," *New York Times*, November 1, 2004.

[9]The text transcribed here retains Lee's punctuation and capitalization. A few modern spelling changes have been adopted.

[10]Lee's note: *The Two Houses of Congress.*

our peaceful quarter of the globe, exempt as it happily has been from any share in the slaughter of the human race, may yet be compelled to abandon her pacific policy, and to risk the doleful casualties of war: what limit is there to the extent of our loss? None within the reach of my words to express; none which your feelings will not disavow.   15

The founder of our federate republic—our bulwark in war, our guide in peace, is no more. Oh that this was but questionable! Hope, the comforter of the wretched, would pour into our agonized hearts its balmy dew. But, alas! There is no hope for us: our Washington is removed forever. Possessing the stoutest frame and purest mind, he had passed nearly to his sixty-eighth year, in the enjoyment of high health, when, habituated   20 by his care of us to neglect of himself, a slight cold, disregarded, became inconvenient on Friday, oppressive on Saturday, and defying every medical interposition, before the morning of Sunday, put an end to the best of men. An end did I say—his fame survives; bounded only by the limits of the earth, and by the extent of the human mind. He survives in our hearts, in the growing knowledge of our children, in the affection of the good   25 throughout the world; and when our monuments shall be done away; when nations now existing shall be no more; when even our young and far-spreading empire shall have perished, still will our Washington's glory unfaded shine, and die not, until love of virtue cease on earth, or earth itself sinks into chaos.

How, my fellow-citizens, shall I signal to your grateful hearts his pre-eminent worth!   30 Where shall I begin in opening to your view a character throughout sublime. Shall I speak of his warlike achievements, all springing from obedience to his country's will—all directed to his country's good?

Will you go with me to the banks of the Monongahela, to see your youthful Washington supporting, in the dismal hour of Indian victory, the ill-fated Braddock, and   35 saving, by his judgment and by his valor, the remains of a defeated army, pressed by the conquering savage foe?[11] Or, when oppressed America, nobly resolving to risk her all in defense of her violated rights, he was elevated by the unanimous voice of Congress to the command of her armies: Will you follow him to the high-grounds of Boston, where to an undisciplined, courageous and virtuous yeomanry, his presence gave the stability   40 of system, and infused the invincibility of love of country; Or shall I carry you to the painful scenes of Long Island, York Island and New Jersey, when combating superior and gallant armies, aided by powerful fleets, he stood the bulwark of our safety; undismayed by disaster; unchanged by change of fortune. Or will you view him in the precarious fields of Trenton, where deep gloom unnerving every arm, reigned triumphant   45 through our thinned, worn down unaided ranks; himself unmoved,—Dreadful was the night; it was about this time of winter—The storm raged—the Delaware rolling furiously with floating ice forbade the approach of man. Washington, self collected, viewed the tremendous scene—his country called; unappalled by surrounding dangers, he passed

---

[11]Lee's references to Native Americans as savages are unacceptable today, but would have been unremarkable in 1799.

50 to the hostile shore: he fought; he conquered. The morning sun cheered an American world. Our country rose on the event; and her dauntless Chief pursuing his blow, completed in the lawns of Princeton, what his vast soul had conceived on the shores of Delaware.

Thence to the strong grounds of Morristown he led his small but gallant band; and
55 through an eventful winter, by the high efforts of his genius, whose matchless force was measurable only by the growth of difficulties, he held in check formidable hostile legions, conducted by a Chief experienced in the art of war, and famed for his valor on the ever memorable heights of Abraham, where fell Wolfe, Montcalm, and since our much lamented Montgomery; all covered with glory. In this fortunate interval, produced
60 by his masterly conduct, our fathers, ourselves, animated by his resistless example, rallied around our country's standard, and continued to follow her beloved Chief, through the various and trying scenes to which the destinies of our union led.

Who is there that has forgotten the vales of Brandywine—the fields of German-town, or the plains of Monmouth; everywhere present, wants of every kind obstructing,
65 numerous and valiant armies encountering, himself a host, he assuaged our sufferings, limited our privations, and upheld our tottering republic. Shall I display to you the spread of the fire of his soul, by rehearsing the praises of the hero of Saratoga, and his much loved compeer of the Carolina's? No; our Washington wears not borrowed glory: To Gates—to Green, he gave without reserve the applause due to their eminent merit;
70 and long may the Chiefs of Saratoga, and of Eutaws, receive the grateful respect of a grateful people.

Moving in his own orbit, he imparted heat and light to his most distant satellites; and combining the physical and moral force of all within his sphere, with irresistible weight he took his course, commiserating folly, disdaining vice, dismaying treason
75 and invigorating despondency, until the auspicious hour arrived, when, united with the intrepid forces of a potent and magnanimous ally, he brought to submission the since conqueror of India; thus finishing his long career of military glory with a luster corresponding to his great name, and in this his last act of war affixing the seal of fate to our nation's birth.

80 To the horrid din of battle sweet peace succeeded, and our virtuous chief, mindful only of the common good, in a moment of tempting personal aggrandizement, hushed the discontents of growing sedition, and surrendered his power into the hands from which he had received it, converted his sword into a ploughshare, teaching an admiring world that to be truly great, you must be truly good.

85 Was I to stop here, the picture would be incomplete, and the task imposed unfinished—Great as was our Washington in war, and much as did that greatness contribute to produce the American Republic, it is not in war alone his pre-eminence stands conspicuous: his various talents combining all the capacities of a statesman with those of the soldier, fitted him alike to guide the councils and the armies of our nation. Scarcely
90 had he rested from his martial toils, while his invaluable parental advice was still sounding in our ears, when he who had been our shield and our sword, was called forth to act a less splendid but a more important part.

Possessing a clear and a penetrating mind, a strong and a sound judgment, calmness and temper for deliberation, with invincible firmness and perseverance in resolutions maturely formed, drawing information from all, acting from himself, with 95 incorruptible integrity and unvarying patriotism: his own superiority and the public confidence alike marked him as the man designated by heaven to lead in the great political as well as military events which have distinguished the aura of his life.

The finger of an over-ruling Providence, pointing at Washington, was neither mistaken nor unobserved; when to realize the vast hopes to which our revolution had given 100 birth, a change of political system became indispensable.

How novel, how grand the spectacle, independent states stretched over an immense territory, and known only by common difficulty, clinging to their union as the rock of their safety, deciding by frank comparison of their relative condition, to rear on that rock, under the guidance of reason, a common government through whose commanding pro- 105 tection, liberty and order, with their long train of blessings should be safe to themselves, and the sure inheritance of their posterity.

This arduous task devolved on citizens selected by the people, from knowledge of their wisdom and confidence in their virtue. In this august assembly of sages and of patriots, Washington of course was found—and, as if acknowledged to be most wise, 110 where all were wise, with one voice he was declared their chief. How well he merited this rare distinction, how faithful were the labors of himself and his compatriots, the work of their hands and our union, strength and prosperity, the fruits of that work, best attest.

But to have essentially aided in presenting to his country this consummation of her 115 hopes, neither satisfied the claims of his fellow-citizens on his talents, nor those duties which the possession of those talents imposed. Heaven had not infused into his mind such an uncommon share of its ethereal spirit to remain unemployed, nor bestowed on him his genius unaccompanied with the corresponding duty of devoting it to the common good. To have framed a constitution, was showing only, without realizing the 120 general happiness. This great work remained to be done, and America, steadfast in her preference, with one voice summoned her beloved Washington, unpracticed as he was in the duties of civil administration, to execute this last act in the completion of the national felicity. Obedient to her call, he assumed the high office with that self-distrust peculiar to his innate modesty, the constant attendant of pre-eminent virtue. What was 125 the burst of joy through our anxious land on this exhilarating event is known to us all. The aged, the young, the brave, the fair, rivaled each other in demonstrations of their gratitude; and this high wrought delightful scene was heightened in its effect, by the singular contest between the zeal of the bestowers and the avoidance of the receiver of the honors bestowed. Commencing his administration, what heart is not charmed with 130 the recollection of the pure and wise principles announced by himself, as the basis of his political life. He best understood the indissoluble union between virtue and happiness, between duty and advantage, between the genuine maxims of an honest and magnanimous policy, and the solid rewards of public prosperity and individual felicity: watching with an equal and comprehensive eye over this great assemblage of communities and 135 interests, he laid the foundations of our national policy in the unerring immutable principles of morality, based on religion, exemplifying the pre-eminence of free government, by all the attributes which win the affections of its citizens or command the respect of the world.

140   "O fortunatos nimium, sua si bona norint!"

Leading through the complicated difficulties produced by previous obligations and conflicting interests, seconded by succeeding houses of Congress, enlightened and patriotic, he surmounted all original obstructions, and brightened the path of our national felicity.

145   The Presidential term expiring, has solicitude to exchange exaltation for humility returned, with a force increased with increase of age, and he had prepared his farewell address to his countrymen, proclaiming his intention, when the united interposition of all around him, enforced by the eventful prospects of the epoch, produced a further sacrifice of inclination to duty. The election of President followed, and Washington, by

150   the unanimous vote of the nation, was called to resume the chief magistracy: what a wonderful fixture of confidence! Which attracts most our admiration, a people so correct, or a citizen combining an assemblage of talents forbidding rivalry, and stifling even envy itself? Such a nation ought to be happy, such a chief must be forever revered.

War, long menaced by the Indian tribes, now broke out; and the terrible conflict

155   deluging Europe with blood, began to shed its baneful influence over our happy land. To the first, outstretching his invincible arm, under the orders of the gallant Wayne, the American Eagle soared triumphant through distant forests. Peace followed victory, and the melioration of the condition of the enemy followed peace. Godlike virtue which uplifts even the subdued savage.

160   To the second he opposed himself. New and delicate was the conjuncture, and great was the stake. Soon did his penetrating mind discern and seize the only course, continuing to us all, the felicity enjoyed. He issued his proclamation of neutrality. This index to his whole subsequent conduct, was sanctioned by the approbation of both houses of Congress and by the approving voice of the people.

165   To this sublime policy he inviolably adhered, unmoved by foreign intrusion, unshaken by domestic turbulence.

"Justum et tenacem propositi virum
Non civium ardor prava jabentium,
Non vultus instantis tyranni

170   Mente quatet solida."

Maintaining his pacific system at the expense of no duty, America faithful to herself and unstained in honor, continued to enjoy the delights of peace, while afflicted Europe mourns in every quarter, under the accumulated miseries of an unexampled war: miseries in which our happy country must have shared, had not our pre-eminent Washington

175   been as firm in council as he was brave in the field.

Pursuing steadfastly his course, he held safe the public happiness, prevented foreign war, and quelling internal discord, till the revolving period of a third election approached, when he executed his interrupted but inextinguishable desire of returning to the humble walks of private life.

The promulgation of his fixed resolution, stopped the anxious wishes of an affectionate people, from adding a third unanimous testimonial of their unabated confidence in the man so long enthroned in their hearts. When, before, was affection like this exhibited on earth? Turn over to the records of ancient Greece—Review the annals of mighty Rome,—examine the volumes of modern Europe; you search in vain. America and her Washington only afford the dignified exemplification.

The illustrious personage called by the national voice in succession to the arduous office of guiding a free people, had new difficulties to encounter: the amicable effort of settling our difficulties with France, begun by Washington, and pursued by his successor in virtue as in station, proving abortive, America took measures of self-defense. No sooner was the public mind roused by prospect of danger, than every eye was turned to the friend of all, though secluded from public view, and grey in public service the virtuous veteran, following his plough,[12] received the unexpected summons with mingled emotions of indignation at the unmerited ill-treatment of his country, and of a determination once more to risk his all in her defense.

The annunciation of these feelings, in his affecting letter to the President accepting the command of the army, concludes his official conduct.

First in war—first in peace—and first in the hearts of his countrymen, he was second to none in the humble and endearing scenes of private life; pious, just, humane, temperate and sincere; uniform, dignified and commanding, his example was as edifying to all around him, as were the effects of that example lasting.

To his equals he was condescending, to his inferiors kind, and to the dear object of his affections exemplarily tender: correct throughout, vice shuddered in his presence, and virtue always felt his fostering hand; the purity of his private character gave effulgence to his public virtues.

His last scene comported with the whole tenor of his life. Although in extreme pain, not a sigh, not a groan escaped him; and with undisturbed serenity he closed his well spent life.—Such was the man America has lost. Such was the man for whom a nation mourns.

Methinks I see his august image, and hear falling from his venerable lips these deep sinking words: Cease Sons of America, lamenting our separation; go on and confirm by your wisdom the fruits of your joint councils, joint efforts, and common dangers: Reverence religion, diffuse knowledge throughout your land, patronize the arts and sciences: let Liberty and Order be inseparable companions; control party spirit, the bane of free governments; observe good faith to, and cultivate peace with all nations, shut up every avenue to foreign influence, contract rather than extend national

180

185

190

195

200

205

210

215

---

[12]Lee's note: *General Washington, though opulent, gave much of his time and attention to practical agriculture.*

connection, rely on yourselves only: Be American in thought, word, and deed—Thus will you give immortality to that union, which was the constant object of my terrestrial labors; thus will you preserve undisturbed to the latest posterity, the felicity of a people to me most dear, and thus will you supply (if my happiness is now aught to you) the only
220 vacancy in the round of pure bliss high heaven bestows.

Source: Lee, Henry. *A Funeral Oration on the Death of George Washington*, London: Bateson, 1800.

DISCUSSION STARTERS

Even though Lee and Washington were friends, Lee does not offer personal information or express personal grief as modern eulogists might be more inclined to do. How does Lee construct a public voice in order to express public emotions? What do you think are the differences between how individuals and groups experience loss? How would these differences affect a eulogy?

EULOGY FOR GLEN E. HOSTETLER
MICHAEL J. HOSTETLER
NOVEMBER 6, 1998

Glen E. Hostetler lived in Indiana his whole life and spent 42 years working in an automobile factory. After that he worked until he was in his eighties as a custodian in the church where his funeral was held and this eulogy was delivered. He was 95 years old when he died. This eulogy was published in the Jacob Hochstetler Family Association Newsletter.

"Altogether, Abraham lived a hundred and seventy-five years. Then Abraham breathed his last and died at a good old age, an old man and full of years; and he was gathered to his people." (Gen. 25:8)

Like Abraham, my grandfather lived a life full of years. His years spanned the 20th Century. On that October day when he was born on the farm in 1903, his 23 year old mother, for whom the 20th Century was brand new, could hardly imagine that her first born son would live almost to see the 21st Century.
5   His life spanned all the changes brought about in this century. Eleven years ago at our home on Chautauqua Lake in New York, my sons and my father and I sat around the fire and listened as Grandpa regaled us with stories of his early life, like when he saw an airplane for the first time.
His life also reflected big changes in our family. We came to this country in 1738,
10   and for seven generations we were farmers until 1920 when Glen left the farm for the city. Since then, our family has gone from the farm to the factory to professions born

in universities. In this way, our story is like the story of so many other Americans in this century.

Whenever a man's life is full of years, we are prone to ask, and rightly so, what exactly were his years full of? What kind of life filled his years? His life was full of quiet faith and hard work. His life was the embodiment of the Scripture to the Thessalonians, which exhorts us to "work in quietness and earn our living. And not to be weary in well-doing." His faith was exactly like that described in the book of James: it was proved by the quality of his life.

Theodore Roosevelt, who was President when Grandpa was born, once said, "Far and away the best prize that life offers is the chance to work hard at work worth doing." Grandpa worked hard at work worth doing, the work that involves helping others: his family, his church, his friends and anyone else who happened to need it. If you hired him to mow your grass for money, he ended up taking care of you in your old age for free. When you get right down to it, he didn't know how not to help others. And he was still doing it right up to the end. After all, in the nursing home, somebody had to wheel the old people to the dining room. This was not in the least bit surprising to anyone who knew him.

I don't believe that a long life, full of good work and well doing, ends just because someone dies. In his book, *Lake Wobegon Days*, Garrison Keillor describes in some detail the death of his aged grandmother in the hospital. As he comes to the end of the story he says, quite simply, "She was 82 years old. Her life was in all of us in the room. Nobody in the room needed to be told that."

Today, my grandfather lives with Christ and in all of us.

DISCUSSION STARTERS

What resources are brought to bear in this eulogy to give tribute to a person who was not rich or famous and who from all appearances led an ordinary life? How are religious themes woven into the fabric of the eulogy?

BIBLIOGRAPHY

Copeland, Cyrus M. *F.arewell, Godspeed: The Greatest Eulogies of Our Time*. New York: Harmony Books, 2003.

Hewitt, Beth L. "The Eulogy: Grief and the Wisdom of the Ancients." In *Sizing up Rhetoric*, Elizabeth Benacka and David Zarefsky, eds. Longrove: Waveland Press, 2008.

Schaeffer, Garry M. *A Labor of Love: How to Write a Eulogy*, 2nd edition. San Diego: GMS Publishing, 1995.

Schaeffer's short book offers nearly step-by-step instructions for composing a eulogy. A professional writer, Schaeffer recommends that eulogists begin by compiling a "cluster outline" to organize their random thoughts about the deceased. Cluster outlining allows the eulogist to map out related issues without having to follow a strictly logical progression of ideas. The last fifty-five pages of the book contain sample eulogies of famous persons and useful poems for inclusion in eulogies.

Theroux, Phyllis, ed. *The Book of Eulogies: A Collection of Memorial Tributes, Poetry, Essays and Letters of Condolence.* New York: Scribner, 1997.

Theroux provides a fine collection of eulogies, mostly from the past two centuries, as well as chapters on letters of condolence and poetry. The book has a bent toward high culture (eulogy for Mozart), as opposed to Copeland's tilt toward pop culture (eulogy for Chet Atkins). Considering the subject matter and the typical circumstances of eulogies in American culture, Theroux's collection is noticeably nonreligious.

Crisis Speeches

ASSIGNMENT

Option One: You are the president of your fraternity (or sorority). One of your fraternity brothers died over the weekend from alcohol poisoning at an off-campus party. You must address this situation in an emergency general meeting of your fraternity. Your university's dean of students will be there along with other university staff members who oversee Greek activities. Construct a six or seven minute speech to address this audience.

Option Two: As the dean of students at your college or university, you must address a recent outbreak of meningococcal meningitis, which has infected a significant number of students. Construct a six to seven minute speech to address students and faculty members in which you try to calm their fears and articulate what steps are being taken to address the outbreak.

COMMENTARY

When unanticipated or potentially dangerous events threaten to disrupt our everyday lives, we often look to our leaders for reassurance and guidance. Whether these events occur in political, business, or social contexts, they are often viewed as crises that demand spoken responses from those in positions of power or authority. As a result, speeches given in times of crisis require thorough understanding of the critical situation, thoughtful analysis of audience perceptions, and clear reassurance that the threat will be addressed as successfully as possible.

You may ask: what kinds of situations should be labeled as crises? Audiences often label threatening events as crises only after those events have been discussed publicly in the news media and by official leaders. Often the media report on a serious event, and then the public assumes that leaders will soon step forward to speak about it. Other times, leaders' speeches about a serious situation precede media coverage. In either case, to identify an event as a crisis gives it special significance and empowers leaders to take control of the situation through the spoken word as well as through other official actions. Communication scholars assert that crises are "primarily rhetorical," meaning that the very existence of a crisis speech is what distinguishes a crisis situation from other less serious circumstances.[1]

Leaders who give crisis speeches typically need to accomplish several goals. Each of these goals depends on speakers establishing their own credibility as competent leaders. If you are going to speak at a time of crisis, your effectiveness will likely depend on your ability to persuade your audience that you are a person who can be trusted and to whom they can turn for guidance. In other words, it is your ethos, your credibility as a leader, which will enable you to accomplish the following objectives, usually in chronological order.

Identify the Parameters of the Crisis Situation

Learn all that you can discover about the dimensions of the crisis. You will not need to tell your audience everything you know, but you will certainly need all the facts at your disposal. When you understand all the factual parameters of the situation to the best of your ability, then you can make informed choices about what to include or omit in your speech. Offering too much detail about the crisis may only confuse your listeners, but offering too little may make you seem uninformed or intentionally withholding key points of information. As you consider the inventional choices for your speech, strike a balance, neither overloading nor underreporting the facts.

Speak at the Right Time

The timing of a crisis speech is very important. While speaking too soon about a crisis is seldom a problem, many leaders make the mistake of waiting too long to address a situation considered to be urgent. Rumors and half-truths about a crisis circulate with astonishing speed through electronic communication channels. Crisis communication may very well require schedules to be abandoned and all-night work sessions to be held.

Demonstrate Your Understanding of the Situation

A large measure of your success as a crisis speaker will come from your ability to show your audience that you understand the situation. Recall that one of your primary goals in these difficult circumstances is to reassure your audience. Demonstrating that you understand the situation and are willing to share this understanding will facilitate a tone of reassurance in your speech. In times of crisis the public frequently places trust in leaders who appear to grasp the gravity of the situation and who are armed with the pertinent facts.

Assert Your Ability to Control or Positively Modify the Situation

Good crisis speakers not only explain facts, demonstrate their understanding of difficult circumstances, and offer reassurance; they also often assert their mastery

---

[1]See, for example, Theodore Otto Windt, Jr., "The Presidency and Speeches on International Crises: Repeating the Rhetorical Past." *Speaker and Gavel* 2 (1) (1973):6–13.

over the crisis. In other words, leaders who speak in times of crisis demonstrate that they are in control or that they are attempting to control a negative situation in a positive manner. We can call this the first "action step" of crisis rhetoric in which the speaker informs the audience about his or her intent to establish measures that will mitigate, improve, or end the troublesome situation.

Announce a Decisive Course of Action for Addressing the Crisis

The second action step of crisis speaking involves the actual announcement of a plan or course of action. You should tell your audience in some degree of detail what you intend to do, or to have others do, to resolve the crisis. It is important to frame your plan of action in terms that match audience perceptions of the crisis and the available options to resolve it. Make sure you explain how your plan will meet the constraints of the situation even as you address any contrary opinions others may hold about what to do.

Argue for Support of Your Crisis Plan

As you approach the end of your speech, you should offer an overt appeal that requests support for your plan of action. Ask audience members to help resolve the problem by embracing your ideas. If there are specific actions or behaviors that you want your listeners to adopt, this is the time to tell them what they are. If you engage your auditors and make them active participants in addressing the crisis, you will likely persuade them that a resolution is possible. You may also want to call on your audience to rise above the circumstances of the situation by encouraging them to be strong and resolute. As philosopher and psychologist William James wrote in 1906, "Great emergencies and crises show us how much greater our vital resources are than we had supposed."[2] Appeals to patriotism, endurance, trust, and goodwill are commonly found in crisis speeches.

Link Public Support for the Crisis Policy to Sound Ethics

Sometimes crisis speeches call on audiences to support particular policies on the basis of sound ethics. In other words, speakers imply that those who possess good character will support the suggested course of action and that those of more dubious ethical standards will not. This linking of crisis policy with ethical behavior is highly situation dependent. It may serve your purposes as a crisis speaker, or it may not. Nonetheless, you should probably consider the appeal to ethics as an inducement to belief as another way to gain audience support.

CLASSICAL CONCEPT: ETHOS

According to Aristotle, the "personal character" of the speaker is one of the three most important factors in persuasion (see *Rhetoric* I, 2 and II, 1). The Greek word

---

[2]William James to Wincenty Lutoslawski, May 6, 1906. *The Letters of William James.* Boston: The Atlantic Monthly Press, 1920.

for this is "ethos," which refers to credibility. Where there are honest differences of opinion and various courses of action available, Aristotle says, we are prone to believe "good men more fully and more readily than others." He goes on to say that a speaker's character "may almost be called the most effective means of persuasion he possesses." Character consists of three components: "good sense, good moral character, and goodwill." Modern researchers have explored the topic of ethos as "source credibility," to a large extent confirming the importance Aristotle attached to it.

Although Aristotle recognized the influence of reputation on credibility, he put a strong emphasis on the idea of developing or constructing credibility through the words of the speech itself. This may seem strange to us unless we remember that in ancient times there were no photographs, no recordings, no newspapers, and few books. Leaders were known to others only by personal acquaintance or by hearsay. As a result, speakers then had more opportunity to create strong credibility by their words than speakers now who carry the heavy baggage of their own words and images recorded in documents, recounted in perpetual news coverage, or replayed a million times on YouTube. For leaders today, credibility may be harder to attain and easier to lose than ever before. This is one possible reason why public discourse today seems insipid and impoverished. Instead of speaking their minds or making provocative proposals, speakers are extremely cautious, viewing successful communication merely in terms of "not making a mistake." Eventually, the very ability not to make a mistake constitutes "good sense" and enhances credibility.

Crowley and Hawhee point out that in ancient times people believed that character could be developed "by the moral practices in which they habitually engaged."[3] Today, however, we tend to think character is revealed in and through our experiences. Think about it. Who would people most likely find credible regarding physical fitness, a man who played for the Chicago Bears in the 1985 Super Bowl or a neighbor who has worked out at the gym five times a week every week since 1985?

EXAMPLES

REMARKS ON IMPROVING HOMELAND SECURITY
Attempted Terrorist Act on Northwest Airlines Flight 253
PRESIDENT BARACK OBAMA
KANEOHE, HAWAII
DECEMBER 28, 2009

On December 25, 2009, a bomb was nearly detonated on international flight from Amsterdam, the Netherlands, to the United States. The suspected bomber,

---

[3]Sharon Crowley and Debra Hawhee, *Ancient Rhetorics for Contemporary Students*, 4th edition. New York: Pearson Longman, 2009, p. 198.

Umar Farouk Abdulmutallab, allegedly attempted to ignite an explosive device in his underwear as the plane was preparing to land at Detroit's Metropolitan Airport. Quick action on the part of passengers aboard the plane prevented a catastrophe from occurring. President Obama's extended remarks about this crisis situation were delivered three days later, while he was vacationing in Hawaii.

Hey, guys. Good morning, everybody. I want to take just a few minutes to update the American people on the attempted terrorist attack that occurred on Christmas Day and the steps we're taking to ensure the safety and security of the country.

The investigation's ongoing, and I spoke again this morning with Attorney General Eric Holder, the Secretary of Homeland Security Janet Napolitano, and my Coun- 5
terterrorism and Homeland Security Adviser, John Brennan. I asked them to keep—continue monitoring the situation, to keep the American people and Members of Congress informed.

Here's what we know so far. On Christmas Day, Northwest Airlines Flight 253 was en route from Amsterdam, Netherlands, to Detroit. As the plane made its final approach 10 to Detroit Metropolitan Airport, a passenger allegedly tried to ignite an explosive device on his body, setting off a fire.

Thanks to the quick and heroic actions of passengers and crew, the suspect was immediately subdued, the fire was put out, and the plane landed safely. The suspect is now in custody and has been charged with attempting to destroy an aircraft. And a full 15
investigation has been launched into this attempted act of terrorism, and we will not rest until we find all who were involved and hold them accountable.

Now, this was a serious reminder of the dangers that we face and the nature of those who threaten our homeland. Had the suspect succeeded in bringing down that plane, it could have killed nearly 300 passengers and crew, innocent civilians preparing 20
to celebrate the holidays with their families and friends.

The American people should be assured that we are doing everything in our power to keep you and your families safe and secure during this busy holiday season. Since I was first notified of this incident, I've ordered the following actions to be taken to protect the American people and to secure air travel. 25

First, I directed that we take immediate steps to ensure the safety of the traveling public. We made sure that all flights still in the air were secure and could land safely. We immediately enhanced screening and security procedures for all flights, domestic and international. We added Federal air marshals to flights entering and leaving the United States. And we're working closely in this country—Federal, State, and local law 30
enforcement—with our international partners.

Second, I've ordered two important reviews, because it's absolutely critical that we learn from this incident and take the necessary measures to prevent future acts of terrorism. The first review involves our watch list system, which our Government has had in place for many years to identify known and suspected terrorists so that we can 35
prevent their entry into the United States.

Apparently, the suspect in the Christmas incident was in this system, but not on a watch list such as the so-called no-fly list. So I've ordered a thorough review not only of

40   how information related to the subject was handled but of the overall watch list system and how it can be strengthened.

The second review will examine all screening policies, technologies, and procedures related to air travel. We need to determine just how the suspect was able to bring dangerous explosives aboard an aircraft and what additional steps we can take to thwart future attacks.

45   Third, I've directed my national security team to keep up the pressure on those who would attack our country. We do not yet have all the answers about this latest attempt, but those who would slaughter innocent men, women, and children must know that the United States will more—do more than simply strengthen our defenses; we will continue to use every element of our national power to disrupt, to dismantle, and

50   defeat the violent extremists who threaten us, whether they are from Afghanistan or Pakistan, Yemen or Somalia, or anywhere where they are plotting attacks against the U.S. homeland.

Finally, the American people should remain vigilant, but also be confident. Those plotting against us seek not only to undermine our security but also the open society and

55   the values that we cherish as Americans. This incident, like several that have preceded it, demonstrates that an alert and courageous citizenry are far more resilient than an isolated extremist. As a nation, we will do everything in our power to protect our country. As Americans, we will never give in to fear or division; we will be guided by our hopes, our unity, and our deeply held values. That's who we are as Americans. That's what

60   our brave men and women in uniform are standing up for as they spend the holidays in harm's way. And we will continue to do everything that we can to keep America safe in the new year and beyond.

Situation in Iran

Before I leave, let me also briefly address the events that have taken place over the

65   last few days in the Islamic Republic of Iran.

The United States joins with the international community in strongly condemning the violent and unjust suppression of innocent Iranian citizens, which has apparently resulted in detentions, injuries, and even death.

For months, the Iranian people have sought nothing more than to exercise their

70   universal rights. Each time they have done so, they have been met with the iron fist of brutality, even on solemn occasions and holy days. And each time that has happened the world has watched with deep admiration for the courage and the conviction of the Iranian people, who are part of Iran's great and enduring civilization.

What's taking place within Iran is not about the United States or any other coun-

75   try; it's about the Iranian people and their aspirations for justice and a better life for themselves. And the decision of Iran's leaders to govern through fear and tyranny will not succeed in making those aspirations go away. As I said in Oslo, it's telling when governments fear the aspirations of their own people more than the power of any other nation.

80   Along with all free nations, the United States stands with those who seek their universal rights. We call upon the Iranian Government to abide by the international

obligations that it has to respect the rights of its own people. We call for the immediate release of all who have been unjustly detained within Iran. We will continue to bear witness to the extraordinary events that are taking place there. And I'm confident that history will be on the side of those who seek justice.   85

    Thank you very much, everybody, and happy New Year.

Source: Barack Obama, "Remarks on Improving Homeland Security in Kaneohe, Hawaii," 28 December 2009. *Daily Compilation of Presidential Documents.* Public domain.

Discussion Starters

President Obama was criticized for waiting three days to give this speech. Was he too late? What does he say to convey that he is in control of the situation? How does he offer reassurance? What else might he have said to address the crisis?

PREPARED TESTIMONY BEFORE THE U.S. CONGRESS, HOUSE OF REPRESENTATIVES COMMITTEE ON OVERSIGHT AND GOVERNMENTAL REFORM

Akio Toyoda, President, Toyota Motor Corporation
February 24, 2010

As concerns about the safety of Toyota automobiles mounted in 2009 and 2010, Akio Toyoda, president of Toyota Motor Corporation, delivered a series of crisis speeches about accelerator and braking problems on various car models manufactured by his company. Most often Toyoda spoke in his native Japan, but this speech was given when he was called to testify before a committee in the U.S. House of Representatives.

    Thank you Chairman Towns.

    I am Akio Toyoda of Toyota Motor Corporation. I would first like to state that I love cars as much as anyone, and I love Toyota as much as anyone. I take the utmost pleasure in offering vehicles that our customers love, and I know that Toyota's 200,000 team members, dealers, and suppliers across America feel the same way. However, in   5 the past few months, our customers have started to feel uncertain about the safety of Toyota's vehicles, and I take full responsibility for that. Today, I would like to explain to the American people, as well as our customers in the U.S. and around the world, how seriously Toyota takes the quality and safety of its vehicles. I would like to express my appreciation to Chairman Towns and Ranking Member Issa, as well as the members of   10 the House Oversight and Government Reform Committee, for giving me this opportunity to express my thoughts today.

I would like to focus my comments on three topics—Toyota's basic philosophy regarding quality control, the cause of the recalls, and how we will manage quality
15   control going forward. First, I want to discuss the philosophy of Toyota's quality control. I myself, as well as Toyota, am not perfect. At times, we do find defects. But in such situations, we always stop, strive to understand the problem, and make changes to improve further. In the name of the company, its long-standing tradition and pride, we never run away from our problems or pretend we don't notice them. By making con-
20   tinuous improvements, we aim to continue offering even better products for society. That is the core value we have kept closest to our hearts since the founding days of the company.

At Toyota, we believe the key to making quality products is to develop quality people. Each employee thinks about what he or she should do, continuously mak-
25   ing improvements, and by doing so, makes even better cars. We have been actively engaged in developing people who share and can execute on this core value. It has been over 50 years since we began selling in this great country, and over 25 years since we started production here. And in the process, we have been able to share this core value with the 200,000 people at Toyota operations, dealers, and suppliers in this country.
30   That is what I am most proud of.

Second, I would like to discuss what caused the recall issues we are facing now. Toyota has, for the past few years, been expanding its business rapidly. Quite frankly, I fear the pace at which we have grown may have been too quick. I would like to point out here that Toyota's priority has traditionally been the following: First, Safety; Second,
35   Quality; and Third, Volume.

These two priorities became confused, and we were not able to stop, think, and make improvements as much as we were able to before, and our basic stance to listen to customers' voices to make better products has weakened somewhat. We pursued growth over the speed at which we were able to develop our people and our organiza-
40   tion, and we should sincerely be mindful of that. I regret that this has resulted in the safety issues described in the recalls we face today, and I am deeply sorry for any accidents that Toyota drivers have experienced.

Especially, I would like to extend my condolences to the members of the Saylor family, for the accident in San Diego. I would like to send my prayers again, and I will do
45   everything in my power to ensure that such a tragedy never happens again.

Since last June, when I first took office, I have personally placed the highest priority on improving quality over quantity, and I have shared that direction with our stakeholders. As you well know, I am the grandson of the founder, and all the Toyota vehicles bear my name. For me, when the cars are damaged, it is as though I am as well. I, more
50   than anyone, wish for Toyota's cars to be safe, and for our customers to feel safe when they use our vehicles. Under my leadership, I would like to reaffirm our values of placing safety and quality the highest on our list of priorities, which we have held to firmly from the time we were founded. I will also strive to devise a system in which we can surely execute what we value.

Third, I would like to discuss how we plan to manage quality control as we go for-   55
ward. Up to now, any decisions on conducting recalls have been made by the Customer
Quality Engineering Division at Toyota Motor Corporation in Japan. This division con-
firms whether there are technical problems and makes a decision on the necessity of
a recall. However, reflecting on the issues today, what we lacked was the customers'
perspective.   60

To make improvements on this, we will make the following changes to the recall
decision making process. When recall decisions are made, a step will be added in the
process to ensure that management will make a responsible decision from the perspective of "customer safety first." To do that, we will devise a system in which customers' voices around the world will reach our management in a timely manner, and also a   65
system in which each region will be able to make decisions as necessary. Further, we
will form a quality advisory group composed of respected outside experts from North
America and around the world to ensure that we do not make a misguided decision.
Finally, we will invest heavily in quality in the U.S., through the establishment of an Auto-
motive Center of Quality Excellence, the introduction of a new position—Product Safety   70
Executive, and the sharing of more information and responsibility within the company for
product quality decisions, including defects and recalls.

Even more importantly, I will ensure that members of the management team actually drive the cars, and that they check for themselves where the problem lies as well
as its severity. I myself am a trained test driver. As a professional, I am able to check   75
on problems in a car, and can understand how severe the safety concern is in a car.
I drove the vehicles in the accelerator pedal recall as well as the Prius, comparing the
vehicles before and after the remedy in various environmental settings. I believe that
only by examining the problems on-site, can one make decisions from the customer
perspective. One cannot rely on reports or data in a meeting room.   80

Three—through the measures I have just discussed, and with whatever results we
obtain from the investigations we are conducting in cooperation with NHTSA, I intend
to further improve on the quality of Toyota vehicles and fulfill our principle of putting the
customer first.

My name is on every car. You have my personal commitment that Toyota will work   85
vigorously and unceasingly to restore the trust of our customers.

Thank you.

Source: Akio Toyoda, "Prepared Testimony of Akio Toyoda before the U.S. Congress,
House of Representatives Committee on Oversight and Government Reform," February
24, 2010. Public domain.

DISCUSSION STARTERS

How do you sense that Mr. Toyoda is attempting to build his credibility with the congressional audience? How does he use implicit references to his honor to bolster his
ethos? Does his statement offer sufficient details about his plans to address the crisis?

BIBLIOGRAPHY

Theodore Otto Windt, Jr. "The Presidency and Speeches on International Crises: Repeating the Rhetorical Past." *Speaker and Gavel* 2, 1 (1973):6–13.

This early treatment of presidential crisis rhetoric is one of the very few published essays that exist on the genre of crisis speeches. The author focuses solely on presidential speechmaking, but the principles he develops can be applied in a variety of contexts. Many of the suggestions in this chapter are based on this essay.

Technical Briefings

ASSIGNMENT

Give a five minute briefing on a technical subject that calls for a visual aid to help the audience understand the subject.

COMMENTARY

Briefings are usually thought of as short information speeches given in a business setting. Sometimes positioned at the beginning of the workday, briefings might be given on a wide range of topics. The focus of this chapter is the technical briefing, a short speech that explains specialized or complex information a speaker knows well. If you know how to approach this kind of speech, you should have confidence in giving other types of briefings involving less complex material. Obviously, briefings should be brief because time constraints weigh heavily in many organizational settings. A briefing is not the occasion for detailed explanations or instructions. Concentrate on clearly organized essential information. Keep in mind the following guidelines when preparing a briefing.

Make the Abstract Concrete

Abstract theories, ideas, and terms demand concrete examples, illustrations, or definitions. Consider this example. In the romantic comedy film *Other People's Money*, Danny DeVito plays the part of a Wall Street corporate raider trying to take over a small company. In his speech to the company's stockholders he says,

> You know the surest way to go broke? Keep getting an increasing share of a shrinking market. Down the tubes! . . . You know, at one time there must have been dozens of companies making buggy whips. And I'll bet the last company around was the one that made the best goddamned buggy whip you ever saw! Now, how would you like to have been a stockholder in that company?[1]

---

[1]*Other People's Money*, Warner Brothers, Inc., 1991.

The idea that it's bad to "get an increasing share of a shrinking market" is an abstraction of economic theory. It remains an abstraction until the speaker gives an example that transforms the abstract principle into something concrete and memorable. This is not to say that good speakers never talk about abstract concepts. On the contrary, good speakers trade in good ideas, but recognize when those ideas need to be explained in concrete terms.

Beware of Statistics

Statistics—a general term encompassing all manner of numerical evidence—are a ubiquitous feature of discourse in American culture. Leaders are expected to invoke statistics in their communication, whether in the areas of business, politics, education, or even religion. Although we read and speak of them all the time, skilled rhetoricians realize that statistics are more likely to start an argument than to settle one. Further complicating our reliance on statistics is widespread ignorance and discomfort with mathematics itself. The mathematician John Allen Paulos has dubbed this problem innumeracy, defined as "an inability to deal comfortably with the fundamental notions of number and chance."[2] When it comes to statistics, public speakers face a dilemma. Audiences have come to rely on and expect statistics even though most people—even educated ones—live and think in a mathematical fog.

Numbers are by nature abstract. Think about it. The word "one," as a noun, indicates nothing until it becomes an adjective as in "one pizza." But even as adjectives, numbers indicating very large or very small quantities are so abstract as to become meaningless. You probably have a pretty good idea of what one hundred dollars is, but how about one trillion dollars? Such a number is utterly abstract. Good speakers should help their audiences through the fog of math. To say that one trillion dollars would be equivalent to so many hundred dollar bills attached end to end to go to the moon and back so many thousands of times is not much help. Don't explain one abstraction with another. Instead of verbally reciting numerical data, emphasize only the most significant or interesting numbers, explaining why they are particularly important. When using statistics for comparisons and contrasts, be sure to magnify the point of comparison or contrast. Keep in mind that numbers are usually not self-explanatory.

Slow Down

Complex subject matter demands a deliberate, measured rate of speaking geared to the audience's familiarity with the material. A deliberate rate is connected to careful preparation. One of the most common reasons speakers end up rushing their delivery is failure to prepare the appropriate amount of information for the time allowed for the speech. If there is too much information to give, the speaker feels pressure to hurry. A well-prepared speaker never has to say, "I'm sorry, I'm running out of time" (unless, of course, the timing of the event has been thrown off by other factors). Trying to rush through complex information is a recipe for miscommunication.

---

[2]John Allen Paulos, *Innumeracy: Mathematical Illiteracy and Its Consequences*, New York: Hill & Wang, 2001, p. 3.

Avoid Jargon

A common complaint of people who have to sit through lots of briefings is the mindless use of acronyms and jargon. The following statement could be heard on any day at the university of one of the authors of this book: "Your PAF has to go to the college P&B before being forwarded to the UPC." New faculty members need the translation: "Your Personnel Action Form (application for promotion) has to be approved by the Personnel and Budget Committee of your college before it can be considered by the University Personnel Committee." The use of acronyms and jargon is perfectly acceptable if you know for sure that everyone in your audience knows what you are talking about. If not, cut the jargon.

Use, but Don't Abuse PowerPoint

The proliferation of Microsoft's PowerPoint software has had a big influence on informational speaking, particularly in business and academic settings. Speaking situations that at one time would not have had enough visual reinforcement now often have too much. In many business and educational settings, a backlash against the overuse of PowerPoint has emerged. For example, PowerPoint has proven to be especially troublesome to the American military where briefings occur frequently and the tidy hierarchy of a bullet-point slide appeals to the audience's sensibility. In response to too many PowerPoint briefings, one general banned them during an important operation in Iraq, declaring that "Some problems in the world are not bulletizable."[3]

One of the most outspoken critics of PowerPoint has been Edward R. Tufte, a Yale University Professor who specializes in analytical design. In his booklet *The Cognitive Style of PowerPoint: Pitching Out Corrupts Within*, Tufte argues that PowerPoint has a distinctive cognitive style that leads to a host of problems:

> foreshortening of evidence and thought, low spatial resolution, an intensely hierarchical single-path structure as the model for organizing every type of content, breaking up narratives and data into slides and minimal fragments, rapid temporal sequencing of thin information rather than focused spatial analysis . . . a preoccupation with format not content, incompetent designs for data graphics and tables, and a smirky commercialism that turns information into a sales pitch and presenters into marketers.[4]

Although it has serious limitations, PowerPoint has valid uses such as the projection of photographs or simple graphic lists like meeting agendas. For complex or technical data, paper handouts may be the best choice for communicating with your audience. Tufte argues that an 11 × 17 inch piece of paper "can show images with 1,200 dpi resolution, up to 60,000 characters of words and numbers . . . or

---

[3]The general was H. R. McMaster, quoted by Elisabeth Bumiller in "We Have Met the Enemy and He Is PowerPoint," *New York Times*, April 27, 2010. See also T. X. Hammes, "Essay: Dumb-Dumb Bullets," *Armed Forces Journal*, July 2009, http://armedforcesjournal.com/2009/07/4061641/. Retrieved November 12, 2010.

[4]Edward R. Tufte, *The Cognitive Style of PowerPoint: Pitching Out Corrupts Within*, 2nd edition, Cheshire, CT: Graphics Press LLC, 2001, p. 4.

1,000 sparkline[5] statistical graphics showing 500,000 numbers. *That one piece of paper shows the content-equivalent of 50–250 typical PP slides.*"[6]

Consider the following suggestions when using PowerPoint:

- Avoid text slides. The worst possible slide is one full of words. Reading slides to an audience is an inexcusable public speaking gaffe. Use slides primarily for maps, graphs, photographs, and video clips.
- Don't mistake your slides for speech organization. Just because you have a series of slides in order—slide #1, slide #2, and so on—does not mean your thoughts are organized in the least. Slides can ramble just as easily as words.
- When the audience is looking at the slide, you have to be talking about the slide, not something else. The same is true of any other visual prop. The visual will not reinforce the verbal if the two are disconnected.
- Fewer is better. A few well-designed slides of visual material are more likely to strengthen a speech than distract from it as invariably happens when you make too many slides. Don't give an inordinate amount of your speech preparation time to making lots of slides that end up having minimal or negative impact.
- Just because you know how to make slides does not mean you know how to incorporate them seamlessly into your speech. Include the slides when practicing your speech, and make sure their projection matches up to what you are saying.
- Remember, the bottom line for using any presentation software is to prevent your content from being distorted or diminished by forcing it into an inappropriate visual format.

CLASSICAL CONCEPT: INARTISTIC PROOF

"Just the facts, ma'am."

Aristotle is credited with the idea that materials available to a speaker can be divided into two types he called "artistic" and "inartistic" (*Rhetoric* I.ii, 1355b). Artistic proofs are the reasoned arguments a speaker invents, while the inartistic are empirical factors connected to the issue being discussed. These factors are sometimes referred to as extrinsic to the mind of the speaker or situated in the case. Aristotle identified five types of inartistic proofs in legal cases: laws, witnesses, contracts, tortures, and oaths (*Rhetoric* 1.xv, 1375a; see Cicero *De Oratore* 2.xxvii). (The renewed debate over the usefulness of torture in the war on terrorism should remind us of the ongoing relevance of the ancient rhetoricians even when, at first, we might dismiss them as hopelessly antiquated).

Speakers today place much more confidence in empirical evidence than the ancients did. Whether or not he ever said it, Detective Joe Friday of the classic TV show *Dragnet* is popularly remembered for the line, "Just the facts, ma'am." The facts, after all, will settle everything. One reason American culture subscribes to this idea is that we trust technology. A bloody knife might be a decisive piece of

---

[5]"Sparkline," meaning "intense, simple, word-sized graphic," is a term invented by Tufte. See his book, *Beautiful Evidence*, Cheshire, CT: Graphics Press, 2006.

[6]Tufte, p. 30.

evidence in a murder trial because with forensic science we can tell that the blood comes from the victim. The ancients had no way of knowing if the blood was from a chicken, a goat, or a human.

Does our confidence in empirical evidence reduce the need for reasoned arguments? Not really. Empirical evidence may increase the need for argument. For example, fingerprints have been used for many years to establish the presence of a person at a crime scene. They seem decisive, but once introduced as evidence they are open to various lines of attack. It can be argued that the prints are ambiguous or smudged; that the technician who gathered them was incompetent, drunk, or deceitful; that the prints were stored in a place where they could be altered or damaged; that the prints were discovered in an untimely manner, too long after the crime; that the expert witness who deciphers the prints is not credible; and so on. Similar arguments can be brought against video surveillance tapes, signed contracts, and laws.

Will more highly technical forms of evidence like DNA be immune from the doubts that can be raised about the human beings who gather, interpret, and use them? Stay tuned. In the meantime, as a leader you need to cite the best authorities and the latest data. By all means project your graph on the screen. But when you do these things, don't be surprised if instead of settling an argument, you start one.

EXAMPLES

Both of the examples that follow were given by officials of the federal government and, due to the nature of their contents, are considerably longer than briefings commonly given in business settings. The first is a briefing by General David Petraeus to the Congress on the situation of the war in Iraq. Notice General Petraeus' presentation of statistical data and the quality of the projected slides that accompanied his briefing. The second example is a press briefing regarding the government's plan to shoot down a disabled satellite that was loaded with a toxic material. The three speakers used no visuals but were successful in avoiding jargon in explaining scientific information in understandable language.

THE STATUS OF THE WAR AND POLITICAL DEVELOPMENTS IN IRAQ

Joint Hearing, House of Representatives,
One Hundred Tenth Congress, First Session

GENERAL DAVID PETRAEUS

SEPTEMBER 10, 2007

GENERAL PETRAEUS: Thank you, Mr. Chairman.

Mr. Chairman, ranking members, members of the committees, thank you for the opportunity to provide my assessment of the security situation in Iraq and to discuss the recommendations I recently provided to my chain of command for the way forward.

At the outset, I would like to note that this is my testimony. Although I have briefed my assessment and recommendations to my chain of command, I wrote this testimony myself. It has not been cleared by nor shared with anyone in the Pentagon, the White House, or the Congress until it was just handed out.

As a bottom line up front, the military objectives of the surge are in large measure being met. In recent months, in the face of tough enemies and the brutal summer heat of Iraq, coalition and Iraqi Security Forces have achieved progress in the security arena. Though the improvements have been uneven across Iraq, the overall number of security incidents in Iraq has declined in 8 of the last 12 weeks, with the number of incidents in the last 2 weeks at the lowest level seen since June 2006.

One reason for the decline in incidents is that coalition and Iraqi forces have dealt significant blows to al Qaeda Iraq. Though al Qaeda and its affiliates in Iraq remain dangerous, we have taken away a number of their sanctuaries and gained the initiative in many areas. We have also disrupted Shi'a militia extremists, capturing the head and numerous other leaders of the Iranian-supported special groups, along with senior Lebanese Hezbollah operative supporting Iran's activities in Iraq.

Coalition and Iraqi operations have helped reduce ethnosectarian violence as well, bringing down the number of ethnosectarian deaths substantially in Baghdad and across Iraq since the height of the sectarian violence last December. The number of overall civilian deaths has also declined during this period, although the numbers in each area are still at troubling levels.

Iraqi Security Forces have also continued to grow and to shoulder more of the load, albeit slowly and amid continuing concerns about the sectarian tendencies of some elements in their ranks. In general, however, Iraqi elements have been standing and fighting and sustaining tough losses, and they have taken the lead in operations in many areas.

Additionally, in what may be the most significant development of the past eight months, the tribal rejection of al Qaeda that started in Anbar Province and helped produce such significant change there has now spread to a number of other locations as well.

Based on all this and on the further progress we believe we can achieve over the next few months, I believe that we will be able to reduce our forces to the presurge level of brigade combat teams by next summer without jeopardizing the security gains that we have fought so hard to achieve. Beyond that, while noting that the situation in Iraq remains complex, difficult, and sometimes downright frustrating, I also believe that it is possible to achieve our objectives in Iraq over time, although doing so will be neither quick nor easy.

Having provided that summary, I would like to review the nature of the conflict in Iraq, recall the situation before the surge, describe the current situation, and explain the recommendations I have provided to my chain of command for the way ahead in Iraq.

The fundamental source of the conflict in Iraq is competition among ethnic and sectarian communities for power and resources. This competition will take place, and its resolution is key to producing long-term stability in the new Iraq. The question is whether the competition takes place more or less violently. This chart shows the security challenges in Iraq.

THE CHAIRMAN: General, let me interrupt you. The Members should have the charts in front of them. The chart over near the wall is very difficult to see from here. So I would urge the Members to look at the charts that have been handed out and should be immediately in front of them.

Thank you, General.

GENERAL PETRAEUS: [Slide: "Major Threats to Iraq"] This chart shows the security challenges in Iraq. Foreign and home-grown terrorists, insurgents, militia extremists, and criminals all push the ethnosectarian competition toward violence. Malign actions by Syria, and especially by Iran, fuel that violence. Lack of adequate governmental capacity, lingering sectarian mistrust, and various forms of corruption add to Iraq's challenges.

In our recent efforts to look to the future, we found it useful to revisit the past. In December 2006, during the height of the ethnosectarian violence that escalated in the wake of the bombing of the Golden Dome Mosque in Samarra, the leaders in Iraq at that time, General George Casey and Ambassador Zalmay Khalilzad, concluded that the coalition was failing to achieve its objectives. Their review underscored the need to protect the population and reduce sectarian violence, especially in Baghdad. As a result, General Casey requested additional forces to enable the coalition to accomplish these tasks, and those forces began to flow in January. In the ensuing months, our forces and our Iraqi counterparts have focused on improving security, especially in Baghdad and the areas around it, wresting sanctuaries from al Qaeda control, and disrupting the efforts of the Iranian-supported militia extremists.

We have employed counterinsurgency practices that underscore the importance of units living among the people they are securing, and accordingly our forces have established dozens of joint security stations and patrol bases manned by coalition and Iraqi forces in Baghdad and in other areas across Iraq.

In mid-June, with all the surge brigades in place, we launched a series of offensive operations focused on expanding the gains achieved in the preceding months in Anbar Province, clearing Baqubah, several key Baghdad neighborhoods, the remaining sanctuaries in Anbar Province, and important areas in the so-called belts around Baghdad, and pursuing al Qaeda in the Diyala River Valley and several other areas. Throughout this period as well, we engaged in dialogue with insurgent groups and tribes, and this led to additional elements standing up to oppose al Qaeda and other extremists.

We also continued to emphasize the development of the Iraqi Security Forces, and we employed nonkinetic means to exploit the opportunities provided by the conduct of our kinetic combat operations, aided in this effort by the arrival of additional provincial reconstruction teams.

The progress our forces have achieved with our Iraqi counterparts has, as I noted at the outset, been substantial. While there have been setbacks as well as successes and tough losses along the way, overall our tactical commanders and I see improvements in the security environment. We do not, however, just rely on gut feel or personal observations. We also conduct considerable data collection and analysis to gauge progress and determine trends. We do this by gathering and refining data from coalition and Iraqi operation centers, using the methodology that has been in place for well over a year, and that has benefited over the past seven months from the increased presence of our forces living among the Iraqi people.

We endeavor to ensure our analysis of that data is conducted with rigor and consistency as our ability to achieve a nuanced understanding of the security environment is dependent on collecting and analyzing data in a consistent way over time. Two U.S. Intelligence agencies recently reviewed our methodology, and they concluded that the data we produce is the most accurate and authoritative in Iraq.

As I mentioned up front, and as the chart before you reflects, [Slide: "Overall Weekly Iraq Attack Trends"] the level of security incidents has decreased significantly since the start of the surge of offensive operations in mid-June, declining in 8 of the past 12 weeks, with the level of incidents in the past 2 weeks the lowest since June 2006, and with the number of attacks this past week the lowest since April 2006. Civilian deaths of all categories, less natural causes, have also declined considerably by over 45 percent Iraq-wide since the height of sectarian violence in December. [Slide: "Iraq Civilian Deaths"] This is shown by the top line in this chart, and the decline by some 70 percent in Baghdad is shown by the bottom line.

Periodic mass casualty attacks by al Qaeda have tragically added to the numbers outside Baghdad in particular. Even without the sensational attacks, however, the level of civilian deaths is clearly still too high and continues to be of serious concern.

As the next chart shows, [Slide: "Ethno-Sectarian Violence"] the number of ethnosectarian deaths, an important subset of the overall civilian casualty figures, has also declined significantly since the height of the sectarian violence in December. Iraq-wide as shown by the top line on this chart, the number of ethnosectarian deaths has come down by over 55 percent, and it would have come down much further were it not for the casualties inflicted by barbaric al Qaeda bombings attempting to reignited sectarian violence.

In Baghdad, as the bottom line shows, the number of ethnosectarian deaths has come down some 80 percent since December. This chart also displays the density of sectarian incidents in various Baghdad neighborhoods, and it both reflects the progress made in reducing ethnosectarian violence in the Iraqi capital and identifies the areas that remain the most challenging.

Now, as we have gone on the offensive in former al Qaeda and insurgent sanctuaries, and as locals have increasingly supported our efforts, we have found a substantially increased number of arms and munition and explosives caches. As this chart shows, [Slide: "Caches Found & Cleared"] we have so far this year already found and cleared over 4,400 caches, nearly 1,700 more than we discovered in all of the last year. This may be a factor in the reduction in the number of overall improvised explosive device attacks in recent months, which, as this chart shows, [Slide: "Improvised Explosive Devices (IEDs)"] has declined sharply by about one-third since June.

The change in the security situation in Anbar Province has, of course, been particularly dramatic. As this chart shows, [Slide: "Anbar Attacks"] monthly attack levels in Anbar have declined from some 1,350 in October of 2006 to a bit over 200 in August of this year. This dramatic decrease reflects the significance of the local rejection of al Qaeda and the newfound willingness of local Anbaris to volunteer to serve in the Iraqi Army and Iraqi Police Service. As I noted earlier, we are seeing similar actions in other locations as well.

To be sure, trends have not been uniformly positive across Iraq, as is shown by this chart [Slide: "Iraq Violence Trends"] depicting violence levels in several key Iraqi provinces. The trend in Ninevah Province, for example, has been much more up and down until a recent decline. And the same is true in Salah ad Din Province, Saddam's former home province, though recent trends there and in Baghdad have been in the right direction recently. In any event, the overall trajectory in Iraq, a steady decline of incidents in the past three months, is still quite significant.

The number of car bombings and suicide attacks has also declined in each of the past 5 months from a high of some 175 in March, as this chart shows, [Slide: "High Profile Attacks"] to about 90 this past month. While this trend in recent months has been heartening, the number of high-profile attacks is still too high, and we continue to work hard to destroy the networks that carry out these barbaric attacks.

Our operations have, in fact, produced substantial progress against al Qaeda and its affiliates in Iraq. As this chart shows, [Slide: "State of Al Qaeda Iraq"] in the past eight months, we have considerably reduced the areas in which al Qaeda enjoyed sanctuary. We have also neutralized five media cells, detained the senior Iraqi leader of al Qaeda Iraq, and killed or captured nearly 100 other key leaders and some 2,500 rank-and-file fighters.

Al Qaeda is certainly not defeated; however, it is off balance, and we are pursuing its leaders and operators aggressively. Of note, as the recent National Intelligence Estimate on Iraq explained, these gains against al Qaeda are a result of the synergy of actions by conventional forces to deny the terrorists sanctuary, intelligence of surveillance and reconnaissance assets to find the enemy, and Special Operations elements to conduct targeted raids. A combination of these assets is necessary to prevent the creation of a terrorist safe haven in Iraq.

In the past six months, we have also targeted Shi'a militia extremists, capturing a number of senior leaders and fighters, as well as the deputy commander of Lebanese

Hezbollah Department 2800, the organization created to support the training, arming, and funding and in some cases direction of the militia extremists by the Iranian Republican Guard's Quds Force. These elements have assassinated and kidnapped Iraqi governmental leaders, killed and wounded our soldiers with advanced explosive devices provided by Iran, and indiscriminately rocketed civilians in the international zone and elsewhere.

It is increasingly apparent to both coalition and Iraqi leaders that Iran, through the use of the Quds Force, seeks to turn the Iraqi Special Groups into a Hezbollah-like force to serve its interests and fight a proxy war against the Iraqi state and coalition forces in Iraq.

The most significant development in the past six months likely has been the increasing emergence of—

[Disturbance in the hearing room.]

THE CHAIRMAN: Let us suspend the—will the entire group that is back there supporting that person be removed.

GENERAL PETRAEUS: The most significant—

THE CHAIRMAN: Just a minute, General

GENERAL PETRAEUS: Yes, sir.

THE CHAIRMAN: Proceed.

GENERAL PETRAEUS: The most significant development in the past six months likely has been the increasing emergence of tribes and local citizens rejecting al Qaeda and other extremists. This has, of course, been most visible in Anbar Province. A year ago the province was assessed as lost politically. Today it is a model of what happens when local leaders and citizens decide to oppose al Qaeda and reject its Taliban-like ideology. While Anbar is unique, and the model it provides cannot be replicated everywhere in Iraq, it does demonstrate the dramatic change in security that is possible with the support and participation of local citizens.

As this chart shows, [Slide: "Tribal Engagement"] other tribes have been inspired by the actions of those in Anbar and have volunteered to fight extremists as well. We have, in coordination with the Iraqi Government's National Reconciliation Committee been engaging these tribes and groups of local citizens who want to oppose extremists and to contribute to local security. Some 20,000 such individuals are already being hired for the Iraqi police. Thousands of others are being assimilated into the Iraqi Army, and thousands more are vying for a spot in Iraq's security forces.

As I noted earlier, Iraqi Security Forces have continued to grow, to develop their capabilities, and to shoulder more of the burdens of providing security for their country. Despite concerns about sectarian influence, inadequate logistics and supporting institutions, and an insufficient number of qualified commissioned and noncommissioned officers, Iraqi units are engaged around the country. As this chart shows, [Slide: "Iraqi Security Forces Capabilities"] there are now nearly 140 Iraqi Army national police and Special Operations Forces battalions in the fight, with about 95 of those capable of taking the lead in operations, albeit with some coalition support.

Beyond that, all of Iraq's battalions have been heavily involved in combat operations that often result in the loss of leaders, soldiers and equipment. These losses are among the shortcomings identified by operational readiness assessments, but we should not take from these assessments the impression that Iraqi forces are not in the fight and contributing. Indeed, despite their shortages, many Iraqi units across Iraq now operate with minimal coalition assistance.

As counterinsurgency operations require substantial numbers of boots on the ground, we are helping the Iraqis expand the size of their security forces. Currently there are some 445,000 individuals on the payrolls of Iraq's Interior and Defense Ministries. Based on recent decisions by Prime Minister Maliki, the number of Iraqi Security Forces will grow further by the end of this year, possibly by as much as 40,000. Given the security challenges Iraq faces, we support this decision, and we will work with the two security ministries as they continue their efforts to expand their basic training capacity, leader development programs, logistical structures and elements, and various other institutional capabilities to support the substantial growth in Iraqi forces.

Significantly, in 2007, Iraq will, as in 2006, spend more on its security forces than it will receive in security assistance from the United States. In fact, Iraq is becoming one of the United States' larger foreign military sales (FMS) customers, committing some 1.6 billion to FMS already, with a possibility of up to 1.8 billion being committed before the end of the year. And I appreciate the attention that some Members of Congress have recently given to speeding up the FMS process for Iraq.

To summarize, the security situation in Iraq is improving, and Iraqi elements are slowly taking on more of the responsibility for protecting their citizens. Innumerable challenges lie ahead; however, coalition and Iraqi Security Forces have made progress toward achieving security. As a result, the United States will be in the position to reduce its forces in Iraq in the months ahead.

Two weeks ago I provided recommendations for the way ahead in Iraq to the members of my chain of command and the Joint Chiefs of Staff. The essence of the approach I recommended is captured in its title: Security While Transitioning: From Leading to Partnering to Overwatch. This approach seeks to build on the security improvements our troopers and our Iraqi counterparts have fought so hard to achieve in recent months. It reflects recognition of the importance of securing the population and the imperative of transitioning responsibilities to Iraqi institutions and Iraqi forces as quickly as possible, but without rushing to failure. It includes substantial support for the continuing development of Iraqi security forces. It also stresses the need to continue the counterinsurgency strategy that we have been employing, but with Iraqis gradually shouldering more of the load. And it highlights the importance of regional and global diplomatic approaches. Finally, in recognition of the fact that this war is not only being fought on the ground in Iraq, but also in cyberspace, it also notes the need to contest the enemy's growing use of that important medium to spread extremism.

The recommendations I provided were informed by operational and strategic considerations. The operational considerations include recognition that military aspects of the surge have achieved progress and generated momentum. Iraqi Security Forces have continued to grow and have slowly been shouldering more of the security burdens in Iraq.

A mission focused on either population security or transition alone will not be adequate to achieve our objectives. Success against al Qaeda-Iraq and Iranian-supported militia extremists requires conventional forces, as well as Special Operations Forces. And the security and local political situations will enable us to draw down the surge forces.

My recommendations also took into account a number of strategic considerations. Political progress will take place only if sufficient security exists. Long-term U.S. ground force viability will benefit from force reductions as the surge runs its course. Regional, global, and cyberspace initiatives are critical to success. And Iraqi leaders understandably want to assume greater sovereignty in their country, although, as they recently announced, they do desire continued presence of coalition forces in Iraq in 2008 under a new U.N. Security Council resolution. And following that, they want to negotiate a long-term security agreement with the United States and other nations.

Based on these considerations, and having worked the battlefield geometry with Lieutenant General Ray Odierno, the Multi-National Corps Commander, to ensure that we retain and build on the gains for which our troopers have fought, I have recommended a drawdown of the surge forces from Iraq. In fact, later this month, the Marine Expeditionary Unit deployed as part of the surge will depart Iraq. Beyond that, if my recommendations are approved, that unit's departure will be followed by the withdrawal of a brigade combat team without replacement in mid-December and the further redeployment without replacement of four other brigade combat teams and the two surge Marine battalions in the first 7 months of 2008 until we reach the presurge levels of 15 brigade combat teams by mid-July 2008.

I would also like to discuss the period beyond next summer. Force reductions will continue beyond the presurge levels of brigade combat teams that we will reach by mid-July 2008. However, in my professional judgment, it would be premature to make recommendations on the pace of such reductions at this time. In fact, our experience in Iraq has repeatedly shown that projecting too far into the future is not just difficult: it can be misleading and even hazardous.

The events of the past six months underscore that point. When I testified in January, for example, no one would have dared to forecast that Anbar Province would have been transformed the way it has in the past six months, nor would anyone have predicted that volunteers and one-time al Qaeda strongholds like Ghazaliyah and western Baghdad were an oddity and eastern Baghdad would seek to join the fight against al Qaeda. Nor would we have anticipated that a Shi'a-led government would accept significant numbers of Sunni volunteers into the ranks of the local police force in Abu Ghraib.

Beyond that, on a less encouraging note, none of us earlier this year appreciated the extent of Iranian involvement in Iraq, something about which we and Iraq's leaders all now have greater concern. In view of this, I do not believe it is reasonable to have an adequate appreciation for the pace of further reductions or mission adjustments beyond the summer of 2008 until about mid-March of next year. We will no later than that time consider factors similar to those on which I have based the current recommendations, having by then, of course, a better feel for the security situation, and the improvements in the capabilities of our Iraqi counterparts and the enemy situation. I will then, as I did in developing the recommendations I have explained here today, also take into consideration the demands on our Nation's ground forces, although I believe that that consideration should once again inform, not drive, the recommendations I make.

This chart [Slide: "Recommended Force Reductions/Mission Shift"] captures the recommendations I have described, showing the recommended reduction of brigade combat teams as the surge runs its course, and illustrating the concept of our units adjusting their missions and transitioning responsibilities to Iraqis as the situation and Iraqi capabilities permit. It also reflects the "no later than" date for recommendations on force adjustments beyond next summer, and provides a possible approach we have considered for the future force structure and missions set in Iraq.

One may argue that the best way to speed the process in Iraq is to change the Multi-National Forces Iraq (MNFI) mission from one that emphasizes population security, counterterrorism and transition to one that is strictly focused on transition and counterterrorism. Making that change now would, in our view, be premature. We have learned before that there is a real danger in handing over tasks to the Iraqi Security Forces before their capacity and local conditions warrant. In fact, the drafters of the recently released National Intelligence Estimate on Iraq recognized this danger when they wrote—and I quote—we asses that changing the mission of coalition forces from a primarily counterinsurgency and stabilization role to a primary countercombat support role of Iraqi forces in counterterrorist operations to prevent al Qaeda Iraq from establishing a safe haven would erode security gains achieved thus far.

In describing the recommendations I have made, I should note, again, that like Ambassador Crocker, I believe Iraq's problems will require a long-term effort. There are no easy answers or quick solutions. And although we both believe this effort can succeed, it will take time. Our assessments underscore, in fact, the importance of recognizing that a premature drawdown of our forces would likely have devastating consequences. That assessment is supported by the findings of the 16 August Defense Intelligence Agency report on the implications of a rapid withdrawal of U.S. forces from Iraq. Summarizing it in an unclassified fashion, it concludes that a rapid withdrawal would result in the further release of the strong centrifugal forces in Iraq and produce a number of dangerous results, including a high risk of disintegration of the Iraqi Security Forces, rapid deterioration of local security initiatives, al Qaeda-Iraq regaining lost ground and freedom of maneuver, a marked increase in violence, and further ethnosectarian displacement and refugee flows, alliances of convenience by Iraqi groups with internal and external forces to gain advantages over their rivals, and exacerbation of already challenging regional dynamics, especially with respect to Iran.

Lieutenant General Odierno and I share this assessment and believe that the best way to secure our national interests and to avoid an unfavorable outcome in Iraq is to continue to focus our operations on securing the Iraqi people while targeting terrorist groups and militia extremists and, as quickly as conditions are met, transitioning security tasks to Iraqi elements.

Before closing, I want to thank you and your colleagues for your support of our men and women in uniform in Iraq. The soldiers, sailors, airmen, marines and coastguardsmen with whom I am honored to serve are the best equipped and very likely the most professional force in our Nation's history. Impressively, despite all that has been asked of them in recent years, they continue to raise their right hands and volunteer to stay in uniform. With 3 weeks to go in this fiscal year, in fact, the Army elements in Iraq of Multi-National Corps Iraq, for example, have achieved well over 130 percent of the reenlistment goals in the initial term and careers categories and nearly 115 percent in the midcareer category. All of us appreciate what you have done to ensure that these great troopers have had what they have needed to accomplish their mission, just as we appreciate what you have done to take care of their families, as they, too, have made significant sacrifices in recent years.

The advances you have underwritten in weapons systems and individual equipment, in munitions and command control, and communications systems, and intelligence surveillance, and reconnaissance capabilities, and vehicles, and counter-improvised explosive device (IED) systems and programs, and in manned and unmanned aircraft have proved invaluable in Iraq. The capabilities that you have funded most recently, especially the vehicles that will provide greater protection against improvised explosive devices, are also of enormous importance. Additionally, your funding of the Commander's Emergency Response Program has given our leaders a critical tool with which to prosecute the counterinsurgency campaign. Finally, we appreciate as well your funding of our new detention programs and rule-of-law initiatives in Iraq.

In closing, it remains an enormous privilege to soldier again in Iraq with America's new greatest generation. Our country's men and women in uniform have done a magnificent job in the most complex and challenging environment imaginable. All Americans should be very proud of their sons and daughters serving in Iraq today. Thank you very much.

Source: U.S. Government Printing Office via GPO Access.

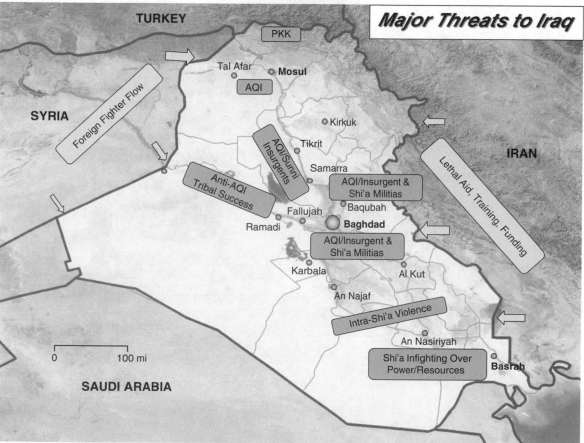

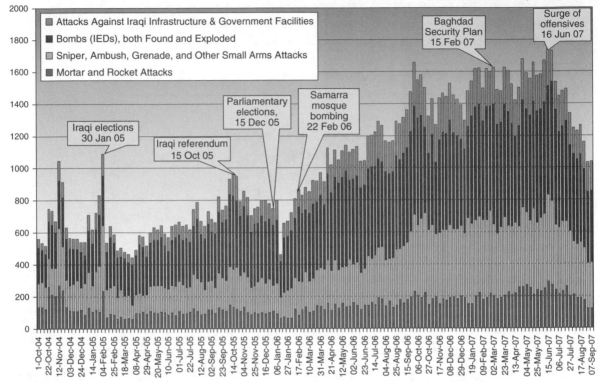

Overall Weekly Iraq Attack Trends

1 October 2004–7 September 2007

Legend:
- Attacks Against Iraqi Infrastructure & Government Facilities
- Bombs (IEDs), both Found and Exploded
- Sniper, Ambush, Grenade, and Other Small Arms Attacks
- Mortar and Rocket Attacks

Annotations on chart:
- Iraqi elections 30 Jan 05
- Iraqi referendum 15 Oct 05
- Parliamentary elections, 15 Dec 05
- Samarra mosque bombing 22 Feb 06
- Baghdad Security Plan 15 Feb 07
- Surge of offensives 16 Jun 07

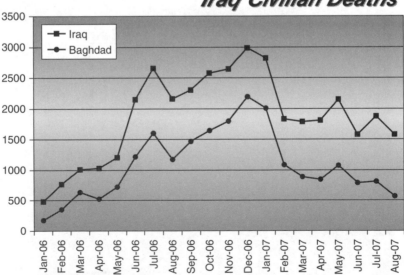

Iraq Civilian Deaths

Legend:
- Iraq
- Baghdad

Source: Coalition and Host National Reporting

As of 31 Aug 07

Ethno-Sectarian Violence

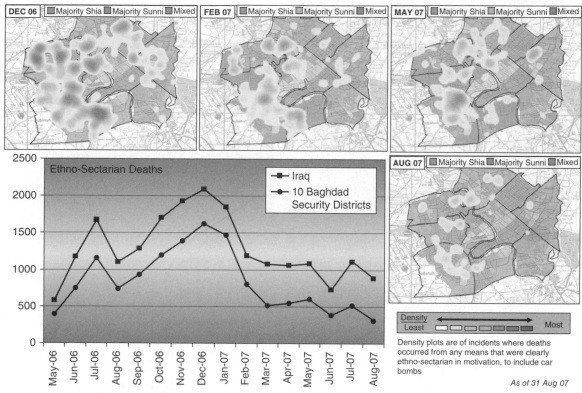

DEC 06	☐ Majority Shia ☐ Majority Sunni ☐ Mixed
FEB 07	☐ Majority Shia ☐ Majority Sunni ☐ Mixed
MAY 07	☐ Majority Shia ☐ Majority Sunni ☐ Mixed
AUG 07	☐ Majority Shia ☐ Majority Sunni ☐ Mixed

Ethno-Sectarian Deaths

- ■ Iraq
- ● 10 Baghdad Security Districts

Density
Least ◄——————► Most

Density plots are of incidents where deaths occurred from any means that were clearly ethno-sectarian in motivation, to include car bombs

As of 31 Aug 07

Caches Found & Cleared

Year	Anbar	Iraq
1 JAN 07–7 SEP 07	2111	4409
2006	1222	2726
2005	1483	3091
2004	692	2691

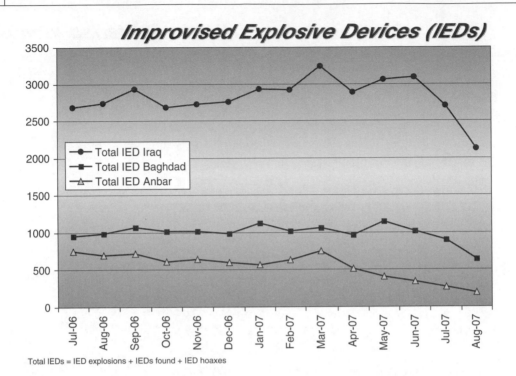

Improvised Explosive Devices (IEDs)

Total IEDs = IED explosions + IEDs found + IED hoaxes

Anbar Attacks

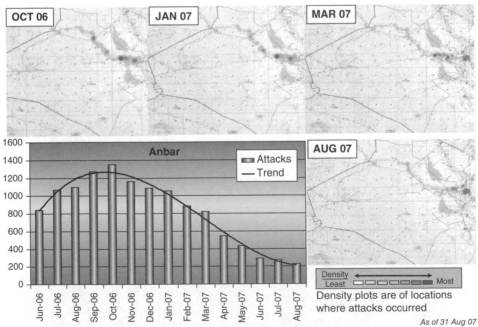

Density plots are of locations where attacks occurred

As of 31 Aug 07

Iraq Violence Trends

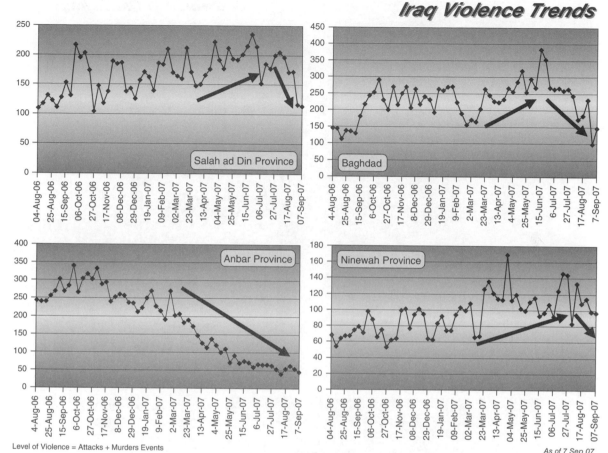

Salah ad Din Province

Baghdad

Anbar Province

Ninewah Province

Level of Violence = Attacks + Murders Events

As of 7 Sep 07

High Profile Attacks

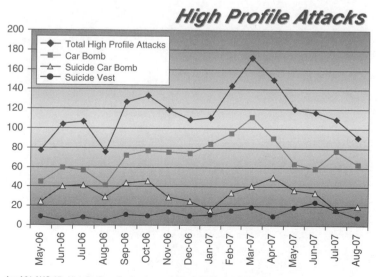

- ◆ Total High Profile Attacks
- ■ Car Bomb
- △ Suicide Car Bomb
- ● Suicide Vest

As of 31 AUG 07; High Profile = Car bombs + suicide car bombs + suicide vests

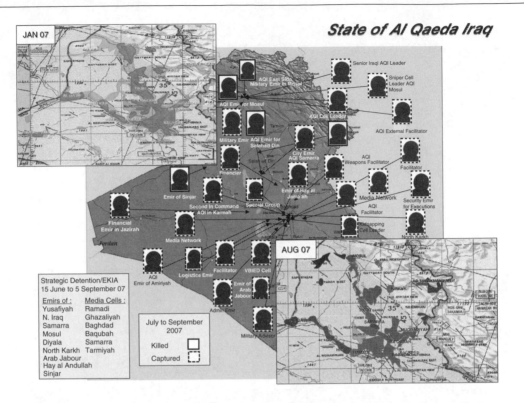

State of Al Qaeda Iraq

JAN 07

AUG 07

Senior Iraqi AQI Leader

AQI East Side Military Emir in Mosul

Sniper Cell Leader AQI Mosul

AQI Emir of Mosul

AQI Cell Leader

AQI External Facilitator

Military Emir AQI Emir for Selahad Din

City Emir AQI Samarra

AQI Weapons Facilitator

Facilitator

Financier

Emir of Sinjar

Emir of Hay al Jama'ah

Media Network AQI Facilitator

Security Emir for Executions

Second In Command AQI in Karmah

Special Group

Financial Emir in Jazirah

Media Network

Kidnapping Cell Leader

North Karkh

AQI Emir of Amiriyah

Logistics Emir

Facilitator

VBIED Cell

Emir of Arab Jabour

Admin Emir

Military Advisor

Strategic Detention/EKIA
15 June to 5 September 07

Emirs of :
Yusafiyah
N. Iraq
Samarra
Mosul
Diyala
North Karkh
Arab Jabour
Hay al Andullah
Sinjar

Media Cells :
Ramadi
Ghazaliyah
Baghdad
Baqubah
Samarra
Tarmiyah

July to September 2007

Killed

Captured

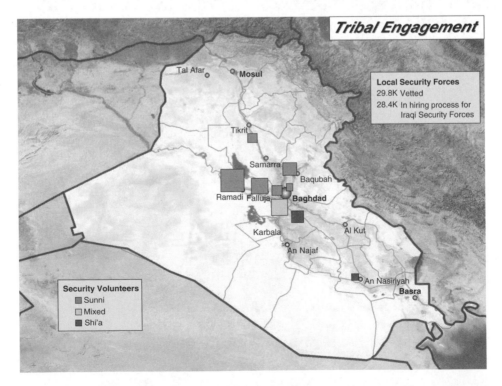

Tribal Engagement

Local Security Forces
29.8K Vetted
28.4K In hiring process for Iraqi Security Forces

Tal Afar
Mosul
Tikrit
Samarra
Baqubah
Ramadi Falluja Baghdad
Karbala
Al Kut
An Najaf
An Nasiriyah
Basra

Security Volunteers
◼ Sunni
◻ Mixed
◼ Shi'a

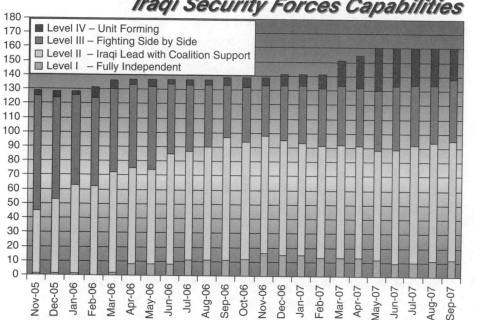

Iraqi Army Battalions, National Police Battalions, and Special Operating Force Battalions

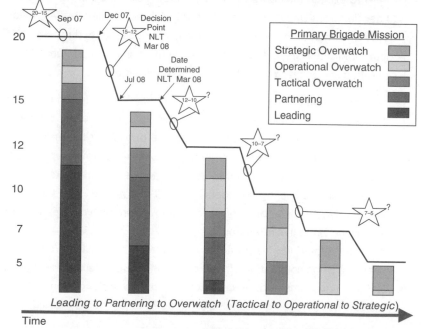

NASA OFFICE OF PUBLIC AFFAIRS
Media Briefing
THURSDAY, FEBRUARY 14, 2008

The Pentagon
"REENTRY OF U.S. SATELLITE"

Speakers:

Ambassador James Jeffrey, Assistant to the President, Deputy National Security Advisor

General James Cartwright, Vice Chair, Joint Chiefs of Staff

Michael Griffin, NASA Administrator

Moderator:

Geoff Morrell, Pentagon Press Secretary

MODERATOR: Good afternoon, and thank you all for joining us today.

As you know, for several weeks now, this Department and many others in the United States Government have been closely monitoring a rapidly decaying U.S. intelligence satellite. Together, we have been looking at options to mitigate any possible risk to human life that could be caused with this satellite reentering the Earth's atmosphere.

Today, we have assembled a group from across the Government to come in here to explain the course of action that President Bush has selected. You will hear first from Deputy National Security Advisor James Jeffrey, followed by the Vice Chairman of the Joint Chiefs, General "Hoss" Cartwright, and NASA Administrator Michael Griffin. Please allow them to finish their statements before chiming in with questions, and with that, Ambassador Jeffrey?

AMBASSADOR JEFFREY: Thank you very much. What I would like to do is sketch a little bit the rationale behind our decision, and then we will talk more about the details of it. We first discussed the satellite publicly at the end of January, after we had determined that it was coming down and as news reports began breaking. Following further decisions, we have decided to, of course, brief you today. We just finished briefing Members and staff of both the House of Representatives and the Senate a little bit earlier today, and we are also doing a diplomatic rollout across the world this afternoon.

What I would like to do again is to sketch some of the background to the decision. Upon notification of the descending NRO satellite, the President and his National and Homeland Security Advisors reviewed the options available to us to mitigate risk from the descending satellite. As background, I would like to note that over the past 30-plus years, there have been many satellites and other manmade objects falling from space, of course. They have fallen with very little damage and no injuries. What makes this case a little bit different, however, and in particular for the President in his consideration was the likelihood that the satellite upon descent to the Earth's surface could release much of its thousand-plus pounds of hydra-zine fuel as a toxic gas. The likelihood of the satellite falling in a populated area is small, and the extent and duration of toxic hydrazine in the atmosphere would be quite limited. Nevertheless, if the satellite did fall in a populated area, it was a pos-sibility of death or injury to human beings beyond that associated with the fall of satellites and other space objects normally, if we can use that word. Specifically there enough of a risk for the President to be quite concerned about human life, and on that basis, he asked us to review our options.

Apart from the normal consequences of mitigation actions that we are prepared to deploy both at home and internationally to deal with the hydrazine, the one viable op-tion we had, we concluded, was to use a tactical missile from an AEGIS ship to strike the satellite in order to reduce the overall risk. This missile was designed, of course, for other missions, but we concluded that it could be reconfigured, both the missile and the various other systems related to it, on a one-time reversible basis to do the shot.

After further review of this option and in particular consideration of the question of saving—reducing injury to human life, the President, on the recommendation of his National and Homeland Security teams, directed the Department of Defense to carry out the intercept.

Let me talk very briefly about the diplomatic side of this, and then I will turn it over to the Vice Chairman. The United States has certain obligations based on treaties and other agreements related to activities in space. The 1967 UN Treaty on Exploration and Use of Outer Space in particular calls on states to keep others informed of activities of potential concern. While we do not believe that we meet the standard of Article 9 of that treaty that says we would have to consult in the case of generating potentially harmful interference with other activities in space, we do believe that it is important to keep other countries informed of what is happening. We let many countries know at the end of January that the satellite was descend-ing, that it would likely have hydrazine, and talked a bit about the consequences of that. Today, we are reaching out to all countries and various organizations—the UN, some of its subordinate agencies, the European Space Agency, and NATO— and inform them of the actions that we are describing to you today. With that, I would like to turn it over to General Cartwright. Thank you very much.

GENERAL CARTWRIGHT: Thank you. Just to re-baseline, this is a National Recon-naissance Office satellite. It was launched on 14 December 2006. It is about, roughly, 5,000 pounds in its weight. Historically, a satellite of this size and that weight, roughly half of it would survive reentry. We are saying in the modeling, somewhere around 2,800 pounds would survive reentry. What is different here is the hydrazine. In this case, we do have some historical background that we can work against for the tank that contains the hydrazine, and we had a similar tank on Columbia that survived reentry. So we have a pretty reasonable understanding that if the tank is left intact, it would survive the reentry.

This satellite essentially went dead for communications and control very shortly after it attained orbit. It was a nominal launch, a nominal insertion into orbit, but then on orbit within the first few hours stopped communicating. A satellite like this, really all of our satellites have fuel that is reserved along with redundant systems to ensure that there is propulsion to allow for what we would call a "controlled deorbit," but the ability to put it, say, in the ocean. But with no communication with this satellite, that is what is different here. That is what distinguishes this particular activity is we have no way to communicate to invoke the safety measures that are already on board the bird.

To take it just a little bit further, hydrazine in this case, normal case, is that when it is used as rocket fuel, it is in a gaseous state. We bring it up to a liquid state with heaters. This has had no benefit of heaters because there is no power on the bird. So this is a frozen state of hydrazine, which leaves for us another unknown, how much of it would melt on the reentry, therefore, would be either a liquid or gaseous phase. In a worse-case scenario for the hydrazine, it is similar to chlorine or ammonia in that when you inhale it, it affects your tissues in your lungs. You know it. It has the burning sensation. If you stay very close to it and inhale a lot of it, it could in fact be deadly, but for the most part here, we are talking an area, say, roughly the size of two football fields that the hydrazine could be dispersed over, and you would at least incur something that would make you go to the doctor. If you stayed inside that zone, if you got very close to it and stayed, you could get to exposures that would be deadly.

So that is a sense of what we are dealing here with Columbia, and I will let the Administrator talk to that, part of it, but with Columbia, the hydrazine tank came down in Texas in a wooded area, unpopulated, and unlike this, we had the mitigating in front of it. They burned most of it. The mission was at its end. So there was almost no hydrazine left. You could walk up very shortly after the event and walk right up to the tank's proximity, and it wouldn't have affected you.

Now, we didn't handle it that way. We treat it as a toxic. Anybody who should encounter something like this ought to treat it as a toxic. Don't approach things like this. Now, having said that, what we tried to do here at the Department was to look at the risks that exist for what we will call a "normal reentry." This is normal for this satellite, not having the ability to deorbit it. It would basically enter the atmosphere. As I said, it would incur the heating. It may break up, and exactly what the pieces look like, all of that, we are not sure. It is very, very unpredictable as to exactly where it would hit the atmosphere. The atmosphere raises and lowers based on heating, but when it encounters the atmosphere, then it would come down, as I said, about 25–2800 pounds worth of mass. Those calculations in that alone would not be reason to take action. In other words, the likelihood of it hitting the land or a person as a hunk of metal or material is relatively low. It is the hydrazine here that is the distinguishing characteristic.

I also, like you, read the blogs. There is some question about the classified side of this. That is really not an issue. Once you go through the atmosphere and the heating and the burning, that would not be an issue in this case. It would not justify using a missile to take it and break it up further. Our objective here was to reduce the risk, could we reduce the risk to space platforms, to airborne platforms, and to terrestrial platforms, the Earth, cities, people, et cetera.

In the first case, one of the first actions that we took together was we believe that the window that we were looking at to intercept this vehicle can be accomplished after we bring the Shuttle down. So we are going to bring the Shuttle down before we even consider this option. The second is that we looked at the various capabilities that we as a nation hold, and what held the highest likelihood of success for us was to move to a mobile platform and a tactical weapon, which we had good understanding of the performance of the weapon. That came to the Standard Missile, a Navy missile that has been in the inventory for several years, has a very solid track record. We understand how to use it and how it works and what its likelihood of performance would be. In addition, it has a mobile platform, and the intent in the mobile platform is—what we would like to be able to do is to intercept this missile at a point at which we could have a high likelihood of bringing it down in an unpopulated area. The second objective is to hit the tank, the hydrazine tank, and rupture it, so that we can off-gas this hydrazine as early as possible, so the least amount of it returns to the Earth. So those are the two key objectives. It is looking at the likelihood of mitigating on orbit, in the air, or on the land.

On the orbit side in space, what we are attempting to do here is to intercept this just prior to it hitting the Earth's atmosphere. That does two things for us. It reduces the amount of debris that would be in space. So, in this case, what we are looking for is to try to have the debris, over 50 percent of it, within the first two orbits or the first 10 or 15 hours would be deorbited. The second piece here is looking at other unmanned bodies in space and low-earth orbit and the Space Station to make sure that we do not increase the risk to other bodies in space. So that was a criteria we're trying to understand.

Next is when the orbit comes down through the air, is there anything that would increase the risk to normal general aviation. We have a set of standards. The FAA has a set of standards that it uses to revector aviation when there is a hazard in the air, would we cause a hazard in the air, if we did, would it be predictable enough that we could revector around. That was a criteria we had to get through.

Then the last criteria was on Earth, can we in any way help mitigate the opportunity for this to come on land, to land in a populated area, and so we worked our way through those. I will let the director talk to the space side of this equation, but suffice it to say, we believe that if we intercept this just prior to entry—and remember, this is not an aerodynamic body. If it were a ballistic missile and had aerodynamic properties, you could see it rising in one hemisphere and predict where it is going to come down in the next and, therefore, that is how you would accomplish an intercept. This has no aerodynamic properties. Once it hits the atmosphere, it tumbles, it breaks apart, it is very unpredictable and next to impossible to engage.

So what we are trying to do here is catch it just prior to the last minute, so it is as absolutely low as possible outside the atmosphere, so that the debris comes down as quickly as possible, A. B, on the intercept, first, if we can hit the satellite, which we believe we have a high confidence we can do, that will slow the satellite down, which means it will deorbit more quickly, and we can predict more accurately where it will deorbit, so we can potentially put it in a position in the ocean. On the land side of the equation, again, the objective would be to breach the tank and let the hydrazine escape. Second is to break apart the satellite at least, so that the pieces can burn up on reentry a little easier and we'd bring them down quicker. The last piece on land, we talked through a little bit, but we have an extensive program that we use regularly with deorbiting bodies that notifies the world that we have something coming in. But this is highly unpredictable. Again, they are not aerodynamic. So we can generally get a quadrant of the Earth down to the last day, but it is down to the last one or two hours before we can tell you potentially a land mass, but not more accurately than that. So this is very difficult because you have a very non-aerodynamic body trying to move through the air.

A couple of the other pieces here to help put a little finer point on some of these, we are using the Standard Missile 3, well understood. It has the ability to get up just beyond the atmosphere. So it has the kinetic energy to be able to reach this satellite as it prepares to reentry. We believe that the window for this activity will start here in the next three or four days and will be open for about maybe as many as seven or eight days. Much of this depends on the heating of the atmosphere. So we are trying to build, knowing that, where would be the best position to be from the Earth to launch a missile to intercept that would drive this down into the ocean, and that is our objective, get rid of the hydrazine and have this fall in the ocean.

We will use one missile with two backups. We will have three ships on station, but it will be one shot. The other missiles are there principally in case something in the launch phase does not work. We will have radars and space sensors pointed at the area, so that we have some sense of whether we were successful or not. In the case that we are not successful with the first shot, we will reassess, but two things will be working against us. One, the satellite will continue to progress across the Earth, and so as it does, we will only have a certain amount of time before. If we shot, we would have a higher likelihood of bringing it down on land, and we are not going to shoot if that is the case.

We have to be able to assess if parts of the satellite came apart, which part is which, and that is a very difficult thing to do. In other words, if the satellite grazed but did not directly impact, how do you decide whether you should take a second shot, and we will work our way through that, but it will be a conscious decision that will take. We will have a window. We believe probably might get us as much as two days to make an assessment and come back before we really find it not feasible to reengage this target and to let it normally decay in its orbit. So it is a relatively small window. We will take one shot and assess, and then we will come back and look. We feel confident that we will be able to assess, but this is not necessarily something that will occur in minutes, and that the challenge is to try to understand what it is we have after we have taken the shot and what it will take to come to the calculus that would say go ahead and reengage again or reengagement will either increase the risk to space, increase the risk to the air, or increase the risk on the ground. If any of those are the case, then we will not take a second shot.

At the end of this, just from my perspective, what to me was compelling as we reviewed the data is that if we fire at the satellite, the worst is that we miss, and then we have a known situation which is where we are today. If we graze the satellite, we are still better off because likely we will still bring it down sooner and, therefore, more predictably. If we hit the hydrazine tank, then we have improved our potential to mitigate that threat. So the regret factor of not acting clearly outweighed the regret factors of acting, and as long as that is the case, we felt that it was the responsibility to go ahead and try to engage the satellite. I will turn it over to the Director for his comments. I'm sorry, Administrator.

ADMINISTRATOR GRIFFIN: Administrator, Director, what difference? [Laughter.]

ADMINISTRATOR GRIFFIN: My colleagues have said almost everything that would need to be said. I will add a couple of quick remarks. The first is that, of course, we have already alluded to the fact that we have a Shuttle on orbit at the moment and a Space Station on orbit permanently with a permanent crew. So we looked very carefully. From the first, NASA has been involved in this. We looked very carefully at increased risks to Shuttle and Station, and broadly speaking, they are negligible. They are at least a factor of 10 smaller than risks we take just being in space anyway in the Shuttle. So they are not significant with respect to the risks we already assumed to fly the Shuttle. On the Space Station, of course, it is a different issue. The Space Station is much more robust than the Shuttle, but even there, the risk posture does not increase significantly, and so we are very comfortable that this is a decision made carefully and objectively and safely.

There are good times to conduct the intercept and poor times to conduct the intercept based on the positioning of the Station, and I and my colleagues will work together to make sure that, if possible, we pick one of the good times, but even the bad times are not too bad, and I would assure all of you that we are conducting this with due regard to the safety of people on orbit. I would make the point that—I want to reinforce the point that General Cartwright made—is that there is a very large amount of uncertainty in predicting the landing zone of an entry object. It is generally acknowledged by specialists in the field that the best you will do is to get within around 10 percent of the remaining lifetime of the bird, and that is the best. So a month ahead of time, you will know when it will land within about three days. That, of course, allows the satellite to make multiple revolutions around the entire surface of the Earth. So, in essence, a month ahead of time, you have no idea. Ten days ahead of time, you will be uncertain by at least a day. Again, it will make 16 revolutions around the Earth in that day. It could land anywhere.

On the day that you land, you will be uncertain by several hours. The satellite will make at least two orbits in that period of time, which again sweeps out a very large fraction of the Earth. So it was necessary to make the decision about whether to engage days, weeks, even longer, if possible, ahead of when it will actually land because it is simply not possible to predict whether it will land in the middle of the Pacific or in a populated area. The decision had to be made before we could be certain where it would go.

I want to again emphasize General Cartwright's point that almost anything that we can do with this turns out to be either neutral or better. Neutral is if we miss. Nothing changes. If we shoot and barely touch it, the satellite is at this point just barely in orbit. Almost anything that you do to it when it is just barely in orbit is going to cause it to reenter within the next couple of orbits, and of course, if we shoot and get a direct hit, then that is a clean kill, and we are in good shape. So there is almost nothing we can do here that makes it worse. Almost everything we can do, technically, makes it better, which was a very strong factor weighting the decision. With that, I will close. I don't think you need to hear more from me.

MEDIA QUESTIONER: Could I ask you a couple quick questions? First of all, you said you have a high confidence that you can do this. Is this a first? Does it employ the same technology you use in Missile Defense and whether you learn anything relative to Missile Defense from this, and how much space debris will be left behind if you are successful?

GENERAL CARTWRIGHT: On the first side of the equation, this is the first time we have used a tactical missile to engage a spacecraft, but not the first time that we have a tactical missile to engage a body that is just reentering. So the leap to move to catching it just before it hits the atmosphere really takes almost no modification at all. What we are talking about here is minor modification to software, both in the AEGIS system and in the missile itself. So that gives us a reasonably high confidence that we understand all of the activities here.

MEDIA QUESTIONER: [Inaudible.]

GENERAL CARTWRIGHT: Well, the missile is designed to—this particular missile, the Standard Missile, is designed to intercept short—and medium-range ballistic missiles. They leave the atmosphere for a short period of time and come back.

MEDIA QUESTIONER: [Inaudible.]

GENERAL CARTWRIGHT: That is correct. So we have the experience there. What we are trying to do is match that period at which the satellite that is most like reentering missile, and so that gives us some sense that all of the work that has been done, the test data that we have over the years and the operational data would be transferable to this activity, but it also makes the window very short for when we could intercept.

MEDIA QUESTIONER: So it does use the Missile Defense technology?

GENERAL CARTWRIGHT: It uses the missile's technology, Missile Defense, and this is a defensive missile. The Standard Missile is a defensive missile, but it does not use that portion of it which is associated with the atmosphere.

MEDIA QUESTIONER: [Inaudible.]

GENERAL CARTWRIGHT: The debris reenters. What we are looking for is to catch it here very close to the Earth's surface. What we are shooting for nominally is about 130 miles up. Those are nautical miles, and these numbers get confusing because some people use kilometers, but 130 nautical miles is what we are trying. In doing that, well over 50 percent of the debris will come in, in the first two revolutions, and so then we are talking weeks, maybe a month for some of the smaller debris to come down, but it is a very finite period of time that we can manage, and it is in an area where we don't have satellites manned or unmanned; in other words, down very low.

MEDIA QUESTIONER: General, first of all, what are the odds? What is the percentage chance that you will succeed, high, low, 70, 80 percent, that you will actually hit?

And secondly, obviously, the U.S. criticized China pretty heavily for their ASAT satellite tests. What makes this difference, and is this just sort of a resurgence of what has been in past years a U.S. anti-satellite program?

GENERAL CARTWRIGHT: Let me start with kind of the first piece here. This missile and what is different here is, one, we are notifying, which is required by treaties and law, and we have started that notification well over a month ago, and we continuing to keep people informed, and we have a Consequence Management Plan that is in place that we will execute. The second here is in looking at comparisons, this is right at the surface of the atmosphere, so to speak. Other intercepts that have occurred substantially higher than the Space Station, as an example, and that means that the debris is up there for 20 to 40 years and has to migrate down through both manned space platforms and unmanned space platforms. That will not be the case here. So those are the types of things that we looked at.

Percentage-wise, percentage that the missile will function normally, very high. Percentage that if it functions normally and gets to the altitude that it would intercept, again, I would give you very high, based on what we know and that this is a well understood asset.

MEDIA QUESTIONER: High, 80, 90?

GENERAL CARTWRIGHT: I will go closer to yours.

ADMINISTRATOR GRIFFIN: I would just comment that the Chinese ASAT test was conducted against a satellite in a circular orbit at around 850 kilometers of altitude. So the debris that was generated could go maybe not anywhere, but a very large swath of Earth orbital space and will be up, as General Cartwright said, for decades. All of the debris from this encounter, as carefully designed as it is, will be done at most within weeks, and most of it will be down in the first couple of orbits afterwards. There is an enormous difference to space-faring nations in the conduct of those two things.

MEDIA QUESTIONER: Where are the ships going to be located when this attempt is made? You can't move them around in space two or three days. Right?

GENERAL CARTWRIGHT: We are holding that close, just for the reasons we are still working the box. We are down in an area, but I will give you the northern hemisphere in the Pacific, and that is about as close as I want to draw it right now.

MEDIA QUESTIONER: General, would there be no danger if you didn't do this and this came down on land and somebody else got to it first if it landed somewhere in China? This would be of no intelligence value to another country?

GENERAL CARTWRIGHT: Our assessment is a high probability that it would not be of any intelligence value. Just the heating, the destruction that occurs on the reentry would leave it in a state that—other than some rare, unforecast happenstance, this would not be of intelligence value.

MEDIA QUESTIONER: But is that rare possibility that—I mean a remote possibility. Is that part of the calculation here?

GENERAL CARTWRIGHT: No. It would not change. It is the hydrazine that makes this different.

Now, I have read the blog space on this also, and I understand, but it is the hydrazine that we are looking at. That is the only thing that breaks it out as worthy of taking extraordinary measures.

MEDIA QUESTIONER: General, I have a quick follow-up to Jamie's question, and then I have a separate question. Are there missiles that are being used in this shoot part of the Missile Defense System? I just wanted to clarify that.

GENERAL CARTWRIGHT: The AEGIS is part of the regional/tactical system of missile defense, and it is netted into the broader system from a sensor standpoint.

MEDIA QUESTIONER: And then in terms of the Shuttle's hydrazine tank that survive [*sic*] the reentry and landed on Earth—but when the Shuttle first reentered, that was a controlled reentry.

GENERAL CARTWRIGHT: Right.

MEDIA QUESTIONER: This reentry would be—even if you don't hit it, it is going to be much more violent. Wouldn't the percentages or the possibility that it would tear itself apart and destroy that hydrazine tank in the atmosphere—

ADMINISTRATOR GRIFFIN: No.

MEDIA QUESTIONER: —increase with that?

ADMINISTRATOR GRIFFIN: No. The analysis that we have done is as certain as any analysis of this type can be. The hydrazine tank will survive intact, and in face, the hydrazine which is in it is frozen, solid as it is now. Not all of it will melt. So you will land on the ground with a tank full of slush hydrazine that would then later evaporate. The tank will have been breached, not probably. The tank will have been breached because the fuel lines will have been ripped out of the main spacecraft, and so that hydrazine will vent. If it lands in a populated area—the General referred to an area the size of a couple of football fields, and loosely, that is what our analysis shows—it is hard to find areas that have any significant population to them where you could put a toxic substance down across a couple of football fields and not have somebody at risk. So we didn't want to create a situation like that. So, in brief, the tank will survive. It will be breached. The hydrazine will reach the ground, and that is not an outcome we want to see.

MEDIA QUESTIONER: Thank you. Can any of you gentlemen put into layman's terms the difficulty in hitting the satellite with one of these tactical missiles?

GENERAL CARTWRIGHT: What you are attempting to do here—correct me if I am wrong, but I think the closing velocities that we are talking about here in rough order of magnitude are about 22,000 miles per hour. So we are at the end of the boost of this missile in a very small box trying to make sure that the sensor can detect the satellite and then maneuver sufficiently to accomplish that intercept. That is a challenge. But I go back to the earlier discussions. We have a missile that is well understood and well known and has a good track record here and a sensor that is part of it. The modifications had been to make it look for something like this satellite in software, and so we have a pretty good idea that we would have a reasonably high opportunity for success, but having said that, we looked at so what happens if we don't or what could be the worst downside. In each case, we really came away with we are better off taking the attempt than not.

Sir, in the back.

MEDIA QUESTIONER: Sir, have you done something similar in the past? This is for the General. How did you brief the international community? Through some organization, or how do you do it?

AMBASSADOR JEFFREY: I will take that. As I said, we have already reached out at the end of January to a large number of nations that do have programs in space to give them an alert. We begin preparing in a national response in the case of the hydrazine coming down as well and alerted our Homeland Security here. What we are doing today is to reach out to the various UN organizations, the UN Headquarters itself, and essentially the entire international community through capitals to let them know more details about the satellite coming down and about our plan to intercept it, and of course, these countries may or may not have comments. They may or may not have supportive statements, and we will see, but we believe in an exchange of information. We believe in keeping them informed, and we believe that we will live up to all of our international obligations in the 1972 and in other treaties.

MEDIA QUESTIONER: As far as the actual dangers of hydrazine, can you help us understand? If you were to inhale it, how quickly would damage be such that you needed hospitalization, and how quickly would damage happen such that you could be at risk of dying?

GENERAL CARTWRIGHT: Very difficult in that it implies that you know what the concentration is, but you could find yourself very close or in a high concentration area, as an example. You are still talking about minutes that you would have to recognize the situation, move yourself, and have enough time to move away from the situation, if you really knew what you were dealing with. The worst scenario is that you have a person who either is not mobile or does not, for whatever reason, sense that they are in danger and, therefore, doesn't take any action, but those variables are very difficult to put minutes or times to.

But we do believe that if you are in this area—and we are talking roughly two football fields—on a standard day with a certain amount of wind—I mean, all of these are calculations that will change with every place on the Earth—that you are at risk to an extent that you will recognize that you are in trouble. You will start to walk to where you feel like you are better off, and you will still need to see a doctor, and that is as close—and if you stay and you are not ambulatory for whatever reason and you stay in a concentrated area, you could eventually get yourself to a point where death would follow.

MEDIA QUESTIONER: Short of death, what would be the other health risks you could have that could happen with short exposure?

GENERAL CARTWRIGHT: Burning sensations, damage to tissue in the lungs.

MEDIA QUESTIONER: Two questions, just to clarify. The Shuttle's schedule will be altered?

ADMINISTRATOR GRIFFIN: No.

MEDIA QUESTIONER: No.

ADMINISTRATOR GRIFFIN: No. The window of engagement is nicely compatible with the nominal end of the Shuttle mission. We expect to have the Shuttle down in the normal course of events, even extending it by a day, as we plan to do, before we need to engage.

MEDIA QUESTIONER: Can you describe what this satellite did, what it was, what its purpose was, why was it up there?

GENERAL CARTWRIGHT: It was a test bird launched by the National Reconnaissance Office. I would direct you towards them. That is as much as I can go into.

MEDIA QUESTIONER: I mean, the question, the reason why I ask is because, as you say, you've read the blogs, and you've read the comments about the classified material aboard. So, presumably, there is some high-level classified information, technology on the satellite.

GENERAL CARTWRIGHT: I will direct you to the National Reconnaissance Office.

MEDIA QUESTIONER: To no extent, this was an answer to the Chinese anti-satellite test? This is not to prove that the U.S. can also do this? That was not part of your consideration?

AMBASSADOR JEFFREY: This is all about trying to reduce the danger to human beings. That was a decision that was taken by the President after listening to all of the technical arguments you have heard today. That was the calculation. Hydrazine equals hazard to human beings, and we tried to do what we could to mitigate it.

GENERAL CARTWRIGHT: But also remember that we did that 20 years ago. There is really no need to go back to that data point, and this is not like that test in technical terms and in terms that talk about the preservation of human life.

MEDIA QUESTIONER: General, can I ask you, on the satellite itself, to be clear, a lot of the taxpayers are going to want to know why did this thing fall within hours? Was this the Lockheed experimental payload satellite?

GENERAL CARTWRIGHT: Again, it wasn't. It is the National Reconnaissance Office's satellite. I direct you to them about its function and its failure mode, other than to tell you there is no power. So it was unresponsive.

MEDIA QUESTIONER: It went into a safe mode because it had a software malfunction?

GENERAL CARTWRIGHT: We don't even know that it is in a safe mode. In other words, it is totally unresponsive. A safe mode implies that you can fly without running into your neighbor, so to speak. This is a totally unresponsive satellite.

MEDIA QUESTIONER: Ambassador Jeffrey, this is a malfunction. This wasn't an act of God or it was up there for years. It was a malfunction shortly after orbit. Is the White House or Pentagon looking at culpability or liability to the contractor on this? Because you are taking extraordinary measures to deal with a flawed bird up in space, and I think taxpayers are going to want to know who is going to get, you know, nailed for this besides the satellite.

AMBASSADOR JEFFREY: For the moment, we are focusing on what is right in front of us, which is to try to mitigate the problems with the hydrazine coming down, and we will continue to review why this happened and what to do about it.

MEDIA QUESTIONER: What about the satellite, sir? Who built this, Lockheed or Boeing?

GENERAL CARTWRIGHT: Sir?

MEDIA QUESTIONER: General, it is our understanding at Space News that the NRO did not recommend that the satellite be destroyed. Is that correct?

GENERAL CARTWRIGHT: Not to my knowledge. They were very much a part of this team. They did much of our analysis on debris and on consequence, contributed largely to understanding what the mechanism would be if we were to intercept and the likelihood of success. I mean, I don't want to speak for them, but they were very much a part of this decision.

MEDIA QUESTIONER: General?

MEDIA QUESTIONER: General?

MEDIA QUESTIONER: General, can you name the three ships that will be involved in this?

GENERAL CARTWRIGHT: I prefer not to.

MEDIA QUESTIONER: Are they the Curtis, [inaudible] the Fitzgerald, and the Shiloh?

GENERAL CARTWRIGHT: I prefer not to.

MEDIA QUESTIONER: [Inaudible] the Curtis, [inaudible] the Fitzgerald, and the Shiloh?

GENERAL CARTWRIGHT: Questions?

MEDIA QUESTIONER: General, if this shot is successful, would it be fair for the international community to regard the Standard Missile now as an anti-satellite-capable weapon, and have you dealt with that issue in the international community already?

GENERAL CARTWRIGHT: A fair question and a good question.

One, this is a modification, yes. In other words, this modification can't coexist with the current configuration. So it is a one-time deal. Does it have the kinetic capability? That is why we picked it, but you would have to go in and do modifications to ships, to missiles, to sensors, and they would be significant. This is an extreme measure for this problem. It would not be transferable to a fleet configuration, so to speak.

MEDIA QUESTIONER: Are you going to have any support of the military international—I mean as a backup or something. Are you going to have the support of some other countries' military just as a backup?

GENERAL CARTWRIGHT: Let me go at it this way. The space network that we use to track assets is an international network, and so from that perspective, people are helping us to make sure that we know what the position, what we would call the "ephemeris data," is because that is a global network of many nations. From the standpoint of the missile itself and the ships, that is in America.

MEDIA QUESTIONER: Could you go back to the second part of my question, though, that I didn't really get an answer to? The international feedback.

GENERAL CARTWRIGHT: I will come back.

MEDIA QUESTIONER: Thanks. The international feedback on whether this is going to be regarded as an ASAT weapon?

MEDIA QUESTIONER: Could you give us some idea of the size of the spacecraft and what the modeling shows, how big the pieces that survive? Will the tank be the biggest, and how big is that?

GENERAL CARTWRIGHT: It is 5,000 pounds, and probably think more along the size of a bus than a pickup truck, the largest piece from the modeling standpoint.

ADMINISTRATOR GRIFFIN: The tank will be the largest intact piece with high confidence. One can never be certain, and the tank is about, what, 40 inches across, something very close to that. It is a spherical tank.

MEDIA QUESTIONER: I'm sorry. I just wanted to see, again, the second part of my question, whether there has been some concern expressed in your diplomatic outreach from any countries about the potential that the Standard Missile could be used again in the future as an ASAT weapon.

AMBASSADOR JEFFREY: We haven't, of course, gotten the feedback yet because we have just gone out today, and I would be very reluctant, over a 30-year career, to predict what one of several hundred countries and international organizations might react to. What I do know is the truth. I know why we are doing this. As explained today, we are very firm in this. We all know why the decision was taken, and we stand by it.

MODERATOR: We will take the last one here.

MEDIA QUESTIONER: Is there an estimated price tag for this operation?

MEDIA QUESTIONER: And the satellite itself?

GENERAL CARTWRIGHT: I would have to go back to the NRO on the satellite. The price tag associated with the missile, if we use one missile, I'd have to go back and dig out the cost, but we have spent about three weeks in modification to software. You would have to kind of calculate the dollars and cents associated with that, but it is an existing round, so we are not off building something new, and we will get you the cost of a Standard Missile.

MEDIA QUESTIONER: I mean the entire operation, not just the missile, but there is a lot of manpower and everything else involved.

MEDIA QUESTIONER: And the satellite, too.

GENERAL CARTWRIGHT: We will come back,

MEDIA QUESTIONER: We are going to call the NRO today, and they are going to blow us off saying it is classified. Can you or Mr. Morrell direct them to give us the name of the contractor and the cost of the satellite roughly? The public deserves an answer on this, since you are taking extraordinary measures to shoot this thing down.

MODERATOR: Your interest is noted, Tony.

All right. Thank you. We appreciate it.

[End of media briefing at the Pentagon on February 14, 2008.]

Source: U.S. Department of Defense Office of the Assistant Secretary of Defense (Public Affairs) "Press Advisories." http://www.defense.gov/advisories/advisory.aspx?advisoryid=2952, Retrieved June 27, 2011.

Discussion Starters

How would you rate General Petraeus' slides for clarity and ease of understanding? In the second example, General Cartwright's comments are much longer than the other two speakers'. If you were the general's speechwriter, how would you suggest to shorten his remarks without reducing their substance? If you were charged with the task of creating visuals for the falling satellite briefing, what kind and how many would you create?

Bibliography

Gamble, Paul R., & Clare E. Kelliher. "Imparting Information and Influencing Behaviour: An Examination of Staff Briefing Sessions." *The Journal of Business Communication* 36, 3 (July 1999):261–279.

The authors conducted an empirical study of a British retailing firm to ascertain the effectiveness of its briefings. Although briefings were considered important in the company, there was much room for improvement in their effectiveness through the introduction of communication training. The authors also provide a fine summary of the literature on business briefings.

Lectures

ASSIGNMENT

Present a ten to fifteen minute lecture about one of the Classical Concepts discussed in this book.

COMMENTARY

A lecture is essentially a form of information speech, usually a long one, forty-five minutes or more. It is a relatively inexpensive and efficient way to convey information to groups of people. The lecture is a more personal means of communication than an essay or online posting because it is delivered in person to a live audience. The medium of a live speaker is intrinsically more interesting and engaging than other forms of communication. Nearly all college-educated persons can remember a teacher they had who was a great lecturer—someone who was interesting, organized, provocative, witty, and altogether unforgettable. We learned from these speakers and aspire to their standard of excellence. However, experienced speakers know that delivering a memorable lecture is much more difficult than it first appears. You might think that someone who knows a lot about a topic should be able to talk about that topic with some degree of success. After all, an expert has a plentiful store of material from which to speak and should do so with confidence. Unfortunately, this is not the case. Superior knowledge does not automatically lead to superior communication. The standard requirements of good speaking apply to lectures—careful preparation, clear organization, engaging delivery, strong introduction and conclusion, and so on. Failing to heed these standards is the most common cause of boring or ineffective lectures.

Lectures can occur in almost any communication setting, but the most common types are academic, public, and commercial lectures.

Academic Lectures

Lectures are probably more common in academic settings than anywhere else. One of the reasons for this is that lectures offer certain advantages over other media.

For one thing, lectures can communicate up to the minute research and information not available in print form. They can also be specifically tailored to particular audiences. For example, in a school of pharmacy, textbook information regarding interpersonal communication can be adapted to the specific challenges faced by pharmacists. In addition, lectures can provide the context and perspective necessary to understand complex readings.[1]

Unfortunately, academic settings are commonly perceived to be where lots of poor lecturing occurs. Many factors contribute to this problem. In the first place, public speaking skill is usually not viewed as a qualification for teaching. As a result, teachers get the same training in public speaking as accountants, engineers, or dentists. In addition, many teachers seem to separate classroom lecturing from public speaking as if they were completely different activities. Finally, there is a danger in giving the same lecture many times. As James Winans points out, "older speakers frequently fall into a perfunctory manner, especially those who speak frequently and in a routine way."[2] The result is a lack of connection with the audience. Most of us have heard lectures where the speaker "covered the material" but did not communicate with the students. These problems are real but not insurmountable. The most important thing teachers can do is view lecturing as public speaking, requiring all the care and attention speaking demands.

Public Lectures

In addition to lectures connected to educational institutions, some business, nonprofit, civic, and other types of organizations sponsor lectures related to their mission and interests. A lecture series may feature an annual presentation over a period of many years. The Royal Institution Christmas Lectures have been held in London every year since they were started by the scientist Michael Faraday in 1825. The lectures have become an annual event in Great Britain with multimedia and interactive features in addition to live audience presentations. American examples would include lecture series sponsored by diverse groups such as the 92nd Street Y in New York City or the annual Erasmus Lecture held by the conservative Institute on Religion and Public Life, also in New York.

Commercial Lectures

What might be called "commercial lecturing" has a long and interesting history in the United States. The Lyceum Movement in the early nineteenth century, followed later by the Chautauqua Movement, helped popularize the paying of admission to hear someone speak. These speeches, like musical concerts or plays, served educational, cultural, and entertainment purposes. A large, vibrant market for paid speakers continues to thrive today. The most popular paid speakers use professional booking agencies to arrange their appearances, often at business meetings and conventions. Frequently these speakers are people who have built

---

[1]Wilbert J. McKeachie et al., *Teaching Tips: Strategies, Research, and Theory for College and University Teachers*, 10th edition, Boston: Houghton Mifflin, 1999, pp. 66–85.

[2]James A. Winans, *Speech-making*, New York: D. Appleton-Century Company, 1938, p. 26.

notable careers in politics, business, or athletics, to name a few, and then take to the lecture circuit when their careers end. A famous example is President Ronald Reagan who, after leaving the White House, created a good deal of controversy for taking huge speaking fees from Japanese companies.

In addition to those who give paid speeches in the wake of a career on which their fame or expertise is built are motivational speakers who are known mostly for their speaking. Motivational speaking as it is currently practiced primarily serves an entertainment function and is marked by several characteristics. Most motivational speakers avoid politically controversial topics. Exhorting people to "unlock their creative potential," for example, is hardly controversial. Who could be against it? Motivational speakers also commonly promote religious inspiration, but with little or no theological content. Finally, this type of speaking relies heavily on tales of "heroic capitalism" in which ordinary people pull themselves up to wealth and celebrity through hard work, providence, and pluck. Frequently the focus of these stories is the speaker himself.

Question and Answer Sessions

Lectures often lend themselves to question and answer (Q&A) sessions. The Q&A session is a good opportunity to interact with the audience, clarify the topic, and leave the audience with a positive feeling toward the speaker and topic. Here are some guidelines for satisfying Q&A sessions.

Prepare. Decide ahead of time if you will have a Q&A time. If you announce it ahead of time, be sure to end your speech in time to accommodate the Q&A session. How long will the Q&A session last? This might be determined by the number of questions allowed or by a set time period. How will questioners be recognized and heard? Will the speaker or the moderator of the meeting recognize questioners? Assistants stationed in the audience and microphones might be needed. To control the situation and provide for appropriate participation, decide on a procedure for fielding questions. Consider the one two rule in which no questioner is permitted to ask a second question until everyone who wants to has been given the chance to ask one question. Will follow-up questions be allowed? Announce these ground rules to the audience at the outset of the question period.

Paraphrase. Before addressing a question, repeat it clearly. This serves several purposes. First, it helps those who may not have clearly heard the question. Second, it clarifies the question and puts you and the questioner on the same page. Paraphrasing also helps you handle the nonquestion question. Sometimes people make a statement under the guise of asking a question. Paraphrasing what was said may help you tease a question out of the statement or in some way affirm the person making the statement without having to deal with the statement. Finally, paraphrasing allows you to defuse hostile questions. Your paraphrase may allow you to control the level of confrontation in the exchange with the questioner. In most, but not all, cases you will probably want to reduce the level of confrontation.

Answer.   Answer, don't evade. If you don't intend to answer questions, then avoid the Q&A session altogether. Some persuaders predetermine a theme or message they want to repeat and emphasize such as, "We need a change." There is nothing wrong with staying on message, but if the answer to every question turns out to be, "We need a change," the message quickly wears thin and damages the speaker's credibility. Your answers should be relevant, short, and directed to the whole audience. Use appropriate eye contact to avoid engaging in a dialogue with the questioner. Finally, if you don't know the answer to a question, say so. Also, be honest with the audience if you are unwilling to discuss a question. This might occur if the answer involves confidential information, leads off-topic, or is too complicated for the time allowed.

End.   If you told the audience you would take ten questions or that the Q&A would last fifteen minutes, then stick with your announcement. If interest is high and you feel like further discussion would be appropriate, offer to continue with questions after the meeting is dismissed.

CLASSICAL CONCEPT: KNOWLEDGE AND ELOQUENCE

In *De Oratore*, Cicero sets up a debate between two prominent Roman lawyers, Crassus and Antonius. Crassus (apparently representing Cicero's own view) argues that, in addition to superior oratorical abilities, a truly eloquent speaker must possess comprehensive knowledge of a host of subjects. He says, "my assertion will be that the complete and finished orator is he who on any matter whatever can speak with fullness and variety" (Book I, 59). Antonius, on the other hand, thinks Crassus impractical, asking too much of an eloquent person. For him, it is enough to combine speaking ability with strong knowledge, not of everything, but of the specific public issue or legal case at hand. He says the comprehensive knowledge Crassus requires "is hard to win," and that the pursuit of it might lead a speaker away from "a style acceptable to the commonalty and suited to advocacy" (I, 81).

Suppose two students, one a freshman and the other a senior, had relatively equal speaking abilities. Does it stand to reason that the senior, with a broader and deeper education, would be more eloquent than the freshman? Or could the freshman be as eloquent as the senior by thoroughly studying the topic or issue at hand? Aside from the topic itself, would the senior's education and knowledge simply make him or her more interesting than the freshman?

Cicero's discussion of the comprehensive knowledge needed to speak eloquently might sound strange to us because we live in an era of intellectual specialization. Focusing our knowledge on ever more narrowly defined topics, however, is a relatively recent phenomenon. Woodrow Wilson's discussion of Adam Smith's lecturing (cited in the bibliography at the end of this chapter) extols Smith for his wide-ranging, comprehensive knowledge. Wilson almost sounds like Crassus when he writes, referring to Smith, "Education and the world of thought need men who, like this man, will dare to know a multitude of things. Without them and their bold synthetic methods, all knowledge and all thought would fall apart into a weak analysis."

EXAMPLES

ACRES OF DIAMONDS
RUSSELL H. CONWELL
1900–1925

Perhaps the most famous lecture in American history is Russell Conwell's, "Acres of Diamonds." The speech was delivered over 5,000 times over a period of years around the turn of the twentieth century. Conwell, a Baptist minister, used the proceeds of the lecture to fund the founding and development of Temple University. The speech is a series of anecdotes all revolving on the themes of self-improvement and success. These are the underlying ideas that form the bedrock of American motivational speaking.

When going down the Tigris and Euphrates rivers many years ago with a party of English travelers I found myself under the direction of an old Arab guide whom we hired up at Baghdad, and I have often thought how that guide resembled our barbers in certain mental characteristics. He thought that it was not only his duty to guide us down those rivers, and do what he was paid for doing, but to entertain us with stories curious and weird, ancient and modern strange, and familiar. Many of them I have forgotten, and I am glad I have, but there is one I shall never forget.

The old guide was leading my camel by its halter along the banks of those ancient rivers, and he told me story after story until I grew weary of his story-telling and ceased to listen. I have never been irritated with that guide when he lost his temper as I ceased listening. But I remember that he took off his Turkish cap and swung it in a circle to get my attention. I could see it through the corner of my eye, but I determined not to look straight at him for fear he would tell another story. But although I am not a woman, I did finally look, and as soon as I did he went right into another story. Said he, "I will tell you a story now which I reserve for my particular friends." When he emphasized the words "particular friends," I listened and I have ever been glad I did. I really feel devoutly thankful, that there are 1,674 young men who have been carried through college by this lecture who are also glad that I did listen.

The old guide told me that there once lived not far from the River Indus an ancient Persian by the name of Ali Hafed. He said that Ali Hafed owned a very large farm; that he had orchards, grain-fields, and gardens; that he had money at interest and was a wealthy and contented man. One day there visited that old Persian farmer one of those ancient Buddhist priests, one of the wise men of the East. He sat down by the fire and told the old farmer how this old world of ours was made.

He said that this world was once a mere bank of fog, and that the Almighty thrust His finger into this bank of fog, and began slowly to move His finger around, increasing the speed until at last He whirled this bank of fog into a solid ball of fire. Then it went rolling through the universe, burning its way through other banks of fog, and condensed the moisture without, until it fell in floods of rain upon its hot surface, and cooled the outward

crust. Then the internal fires bursting outward through the crust threw up the mountains   30
and hills, the valleys, the plains and prairies of this wonderful world of ours. If this internal
molten mass came bursting out and cooled very quickly, it became granite; less quickly
copper, less quickly silver, less quickly gold, and, after gold, diamonds were made. Said
the old priest, "A diamond is a congealed drop of sunlight." Now that is literally scientifi-
cally true, that a diamond is an actual deposit of carbon from the sun.   35

The old priest told Ali Hafed that if he had one diamond the size of his thumb he
could purchase the county, and if he had a mine of diamonds he could place his children upon thrones through the influence of their great wealth. Ali Hafed heard all about
diamonds, how much they were worth, and went to his bed that night a poor man. He
had not lost anything, but he was poor because he was discontented, and discontented   40
because he feared he was poor. He said, "I want a mine of diamonds," and he lay awake
all night. Early in the morning he sought out the priest. I know by experience that a priest
is very cross when awakened early in the morning, and when he shook that old priest out
of his dreams, Ali Hafed said to him:

"Will you tell me where I find diamonds?"   45

"Diamonds! What do you want with diamonds?"

"Why, I wish to be immensely rich."

"Well, then, go along and find them. That is all you have to do; go and find them,
and then you have them."

"But I don't know where to go."   50

"Well, if you will find a river that runs through white sands, between high mountains,
in those white sands you will always find diamonds."

"I don't believe there is any such river."

"Oh yes, there are plenty of them. All you have to do is to go and find them, and
then you have them."   55

Said Ali Hafed, "I will go."

So he sold his farm, collected his money, left his family in charge of a neighbor, and
away he went in search of diamonds. He began his search, very properly to my mind, at
the Mountains of the Moon. Afterward he came around into Palestine, then wandered on
into Europe, and at last when his money was all spent and he was in rags, wretchedness,   60
and poverty, he stood on the shore of that bay at Barcelona, in Spain, when a great tidal
wave came rolling in between the pillars of Hercules, and the poor, afflicted, suffering,
dying man could not resist the awful temptation to cast himself into that incoming tide,
and he sank beneath its foaming crest, never to rise in this life again.

Then after that old guide had told me that awfully sad story, he stopped the camel   65
I was riding on and went back to fix the baggage that was coming off another camel,
and I had an opportunity to muse over his story while he was gone. I remember saying to
myself, "Why did he reserve that story for his 'particular friends'?" There seemed to be
no beginning, no middle, no end, nothing to it.

That was the first story I had ever heard told in my life, and would be the first one   70
I ever read, in which the hero was killed in the first chapter. I had but one chapter of that
story, and the hero was dead. When the guide came back and took up the halter of my

camel, he went right ahead with the story, into the second chapter, just as though there had been no break.

75 The man who purchased Ali Hafed's farm one day led his camel into the garden to drink, and as that camel put its nose into the shallow water of that garden brook, Ali Hafed's successor noticed a curious flash of light from the white sands of the stream. He pulled out a black stone having an eye of light reflecting all the hues of the rainbow. He took the pebble into the house and put it on the mantel which covers the central fires,
80 and forgot all about it.

A few days later this same old priest came in to visit Ali Hafed's successor, and the moment he opened that drawing-room door he saw that flash of light on the mantel, and he rushed up to it, and shouted:

"Here is a diamond! Has Ali Hafed returned?"

85 "Oh no, Ali Hafed has not returned, and that is not a diamond. That is nothing but a stone we found right out here in our own garden."

"But," said the priest, "I tell you I know a diamond when I see it. I know positively that is a diamond."

Then together they rushed out into that old garden and stirred up the white sands
90 with their fingers, and lo! There came up other more beautiful and valuable gems than the first. "Thus," said the guide to me, "was discovered the diamond-mine of Golconda, the most magnificent diamond-mine in all the history of mankind, excelling the Kimberly itself. The Kohinoor, and the Orloff of the crown jewels of England and Russia, the largest on earth, came from that mine."

95 When that old Arab guide told me the second chapter of his story, he then took off his Turkish cap and swung it around in the air again to get my attention to the moral. Those Arab guides have morals to their stories, although they are not always moral. As he swung his hat, he said to me, "Had Ali Hafed remained at home and dug in his own cellar, or underneath his own wheat fields or in his own garden, instead of wretched-
100 ness, starvation, and death by suicide in a strange land, he would have had 'acres of diamonds.' For every acre of that old farm, yes, every shovelful, afterward revealed gems which since have decorated the crowns of monarchs."

When he had added the moral of his story I saw why he reserved it for "his particular friends." But I did not tell him that I could see it. It was that mean old Arab's way of going
105 around a thing like a lawyer, to say indirectly what he did not dare say directly, that "in his private opinion there was a certain young man then traveling down the Tigris River that might better be at home in America." I did not tell him I could see that, but I told it to him quick, and I think I will tell it to you.

I told him of a man out in California in 1847, who owned a ranch. He heard they had
110 discovered gold in southern California, and so with a passion for gold he sold his ranch to Colonel Sutter, and away he went, never to come back. Colonel Sutter put a mill upon a stream that ran through that ranch, and one day his little girl brought some wet sand from the raceway into their home and sifted it through her fingers before the fire, and in that falling sand a visitor saw the first shining scales of real gold that were ever discov-
115 ered in California. The man who had owned that ranch wanted gold, and he could have

secured it for the mere taking. Indeed, thirty-eight millions of dollars has been taken out of a very few acres since then.

About eight years ago I delivered this lecture in a city that stands on that farm, and they told me that a one-third owner for years and years had been getting one hundred and twenty dollars in gold every fifteen minutes, sleeping or waking, without taxation. 120 You and I would enjoy an income like that—if we didn't have to pay an income tax.

But a better illustration really than that occurred here in our town of Pennsylvania. If there is anything I enjoy above another on the platform, it is to get one of these German audiences in Pennsylvania, and fire that at them, and I enjoy it tonight. There was a man living in Pennsylvania, not unlike some Pennsylvanians you have seen, who owned 125 a farm, and he did with that farm just what I should do with a farm if I owned one in Pennsylvania—he sold it. But before he sold it he decided to secure employment collecting coal-oil for his cousin, who was in the business in Canada, where they first discovered oil on this continent. They dipped it from the running streams at that early time. So this Pennsylvania farmer wrote to his cousin asking for employment. You see, friends, 130 this farmer was not altogether a foolish man. No, he was not. He did not leave his farm until he had something else to do. Of all the simpletons the stars shine on I don't know of a worse one than the man who leaves one job before he has gotten another. That has especial reference to my profession, and has no reference whatever to a man seeking a divorce. When he wrote to his cousin for employment, his cousin replied, "I cannot 135 engage you because you know nothing about the oil business." Well, then the old farmer said, "I will know," and with most commendable zeal (characteristic of the students of Temple University) he sat himself at the study of the whole subject. He began away back at the second day of God's creation when this world was covered thick and deep with that rich vegetation which since has turned to the primitive beds of coal. He studied 140 the subject until he found that the drainings really of those rich beds of coal furnished the coal-oil that was worth pumping, and then he found how it came up with the living springs. He studied until he knew what it looked like, smelled like, tasted like, and how to refine it. Now said he in his letter to his cousin, "I understand the oil business." His cousin answered, "All right, come on." 145

So he sold his farm, according to the county record, for $833 (even money, "no cents"). He had scarcely gone from that place before the man who purchased the spot went out to arrange for the watering of the cattle. He found the previous owner had gone out years before and put a plank across the brook back of the barn, edgewise into the surface of the water just a few inches. The purpose of that plank at that sharp angle 150 across the brook was to throw over to the other bank a dreadful-looking scum through which the cattle would not put their noses. But with that plank there to throw it all over to one side, the cattle would drink below, and thus that man who had gone to Canada had been himself damming back for twenty-three years a flood of coal-oil which the state geologists of Pennsylvania declared to us ten years later was even then worth a hundred 155 millions of dollars to our state, a thousand millions of dollars. The man who owned that territory on which the city to Titusville now stands, and those Pleasantville valleys, had studied the subject from the second day of God's creation clear down to the present

160   time. He studied it until he knew all about it, and yet he is said to have sold the whole of it for $833, and again I say, "no sense."

But I need another illustration. I found it in Massachusetts, and I am sorry I did because that is the state I came from. This young man in Massachusetts furnishes just another phase of my thought. He went to Yale College and studied mines and mining, and became such an adept as a mining engineer that he was employed by the authori-
165   ties of the university to train students who were behind their classes. During his senior years he earned $15 a week for doing that work. When he graduated they raised his pay from $15 to $45 a week, and offered him a professorship, as soon as they did he went right home to his mother. If they had raised that boy's pay from $14 to $15.60 he would have stayed and been proud of the place, but when they put it up to $45 at one
170   leap, he said, "Mother, I won't work for $45 a week. The idea of a man with a brain like mine working for $45 a week! Let's go out to California and stake out gold-mines and silver-mines, and be immensely rich." Said his mother, "Now, Charlie, it is just as well to be happy as it is to be rich." "Yes," said Charlie, "But it is just as well to be rich and happy too." And they were both right about it. As he was an only son and she a widow,
175   of course he had his way. They always do.

They sold out in Massachusetts, and instead of going to California they went to Wisconsin, where he went into the employ of the superior Copper Mining Company at $15 a week again, but with the proviso in his contract that he should have an interest in any mines he should discover for the company. I don't believe he ever discovered a
180   mine, and if I am looking in the face of any stockholder of that copper company you wish he had discovered something or other. I have friends who are not here because they could not afford a ticket, who did have stock in that company at the time this young man was employed there. This young man went out there and I have not heard a word from him. I don't know what became of him, and I don't know whether he found any mines or
185   not, but I don't believe he ever did.

But I do know the other end of the line. He had scarcely gotten the other end of the old homestead before the succeeding owner went out to dig potatoes. The potatoes were already growing in the ground when he bought the farm, and as the old farmer was bringing in a basket of potatoes it hugged very tight between the ends of the stone
190   fence. You know in Massachusetts our farms are nearly all stone wall. There you are obliged to be very economical of front gateways in order to have some place to put the stone. When that basket hugged so tight he set it down on the ground, and then dragged on one side, and pulled on the other side, and as he was dragging that basket through this farmer noticed in the upper and outer corner of that stone wall, right next
195   the gate, a block of native silver eight inches square. That professor of mines, mining, and mineralogy who knew so much about the subject that he would not work for $45 a week, when he sold that homestead in Massachusetts sat right on that silver to make the bargain. He was born on that homestead, was brought up there, and had gone back and forth rubbing the stone with his sleeve until it reflected his countenance, and seemed
200   to say, "Here is a hundred thousand dollars right down here just for the taking." But he would not take it. It was in a home in Newburyport, Massachusetts, and there was no

silver there, all away off-well, I don't know where, and he did not, but somewhere else, and he was a professor of mineralogy.

My friends, that mistake is very universally made, and why should we even smile at him. I often wonder what has become of him. I do not know at all, but I will tell you what I "guess" as a Yankee. I guess that he sits out there by his fireside to-night with his friends gathered around him, and he is saying to them something like this: "Do you know that man Conwell who lives in Philadelphia?" "Oh yes, I have heard of him." "Do you know of that man Jones that lives in Philadelphia?" "Yes, I have heard of him, too."

Then he begins to laugh, and shakes his sides, and says to his friends, "Well, they have done just the same thing I did, precisely"—and that spoils the whole joke, for you and I have done the same thing he did, and while we sit here and laugh at him he has a better right to sit out there and laugh at us. I know I have made the same mistakes, but, of course, that does not make any difference, because we don't expect the same man to preach and practice, too.

As I come here to-night and look around this audience I am seeing again what through these fifty years I have continually seen—men that are making precisely that same mistake. I often wish I could see the younger people, and would that the Academy had been filled to-night with our high school scholars and our grammar-school scholars, that I could have them to talk to. While I would have preferred such an audience as that, because they are most susceptible, as they have not gotten into any custom that they cannot break, they have not met with any failures as we have; and while I could perhaps do such an audience as that more good than I can do grown-up people, yet I will do the best I can with the material I have. I say to you that you have "acres of diamonds" in Philadelphia right where you now live. "Oh," but you will say, "you cannot know much about your city if you think there are any 'acres of diamonds' here."

I was greatly interested in that account in the newspaper of the young man who found that diamond in North Carolina. It was one of the purest diamonds that has ever been discovered, and it has several predecessors near the same locality. I went to a distinguished professor in mineralogy and asked him where he thought those diamonds came from. The professor secured the map of the geologic formations of our continent, and traced it. He said it went either through the underlying carboniferous strata adapted for such production, westward through Ohio and the Mississippi, or in more probability came eastward through Virginia and up the shore of the Atlantic Ocean. It is a fact that the diamonds were there, for they have been discovered and sold; and that they were carried down there during the drift period, from some northern locality. Now who can say but some person going down with his drill in Philadelphia will find some trace of a diamond-mine yet down here? Oh, friends! You cannot say that you are not over one of the greatest diamond-mines in the world, for such a diamond as that only comes from the most profitable mines that are found on earth.

But it serves simply to illustrate my thought, which I emphasize by saying if you do not have the actual diamond-mines literally you have all that they would be good for to you. Because now that the Queen of England has given the greatest compliment ever conferred upon American woman for her attire because she did not appear with any

245   jewels at all at the late reception in England, it has almost done away with the use of diamonds anyhow. All you would care for would be the few you would wear if you wish to be modest, and the rest of you would sell for money.

      Now then, I say again that the opportunity to get rich, to attain unto great wealth, is here in Philadelphia now, within the reach of almost every man and woman who hears

250   me speak to-night, and I mean just what I say. I have not come to this platform even under these circumstances to recite something to you. I have come to tell you what in God's sight I believe to be the truth, and if the years of life have been of any value to me in the attainment of common sense, I know I am right; that the men and women sitting here, who found it difficult perhaps to buy a ticket to this lecture or gathering to-night,

255   have within their reach "acres of diamonds," opportunities to get largely wealthy. There never was a place on earth more adapted than the city of Philadelphia to-day, and never in the history of the world did a poor man without capital have such an opportunity to get rich quickly and honestly as he has now in our city. I say it is the truth, and I want you to accept it as such; for if you think I have come to simply recite something, then

260   I would better not be here. I have no time to waste in any such talk, but to say the things I believe, and unless some of you get richer for what I am saying to night my time is wasted.

      I say that you ought to get rich, and it is our duty to get rich. How many of my pious brethren say to me, "Do you, a Christian minister, spend your time going up and

265   down the country advising young people to get rich, to get money?" "Yes, of course I do." They say, "Isn't that awful! Why don't you preach the gospel instead of preaching about man's making money?" "Because to make money honestly is to preach the gospel." That is the reason. The men who get rich may be the most honest men you find in the community. "Oh," but says some young man here to-night, "I have been told all

270   my life that if a person has money he is very dishonest and dishonorable and mean and contemptible."

      My friend, that is the reason why you have none, because you have that idea of people. The foundation of your faith is altogether false. Let me say here clearly, and say it briefly, though subject to discussion which I have not time for here, ninety-eight out of

275   one hundred of the rich men of America are honest. That is why they are rich. That is why they carry on great enterprises and find plenty of people to work with them. It is because they are honest men.

      Says another young man, "I hear sometimes of men that get millions of dollars dishonestly." Yes, of course you do, and so do I. But they are so rare a thing in fact that the

280   newspapers talk about them all the time as a matter of news until you get the idea that all the other rich men got rich dishonestly.

      My friend, you take and drive me—if you furnish the auto—out into the suburbs of Philadelphia, and introduce me to the people who own their homes around this great city, those beautiful homes with gardens and flowers, those magnificent homes so lovely

285   in their art, and I will introduce you to the very best people in character as well as in enterprise in our city, and you know I will. A man is not really a true man until he owns his own home, and they that own their homes are made more honorable and honest and pure, true and economical and careful, by owning the home.

For a man to have money, even in large sum, is not an inconsistent thing. We preach against covetousness, and you know we do, in the pulpit, and oftentimes preach against it so long and use the terms about "filthy lucre" so extremely that Christians get the idea that when we stand in the pulpit we believe it is wicked for any man to have money—until the collection-basket goes around, and then we almost swear at the people because they don't give more money. Oh, the inconsistency of such doctrines as that!

290

Money is power, and you ought to be reasonably ambitious to have it. You ought because you can do more good with it than you could without it. Money printed your Bible, money builds your churches, money sends your missionaries, and money pays your preachers, and you would not have many of them, either, if you did not pay them. I am always willing that my church should raise my salary, because the church that pays the largest salary always raises it the easiest. You never knew an exception to it in your life. The man who gets the largest salary can do the most good with the power that is furnished to him. Of course he can if his spirit be right to use it for what it is given to him.

295

300

I say, then, you ought to have money. If you can honestly attain unto riches in Philadelphia, it is our Christian and godly duty to do so. It is an awful mistake of these pious people to think you must be awfully poor in order to be pious.

305

Some men say, "Don't you sympathize with the poor people?" of course I do, or else I would not have been lecturing these years. I won't give in but what I sympathize with the poor, but the number of poor who are to be with is very small. To sympathize with a man whom God has punished for his sins, thus to help him when God would still continue a just punishment, is to do wrong, no doubt about it, and we do that more than we help those who are deserving. While we should sympathize with God's poor—that is, those who cannot help themselves—let us remember that is not a poor person in the United States who was not made poor by his own shortcomings, or by the shortcomings of some one else. It is all wrong to be poor, anyhow. Let us give in to that argument and pass that to one side.

310

315

A gentleman gets up back there, and says, "Don't you think there are some things in this world that are better than money?" Of course I do, but I am talking about money now. Of course there are some things higher than money. Oh yes, I know by the grave that has left me standing alone that there are some things in this world that are higher and sweeter and purer than money. Well do I know there are some things higher and grander than gold. Love is the grandest thing on God's earth, but fortunate the lover who has plenty of money. Money is power, money is force, money will do good as harm. In the hands of good men and women it could accomplish, and it has accomplished, good.

320

I hate to leave that behind me. I heard a man get up in a prayer-meeting in our city and thank the Lord he was "one of God's poor." Well, I wonder what his wife thinks about that? She earns all the money that comes into that house, and he smokes a part of that on the veranda. I don't want to see any more of the Lord's poor of that kind, and I don't believe the Lord does. And yet there are some people who think in order to be pious you must be awfully poor and awfully dirty. That does not follow at all. While we sympathize with the poor, let us not teach a doctrine like that.

325

330

Yet the age is prejudiced against advising a Christian man (or, as a Jew would say, a godly man) from attaining unto wealth. The prejudice is so universal and the years are

far enough back, I think, for me to safely mention that years ago up at Temple University there was a young man in our theological school who thought he was the only pious stu-
335 dent in that department. He came into my office one evening and sat down by my desk, and said to me: "Mr. President, I think it is my duty sir, to come in and labor with you." "What has happened now?" Said he, "I heard you say at the Academy, at the Pierce School commencement, that you thought it was an honorable ambition for a young man to desire to have wealth, and that you thought it made him temperate, made him anxious
340 to have a good name, and made him industrious. You spoke to make him a good man. Sir, I have come to tell you the Holy Bible says that 'money is the root of all evil.'" I told him I had never seen it in the Bible, and advised him to go out into the chapel and get the Bible, and show me the place. So out he went for the Bible, and soon he stalked into my office with the Bible open, with all the bigoted pride of the narrow sectarian, of one
345 who founds his Christianity on some misinterpretation of Scripture. He flung the Bible down on my desk, and fairly squealed into my ear: "There it is Mr. President; you can read it yourself." I said to him: "Well young man, you will learn when you get a little older that you cannot trust another denomination to read the Bible for you. You belong to another denomination. You are taught in the theological school, however, that emphasis
350 is the exegesis. Now, will you take that Bible and read it yourself, and give the proper emphasis to it?"

He took the Bible, and proudly read, "The love of money is the root of all evil." Then he had it right, and when one does quote aright from that same old Book he quotes the absolute truth. I have lived through fifty years of the mightiest battle that old Book has
355 ever fought, and I have lived to see its banners flying free; for never in the history of this world did the great minds of earth so universally agree that the Bible is true-all true-as they do at this very hour.

So I say that when he quoted right, of course he quoted the absolute truth. "The love of money is the root of all evil." He who tries to attain unto it too quickly, or dishon-
360 estly, will fall into many snares, no doubt about that. The love of money. What is that? It is making an idol of money, and idolatry pure and simple everywhere is condemned by the Holy Scriptures and by man's common sense. The man that worships the dollar instead of thinking of the purposes for which it ought to be used, the man who idolizes simply money, the miser that hordes his money in the cellar, or hides it in his staking, or
365 refuses to invest it where it will do the world good, that man who hugs the dollar until the eagle squeals has in him the root of all evil.

I think I will leave that behind me now and answer the question of nearly all of you who are asking, "Is there opportunity to get rich in Philadelphia?" Well, now, how simple a thing it is to see where it is, and the instant you see where it is it is yours. Some old
370 gentleman gets up back there and says, "Mr. Conwell, have you lived in Philadelphia for thirty-one years and don't know that the time has gone by when you can make anything in this city?" "No, I don't think it is." "Yes, it is; I have tried it."

"What business are you in?" "I kept a store here for twenty years, and never made a thousand dollars in the whole twenty years." "Well, then, you can measure the good
375 you have been to this city by what this city has paid you, because a man can judge very

well what he is worth by what he receives, that is, in what he is to the world at this time. If you have not made over a thousand dollars in twenty years in Philadelphia, it would have been better for Philadelphia if they had kicked you out of the city nineteen years and nine months ago. A man has no right to keep a store in Philadelphia twenty years and not make at least five hundred thousand dollars, even thought it be a corner grocery-up-town." You say, "You cannot make five hundred thousand dollars in a store now." Oh, my friends, if you will just take only four blocks around you, and find out what the people want and what you ought to supply them, you would very soon see it. There is wealth right within the sound of your voice. 380

Some one says: "You don't know anything about business. A preacher never knows a thing about business." Well, then I will have to prove that I am an expert. I don't like to do this, but I have to do it because my testimony will not be taken if I am not an expert. My father kept a country store, and if there is any place under the stars where a man gets all sorts of experience in every kind of mercantile transactions, it is in the country store. I am not proud of my experience, but sometimes when my father was away he would leave me in charge of the store, thought fortunately for him that was not very often. But this did occur many times, friends: A man would come onto the store, and say to me, "Do you keep jack-knives?" "No we don't keep jack-knives," and I went off whistling a tune. What did I care about that man, anyhow? 385 390

Then another farmer would come in and say, "Do you keep jack-knives?" "No, we don't keep jack-knives." Then I went away and whistled another tune. Then a third man came right in the same door and said, "Do you keep jack-knives?" "No. Why is every one around here asking for jack-knives? Do you suppose we are keeping this store to supply the whole neighborhood with jack-knives?" Do you carry on your store like that in Philadelphia? The difficulty was I had not then learned that the foundation of godliness and the foundation principle of success in business are both the same precisely. The man who says, "I cannot carry my religion into business" advertises himself either as being an imbecile in business, or on the road to bankruptcy, or a thief, one of the three, sure. He will fail within a very few years. He certainly will if he doesn't carry his religion into business. If I had been carrying on my father's store on a Christian plan, godly plan, I would have had a jack-knife for the third man when he called for it. Then I would have actually done him a kindness, and I would have received a reward myself, which it would have been my duty to take. 395 400 405

There are some over-pious Christian people who think if you take any profit on anything you sell that you are an unrighteous man. On the contrary, you would be a criminal to sell goods for less than they cost. You have no right to do that. You cannot trust a man with your money who cannot take care of his own. You cannot trust a man in your family that is not true to his wife. You cannot trust a man in the world that does not begin with his own heart, his own character, and his own life. It would have been my duty to have furnished a jack-knife to the third man, or to the second, and to have sold it to him and actually profited myself. I have no more right to sell goods without making a profit on them than I have to overcharge him dishonestly beyond what they are worth. But I should so sell each bill of goods that the person to whom I sell shall make as much as I make. 410 415

To live and let live is the principle of the gospel, and the principle of every-day com-
420 mon sense. Oh, young man, hear me; live as you go along. Do not wait until you have
reached my years before you begin to enjoy anything of this life. If I had the millions
back, of fifty cents of it, which I have tried to earn in these years, it would not do me anything like the good that it does me now in this almost sacred presence to-night. Oh, yes,
I am paid over and over a hundredfold to-night for dividing as I have tried to do in some
425 measure as I went along through the years. I ought not to speak that way, it sounds egotistic, but I am old enough now to be excused for that. I should have helped my fellow-
men, which I have tried to do, and everyone should try to do, and get the happiness of it.
The man who goes home with the sense that he has stolen a dollar that day, that he has
robbed a man of what was his honest due, is not going home to sweet rest. He arises
430 tired in the morning, and goes with an unclean conscience to his work the next day. He
is not a successful man at all, although he may have laid up millions. But the man who
has gone through life dividing always with his fellow-men, making and demanding his
own rights and his own profits, and giving to every other man his rights and profits, lives
every day, and not only that, but it is the royal road to great wealth. The history of the
435 thousands of millionaires shows that to be the case.

Then man over there who said he could not make anything in a store in Philadelphia
has been carrying on his store on the wrong principle. Suppose I go into your store
to-morrow morning and ask, "Do you know a neighbor A, who lives one square away, at
house No. 1240?" "Oh yes, I have met him. He deals here at the corner store." "Where
440 did he come from?" "I don't know." "How many does he have in his family?" "I don't
know." "What ticket does he vote?" "I don't know." "What church does he go to?"
"I don't know, and don't care. What are you asking all these questions for?"

If you had a store in Philadelphia would you answer me like that? If so, then you
are conducting your business just as I carried on my father's business in Worthington,
445 Massachusetts. You don't know where your neighbor came from when he moved to
Philadelphia, and you don't care. If you had cared you would be rich by now. If you had
cared enough about him to take an interest in his affairs, to find out what he needed, you
would have been rich. But you go through the world saying, "No opportunity to get rich,"
and there is the fault right at your door.

450 But another young man gets up over there and says, "I cannot take the mercantile
business" (While I am talking of trade it applies to every occupation.), "Why can't you go
into the mercantile business?" "Because I haven't any capital." Oh, the weak and dudish
creature that can't see over its collar! It makes a person weak to see these little dudes
standing around the corners and saying, "Oh, if I had plenty of capital, how rich would I
455 get." "Young man, do you think you are going to get rich on capital?" "Certainly." Well,
I say, "Certainly not." If your mother has plenty of money, and she will set you up in business, you will "set her up in business," supplying you with capital.

The moment a young man or woman gets more money than he or she has grown to
by practical experience, that moment he has gotten a curse. It is no help to a young man or
460 woman to inherit money. It is no help to your children to leave them money, but if you leave
them education, if you leave them Christian and noble character, if you leave them a wide

circle of friends, if you leave them an honorable name, it is far better than that they should have money. It would be worse for them, worse for the nation, that they should have any money at all. Oh, young man, if you have inherited money, don't regard it as a help. It will curse you through your years, and deprive you of the very best things of human life. There 465
is no class of people to be pitied so much as the inexperienced sons and daughters of the rich of our generation. I pity the rich man's son. He can never know the best things in life.

One of the best things in our life is when a young man has earned his own living, and when he becomes engaged to some lovely young woman, and makes up his mind to have a home of his own. Then with that same love comes also that divine inspiration 470
toward better things, and he begins to save his money. He begins to leave off his bad habits and put money in the bank. When he has a few hundred dollars he goes out in the suburbs to look for a home. He goes to the savings-bank, perhaps, for half of the value, and then goes for his wife, and when he takes his bride over the threshold of that door for the first time he says in words of eloquence my voice can never touch: "I have earned 475
this home myself. It is all mine, and I divide with thee." That is the grandest moment a human heart may ever know.

But a rich man's son can never know that. He takes his bride into a finer mansion, it may be, but he is obliged to go all the way through it and say to his wife, "My mother gave me that, my mother gave me that, and my mother gave me this," until his wife 480
wishes she had married his mother. I pity the rich man's son.

The statistics of Massachusetts showed that not one rich man's son out of seventeen ever dies rich. I pity the rich man's sons unless they have the good sense of the elder Vanderbilt, which sometimes happens. He went to his father and said, "Did you earn all your money?" "I did, my son. I began to work on a ferry-boat for twenty-five 485
cents a day." "Then," said his son, "I will have none of your money," and he, too, tried to get employment on a ferry-boat that Saturday night. He could not get one there, but he did get a place for three dollars a week. Of course, if a rich man's son will do that, he will get the discipline of a poor boy that is worth more than a university education to any man. He would then be able to take care of the millions of his father. But as a rule the 490
rich men will not let their sons do the very thing that made them great. As a rule, the rich man will not allow his son to work—and his mother! Why, she would think it was a social disgrace if her poor, weak, little lily-fingered, sissy sort of a boy had to earn his living with honest toil. I have no pity for such rich men's sons.

I remember one at Niagara Falls. I think I remember one a great deal nearer. I think 495
there are gentlemen present who were at a great banquet, and I beg pardon of his friends. At a banquet here in Philadelphia there sat beside me a kind-hearted young man, and he said, "Mr. Conwell, you have been sick for two or three years. When you go out, take my limousine, and it will take you up to your house on Broad Street." I thanked him very much, and perhaps I ought not to mention the incident in this way, but I follow the facts. 500
I got on to the seat with the driver of that limousine, outside, and when we were going up I asked the driver, "How much did this limousine cost?" "Six thousand eight hundred, and he had to pay the duty on it." "Well," I said, "does the owner of this machine ever drive it himself?" At that the chauffeur laughed so heartily that he lost control of

505 his machine. He was so surprised at the question that he ran up on the sidewalk, and around a corner lamp-post into the street again.

And when he got into the street he laughed till the whole machine trembled. He said: "He drive this machine! Oh, he would be lucky if he knew enough to get out when we get there."

510 I must tell you about a rich man's son at Niagara Falls. I came in from the lecture to the hotel, and as I approached the desk of the clerk there stood a millionaire's son from New York. He was an indescribable specimen of anthropologic potency. He had a skull-cap on one side of his head, with a gold tassel in the top of it, and a gold-headed cane under his arm with more in it than in his head. It is a very difficult thing to describe

515 that young man. He wore an eye-glass that he could not see through, patent-leather boots that he could not walk in, and pants that he could not sit down in-dressed like a grasshopper. This human cricket came up to the clerk's desk just as I entered, adjusted his unseeing eye-glass, and spake in this wise to the clerk. You see, he thought it was "Hinglish, you know," to lisp. "Thir, will you have the kindness to supply me with thome

520 papah and enwelophs!" The hotel clerk measured the man quick, and he pulled the envelopes and paper out of a drawer, threw them across the counter toward the young man, and then turned away to his books. You should have seen that young man when those envelopes came across that counter.

He swelled up like a gobbler turkey, adjusted his unseeing eye-glass, and yelled:

525 "Come right back here. Now, thir, will you order a thervant to take that papah and enwelophs to yondah dethk." Oh, the poor, miserable, contemptible American monkey! He could not carry paper and envelopes twenty feet. I suppose he could not get his arms down to do it. I have no pity for such travesties upon human nature. If you have not capital, young man, I am glad of it. What you need is common sense, not copper cents.

530 The best thing I can do is to illustrate by actual facts well known to you all. A.T. Stewart, a poor boy in New York, had $1.50 to begin life on. He lost 87 ½ cents of that on the very first venture. How fortunate that young man who loses the first time he gambles. That boy said, "I will never gamble again in business," and he never did.

How came he to lose 87 ½ cents? You probably all know the story how he lost

535 it—because he bought some needles, threads, and buttons to sell which people did not want, and had them left on his hands, a dead loss. Said the boy, "I will not lose any more money in that way." Then he went around first to the doors and asked the people what they did want. Then when he had found out what they wanted he invested his 62 ½ cents to supply a known demand. Study it wherever you choose-in business, in your

540 profession, in your housekeeping, whatever your life, that one thing is the secret of success. You must first know the demand. You must first know what people need, and then invest yourself where you are most needed. A.T. Stewart went on that principle until he was worth what amounted afterward to forty millions of dollars, owning the very store in which Mr. Wanamaker carries on his great work in New York.

545 His fortune was made by his losing something, which taught him the great lesson that he must only invest himself or his money in something that people need. When will you salesmen learn it? When will you manufactures learn that you must know the

changing needs of humanity if you would succeed in life? Apply yourselves, all you Christian people, as manufactures or merchants or workmen to supply that human need. It is a great principle as broad as humanity and as deep as the Scripture itself. 550

The best illustration I ever heard was of John Jacob Astor. You know that he made the money of the Astor family when he lived in New York. He came across the sea in debt for his fare. But that poor boy with nothing in his pocket made the fortune of the Astor family on one principle. Some young man here to-night will say, "Well, they could make these over in New York, but they could not do it in Philadelphia!" My friends, 555 did you ever read that wonderful book of Riss (his memory is sweet to us because of his recent death), wherein is given his statistical account of the records taken in 1889 of 107 millionaires of New York. If you read the account you will see that out of the 107 millionaires only seven made their money in New York. Out of the 107 millionaires worth ten million dollars in real estate then, 67 of them made their money in towns of less 560 than 3,500 inhabitants. The richest man in this country to-day, if you read the real-estate values, has never moved away from a town of 3,500 inhabitants.

It makes not so much difference where you are as who you are. But if you cannot get rich in Philadelphia you certainly cannot do it in New York. Now John Jacob Astor illustrated what can be done anywhere. He had a mortgage once on a millinery-store, 565 and they could not sell bonnets enough to pay the interest on his money. So he foreclosed that mortgage, took possession of the store, and went in to partnership with the very same people, in the very same store, with the same capital. He did not give them a dollar of capital. They had to sell goods to get any money. Then he left them alone in the store just as they had been before, and he went out and sat down on a bench in the park 570 in the shade. What was John Jacob Astor doing out there, and in partnership with people who had failed on his own hands? Had the most important and, to my mind, the most pleasant part of that partnership on his hands. For as John Jacob Astor sat on that bench he was watching the ladies as they went by; and where is the man who would not get rich at that business? As he sat on the bench if a lady passed him with her shoulders back and 575 head up, and looked straight to the front, as if she did not care if all the world did gaze on her, then he studied her bonnet, and by the time it was out of sight he know the shape of the frame, the color of the trimmings, and the crinklings in the feather. I sometimes try to describe a bonnet, but not always. I would not try to describe a modern bonnet.

Where is the man that could describe one? This aggregation of all sorts of driftwood 580 stuck on the back of the head, or the side of the neck, like a rooster with only one tail feather left. But in John Jacob Astor's day there was some art about the millinery business, and he went to the millinery-store and said to them: "Now put into the show-window just such a bonnet as I describe to you, because I have already seen a lady who likes such a bonnet. Don't make up any more until I come back." Then he went out and 585 sat down again, and another lady passed him of a different form, of a different complexion, with a different shape and color of bonnet. "Now," said he, "put such a bonnet as that in the show-window." He did not fill his show-window up-town with a lot of hats and bonnets to drive people away, and then sit on the back stairs and bawl because people went to Wanamaker's to trade. He did not have a hat or a bonnet in that show-window 590

but what some lady liked before it was made up. The tide of custom began immediately to turn in, and that has been the foundation of the greatest store in New York in that line, and still exists as one of three stores. Its fortune was made by John Jacob Astor after they had failed in business, not by giving them any more money, but by finding out what
595   the ladies liked for bonnets before they wasted any material in making them up. I tell you if a man could foresee the millinery business he could foresee anything under heaven!

Suppose I were to go through this audience to-night and ask you in this great manufacturing city if there are not opportunities to get rich in manufacturing. "Oh yes, "some young man says, "there are opportunities here still if you build with some trust and if you
600   have two or three millions of dollars to begin with as capital." Young man, the history of the breaking up of the trusts by that attack upon "big business" is only illustrating what is now the opportunity of the smaller man. The time never came in the history of the world when you could get rich so quickly manufacturing without capital as you can now.

But you will say, "You cannot do anything of the kind. You cannot start without capi-
605   tal." Young man, let me illustrate for a moment. I must do it. It is my duty to every young man, and woman, because we are all going into business very soon on the same plan. Young man, remember if you know what people need you have gotten more knowledge of a fortune than any amount of capital can give you.

There was a poor man out of work living in Hingham, Massachusetts. He lounged
610   around the house until one day his wife told him to get out and work, and, as he lived in Massachusetts, he obeyed his wife. He went out and sat down on the shore of the bay, and whittled a soaked shingle into a wooden chain. His children that evening quarreled over it, and he whittled a second one to keep peace. While he was whittling the second one a neighbor came in and said: "Why don't you whittle toys and sell them? You could
615   make money doing that." "Oh," he said, "I would not know what to make." "Why don't you ask your own children right here in your own house what to make?" "What is the use of trying that?" said the carpenter. "My children are different from other people's children." (I used to see people like that when I taught school.) But he acted upon the hint, and the next morning when Mary came down the stairway, he asked, "What do you
620   want for a toy?" She began to tell him she would like a doll's bed, a doll's washstand, and went on with a list of things that would take him a lifetime to supply. So, consulting his own children, in his own house, he took the firewood, for he had no money to buy lumber, and whittled those strong, unpainted Hingham toys that were that were for so many years known all over the world. That man began to make those toys for his own
625   children, and then made copies and sold them through the boot-and-shoe store next door. He began to make a little money, and then a little more, and Mr. Lawson, in his Frenzied Finance says that man is the richest man in old Massachusetts, and I think it is the truth. And that man is worth a hundred millions of dollars to-day, and has been only thirty-four years making it on that one principle—that one must judge that what his own
630   children like at home other people's children would like in their homes, too; to judge the human heart by oneself, by one's wife or by one's children. It is the royal road to success in manufacturing.

"Oh," But you say, "didn't he have any capital?" Yes, a penknife, but I don't know that he had paid for that.

I spoke thus to an audience in New Britain, Connecticut, and a lady four seats back 635
went home and tried to take off her collar, and the collar-button stuck in the buttonhole.
She threw it out and said, "I am going to get up something better than that to put on col-
lars." Her husband said: "After what Conwell said to-night, you see there is a need of an
improved collar-fastener that is easier to handle. There is a human need; there is a great
fortune. Now, then, get up a collar-button and get rich." He made fun of her, and conse- 640
quently made fun of me, and that is one of the saddest things which comes over me like
a deep cloud of midnight sometimes—although I have worked so hard for more than half
a century, yet how little I have ever really done. Notwithstanding the greatness and the
handsomeness of your compliment to-night, I do not believe there is one in ten of you
that is going to make a million of dollars because you are here to-night; but it is not my 645
fault, it is yours. I say that sincerely. What is the use of my talking if people never do what
I advise them to do? When her husband ridiculed her, she made up her mind she would
make a better collar-button, and when a woman makes up her mind "she will," and does
not say anything about it, she does it. It was that New England woman who invented the
snap button which you can find anywhere now. It was a collar-button with a spring cap 650
attached to the outer side. Any of you who wear modern waterproofs know the button
that simply pushes together, and when you unbutton it you simply pull it apart. That is
the button to which I refer, and which she invented. She afterward invented several other
buttons, and then invested in more, and then was taken into partnership with great fac-
tories. Now that woman goes over the sea every summer in her private steamship—yes, 655
and takes her husband with her! If her husband were to die, she would have money
enough to buy a foreign duke or count or some such title as that at the latest quotations.

Now what is my lesson in that incident? It is this: I told her then, though I did not
know her, what I say to you, "Your wealth is too near to you. You are looking right over
it"; and she had to look over it because it was right under her chin. 660

I have read in the newspaper that a woman never invented anything. Well, that newspaper ought to begin again. Of course, I do not refer to gossip—I refer to machines—and
if I did I might better include the men. That newspaper could never appear if women had
not invented something. Friends, think. Ye women, think! You say you cannot make a
fortune because you are in some laundry, or running a sewing-machine it may be, or 665
walking before some loom, and yet you can be a millionaire if you will but follow this
almost infallible direction.

When you say a woman doesn't invent anything, I ask, Who invented the Jacquard
loom that wove every stitch you wear? Mrs. Jacquard. The printer's roller, the printing
press, was invented by farmers' wives. Who invented the cotton-gin of the South that 670
enriched our country so amazingly? Mrs. General Green invented the cotton gin and
showed the idea to Mr. Whitney, and he like a man, seized it. Who was it that invented
the sewing-machine? If I would go to school tomorrow and ask your children they would
say, "Elias Howe."

He was in the Civil War with me, and often in my tent, and I often heard him say that 675
he worked fourteen years to get up that sewing-machine. But his wife made up her mind
one day they would starve to death if there wasn't something or other invented pretty
soon, and so in two hours she invented the sewing-machine. Of course he took out the

680 patent in his name. Men always do that. Who was it that invented the mower and the reaper? According to Mr. McCormick's confidential communication, so recently published, it was a West Virginia woman, who, after his father and he had failed altogether in making a reaper and gave it up, took a lot of shears and nailed them together on the edge of a board, with one shaft of each pair loose, and then wired them so that when she pulled the wire the other way it opened them, and there she had the principle of the

685 mowing-machine. If you look at a mowing-machine, you will see it is nothing but a lot of shears. If a woman can invent a mowing-machine, if a woman can invent a Jacquard loom, if a woman can invent a cotton-gin, if a woman can invent a trolley switch—as she did and made the trolleys possible; if a woman can invent, as Mr. Carnegie said, the great iron squeezers that laid the foundation of all the steel millions of the United States, "we

690 men" can invent anything under the stars! I say that for the encouragement of the men.

Who are the great inventors of the world? Again this lesson comes before us. The great inventor sits next to you, or you are the person yourself. "Oh," but you will say, "I have never invented anything in my life." Neither did the great inventors until they discovered one great secret. Do you think that it is a man with a head like a bushel

695 measure or a man like a stroke of lightning? It is neither. The really great man is a plain, straightforward, every-day, common-sense man. You would not dream that he was a great inventor if you did not see something he had actually done. His neighbors do not regard him so great.

You never see anything great over your back fence. You say there is no greatness

700 among your neighbors. It is all away off somewhere else. Their greatness is ever so simple, so plain, so earnest, so practical, that the neighbors and friends never recognize it.

True greatness is often unrecognized. That is sure. You do not know anything about the greatest men and women. I went out to write the life of General Garfield, and a neighbor, knowing I was in a hurry, and as there was a great crowd around the front door, took

705 me around to General Garfield's back door and shouted, "Jim! Jim!" And very soon "Jim" came to the door and let me in, and I wrote the biography of one of the grandest men of the nation, and yet he was just the same old "Jim" to his neighbor. If you know a great man in Philadelphia and you should meet him to-morrow, you would say, "How are you, Sam?" or "Good morning, Jim." Of course you would. That is just what you would do.

710 One of my soldiers in the Civil War had been sentenced to death, and I went up to the White House in Washington—sent there for the first time in my life—to see the President. I went into the waiting-room and sat down with a lot of others on the benches, and the secretary asked one after another to tell him what they wanted. After the secretary had been through the line, he went in, and then came back to the door and motioned

715 for me. I went up to that anteroom, and the secretary said: "That is the President's door right over there. Just rap on it and go right in." I was never so taken aback, friends, in all my life, never. The secretary himself made it worse for me, because he had told me how to go in and then went out another door to the left and shut that. There I was, in the hallway by myself before the President of the United States of America's door. I had

720 been on fields of battle, where the shells did sometimes shriek and the bullets did sometimes hit me, but I always wanted to run. I have no sympathy with the old man who says,

"I would just as soon march up into the cannon's mouth as eat my dinner." I have no faith in a man who doesn't know enough to be afraid when he is being shot at. I never was so afraid when the shells came around us at Antietam as I was when I went into that room that day; but I finally mustered the courage—I don't know how I ever did—and at arm's length tapped on the door. The man inside did not help me at all, but yelled out, "Come in and sit down!"

Well, I went in and sat down on the edge of a chair, and wished I were in Europe, and the man at the table did not look up. He was one of the world's greatest men, and was made great by one single rule. Oh, that all the young people of Philadelphia were before me now and I could say just this one thing, and that they would remember it. I would give a lifetime for the effect it would have on our city and on civilization. Abraham Lincoln's principle for greatness can be adopted by nearly all. This was his rule: Whatsoever he had to do at all, he put his whole mind in to it and held it and held it all there until that was all done. That makes men great almost anywhere. He stuck to those papers at that table and did not look up at me, and I sat there trembling. Finally, when he put the string around his papers, he pushed them over to one side and looked over at me, and a smile came over his worn face. He said: "I am a very busy man and have only a few minutes to spare. Now tell me in the fewest words what it is you want." I began to tell him, and mentioned the case, and he said: "I have heard all about it and you do not need to say any more. Mr. Stanton was talking to me only a few days ago about that. You can go to the hotel and rest assured that the President never did sign an order to shoot a boy under twenty years of age, and never will. You can say that to his mother anyhow."

Then he said to me, "How is it going in the field?" I said, "We sometimes get discouraged." And he said: "It is all right. We are going to win out now. We are getting very near the light. No man ought to wish to be President of the United States, and I will be glad when I get through; the Tad and I are going out to Springfield, Illinois. I have bought a farm out there and I don't care if I again earn only twenty-five cents a day. Tad has a mule team, and we are going to plant onions."

Then he asked me, "Were you brought up on a farm?" I said, "Yes; in the Berkshire Hills of Massachusetts." He then threw his leg over the corner of the big chair and said, "I have heard many a time, ever since I was young, that up there in those hills you have to sharpen the noses of the sheep in order to get down to the grass between the rocks." He was so familiar, so everyday, so farmer-like, that I felt right at home with him at once.

He then took hold of another roll of paper, and looked up at me and said, "Good morning." I took the hint then and got up and went out. After I had gotten out I could not realize I had seen the President of the United States at all. But a few days later, when still in the city, I saw the crowd pass through the East Room by the coffin of Abraham Lincoln, and when I looked at the upturned face of the murdered President I felt then that the man I had seen such a short time before, who, so simple a man, so plain a man, was one of the greatest men that God ever raised up to lead a nation on to ultimate liberty. Yet he was only "Old Abe" to his neighbors. When they had the second funeral, I was invited among others, and went out to see that some coffin put back in the tomb at Springfield. Around the tomb stood Lincoln's old neighbors, to whom he was just "Old Abe."

765   Of course that is all they would say. Did you ever see a man who struts around altogether too large to notice an ordinary working mechanic? Do you think he is great? He is nothing but a puffed-up balloon, held down by his big feet. There is no greatness there. Who are the great men and women? My attention was called the other day to the history of a very little thing that made the fortune of a very poor man. It was an awful

770   thing, and yet because of that experience he—not a great inventor or genius—invented the pin that now is called the safety-pin, and out of that safety-pin made the fortune of one of the great aristocratic families of this nation.

A poor man in Massachusetts who had worked in the nail-works was injured at thirty-eight, and he could earn but little money. He was employed in the office to rub out the

775   marks on the bills made by pencil memorandums, and he used a rubber until his hand grew tired. He then tied a piece of rubber on the end of a stick and worked it like a plane. His little girl came and said, "Why, you have a patent, haven't you?" The father said afterward, "My daughter told me when I took the stick and put the rubber on the end that there was a patent, and that was the first thought of that." He went to Boston and applied

780   for his patent, and every one of you that has a rubber-tipped pencil in your pocket is now paying tribute to the millionaire. All was income, all the way up into the millions.

But let me hasten to one other greater thought. "Show me the great men and women who live in Philadelphia." A gentleman over there will get up and say: "We don't have any great men in Philadelphia. They don't live here. They live away off in Rome or

785   St. Petersburg or London or Manayunk, or anywhere else but here in our town." I have come now to the apex of my thought. I have come now to the heart of the whole matter and to the center of my struggle: Why isn't Philadelphia a greater city in its greater wealth? Why does New York excel Philadelphia? People say, "Because of her harbor." Why do many other cities of the United States get ahead of Philadelphia now? There

790   is only one answer, and that is because our own people talk down their own city. If there ever was a community on earth that has to be forced ahead, it is the city of Philadelphia. If we are to have a boulevard, talk it down; if we are going to have better schools, talk them down; if you wish to have wise legislation, talk it down; talk all the proposed improvements down. That is the only great wrong that I can lay at the feet of

795   the magnificent Philadelphia that has been so universally kind to me. I say it is time we turn around in our city and begin to talk up the things that are in our city, and begin to set them before the world as the people of Chicago, New York, St. Louis, and San Francisco do. Oh, if we only could get that spirit out among our people, that we can do things in Philadelphia and do them well!

800   Arise, you millions of Philadelphians, trust in God and man, and believe in the great opportunities that are right here—not over in New York or Boston, but here—for business, for everything that is worth living for on earth. There was never an opportunity greater. Let us talk up our own city.

But there are two other young men here to-night, and that is all I will venture to say,

805   because it is too late. One over there gets up and says, "There is going to be a great man in Philadelphia, but never was one." "Oh, is that so? When are you going to be great?" "When I am elected to some political office." Young man, won't you learn a lesson in

the primer of politics that is a prima facie evidence of littleness to hold office under our form of government? Great men get into office sometimes, but what this country needs is men that will do what we tell them to do. This nation—Where the people rule—is gov-   810
erned by the people, for the people, and so long as it is, then the office-holder is but the servant of the people, and the Bible says the servant cannot be greater than the master. The Bible says, "He that is sent cannot be greater than Him who sent Him." The people rule, or should rule; and if they do, we do not need the greater men in office. If the great men in America took our offices, we would change to an empire in the next ten years.   815

I know of a great many young women, now that woman's suffrage is coming, who say, "I am going to be President of the United States some day." I believe in woman's suffrage, and there is no doubt but what is coming, and I am getting out of the way, any-how. I may want an office by and by myself; but if the ambition of an office influences the women in their desire to vote, I want to say right here what I say to the young men, that if   820
you only get the privilege of casting one vote, you don't get anything that is worth while. Unless you can control more than one vote, you will be unknown, and your influence so dissipated as practically not to be felt. This country is not run by votes. Do you think it is? It is governed by influence. It is governed by the ambitions and the enterprises which control votes. The young woman that thinks she is going to vote for the sake of holding   825
an office is making an awful blunder.

That other young man gets up and says, "There are going to be great men in this country and in Philadelphia." "Is that so? When?" "When there comes a great war, when we get into difficulty through watchful waiting in Mexico; when we get into war with England over some frivolous deed, or with Japan or China or New Jersey or some dis-   830
tant country. Then I will march up to the cannon's mouth; I will sweep up among the glistening bayonets; I will leap into the arena and tear down the flag and bear it away in triumph. I will come home with stars on my shoulder, and hold every office in the gift of the nation, and I will be great." No, you won't. You think you are going to be made great by an office, but remember that if you are not great before you get the office, you won't   835
be great when you secure it. It will only be a burlesque in that shape.

We had a Peace Jubilee here after the Spanish War. Out West they don't believe this, because they said, "Philadelphia would not have heard of any Spanish War until fifty years hence." Some of you saw the procession go up Broad Street, I was away, but the family wrote to me that the tally-ho coach with Lieutenant Hobson upon it stopped right   840
at the front door and the people shouted, "Hurrah for Hobson!" and if I had been there I would have yelled too, because he deserves much more of his country than he has ever received. But suppose I go into school and say, "Who sunk the Merrimac at Santiago?" and if the boys answer me, "Hobson," they will tell me seven-eighths of a lie. There were seven other heroes on that steamer, and they, by virtue of their position, were continually   845
exposed to the Spanish fire, while Hobson, as an officer, might reasonably be behind the smoke-stack. You have gathered in this house your most intelligent people, and yet, perhaps, not one here can name the other seven men.

We ought not to so teach history. We ought to teach that, however humble a man's station may be, if he does his full duty in that place he is just as much entitled to the   850

American people's honor as is the king upon his throne. But we do not so teach. We are now teaching everywhere that the generals do all the fighting.

I remember that, after the war, I went down to see General Robert E. Lee, that mag-nificent Christian gentleman of whom both North and South are now proud as one of our great Americans. The general told me about his servant, "Rastus," who was an enlisted colored soldier. He called him in one day to make fun of him, and said, "Rastus, I hear that all the rest of your company are killed, and why are you not killed?" Rastus winked at him and said, "'Cause when there is any fightin' goin' on I stay back with the generals."

I remember another illustration. I would leave it out but for the fact that when you go to the library to read this lecture, you will find this has been printed in it for twenty-five years. I shut my eyes—shut them close—and lo! I see the faces of my youth. Yes, they sometimes say to me, "You hair is not white; you are working night and day without seeming ever to stop; you can't be old." But when I shut my eyes, like any other man of my years, oh, then come trooping back the faces of the loved and lost of long ago, and I know, whatever men may say, it is evening-time.

I shut my eyes now and look back to my native town in Massachusetts, and I see the cattle-show ground on the mountain-top; I can see the horse-sheds there. I can see the Congregational church; see the town hall and mountaineers' cottages; see a great assembly of people turning out, dressed resplendently, and I can see flags flying and handkerchiefs waving and hear bands playing. I can see that company of soldiers that had re-enlisted marching up on that cattle-show ground. I was but a boy, but I was cap-tain of that company and puffed out with pride. A cambric needle would have burst me all to pieces. Then I thought it was the greatest event that ever came to man on earth. If you have ever thought you would like to be king or queen, you go and be received by the mayor.

The bands played, and all the people turned out to receive us. I marched up that Common so proud at the head of my troops, and we turned down into the town hall. Then they seated my soldiers down the center aisle and I sat down on the front seat. A great assembly of people—a hundred or two—came in to fill the town hall, so that they stood up all around. Then the town officers came in and formed a half-circle. The mayor of the town sat in the middle of the platform. He was a man who had never held office before; but he was a good man, and his friends have told me that I might use this without giving them offense. He was a good man, but he thought an office made a man great. He came up and took his seat, adjusted his powerful spectacles, and looked around, when he suddenly spied me sitting there on the front seat.

He came right forward on the platform and invited me up to sit with the town offic-ers. No town officer ever took any notice of me before I went to war, except to advise the teacher to thrash me, and now I was invited up on the stand with the town officers. Oh my! The town mayor was then the emperor, the kind of our day and our time. As I came up on the platform they gave me a chair about this far, I would say, from the front.

When I had got seated, the chairman of the Selectmen arose and came forward to the table, and we all supposed he would introduce the Congregational minister, who was the only orator in town, and that he would give the oration to the returning soldiers.

But, friends, you should have seen the surprise which ran over the audience when they discovered that the old fellow was going to deliver that speech himself. He had never 895 made a speech in his life, but he fell into the same error that hundreds of other men have fallen into. It seems so strange that a man won't learn he must speak his piece as a boy if he intends to be an orator when he is grown, but he seems to think all he has to do is to hold an office to be a great orator.

So he came up to the front, and brought with him a speech which he had learned by 900 heart walking up and down the pasture, where he had frightened the cattle. He brought the manuscript with him and spread it out on the table so as to be sure he might see it. He adjusted his spectacles and leaned over it for a moment and marched back on that platform, and then came forward like this—tramp, tramp, tramp. He must have studied the subject a great deal, then you come to think of it, because he assumed an "elocu- 905 tionary" attitude. He rested heavily upon his left heel, threw back his shoulders, slightly advanced the right foot, opened the organs of speech, and advanced his right foot at an angle of forty-five. As he stood in that elocutionary attitude, friends, this is just the way that speech went. Some people say to me, "Don't you exaggerate?" That would be impossible. But I am here for the lesson and not for the story, and this is the way it 910 went "Fellow-citizens"—As soon as he heard his voice his fingers began to go like that, his knees begin to shake, and then he trembled all over. He choked and swallowed and came around to the table to look at the manuscript. Then he gathered himself up with clenched fists and came back "Fellow-citizens, we are—Fellow-citizens, we are—we are—we are—we are—we are—we are—we are very happy—we are very happy—we are very 915 happy. We are very happy to welcome back to their native town these soldiers who have fought and bled—and come back again to their native town. We are especially—we are especially—we are especially. We are especially pleased to see with us to-day this young hero" (that meant me)—"this young hero who in imagination" (friends remember he said that if he had not said "in imagination" I would have not be egotistic enough to 920 refer to it at all)—"this young hero who in imagination we have seen leading—we have seen leading—leading. We have seen leading his troops on the deadly breach. We have seen his shining—we have seen his shining—his shining—his shining sword—flashing. Flashing in the sunlight, as he shouted to his troops, 'Come on'!"

Oh dear, dear, dear! How little that good man knew about war. If he had known 925 anything about war at all he ought to have known what any of my G. A. R. comrades here to-night will tell you is true, that it is next to a crime for an officer of infantry ever in time of danger to go ahead of his men. "I, with my shining sword flashing in the sunlight, shouting to my troops, 'Come on'!" I never did it. Do you suppose I would get in front of my men to be shot in front by the enemy and in the back by my own men? That is no 930 place for an officer. The place for the officer in actual battle is behind the line. How often, as a staff officer, I rode down the line, when our men were suddenly called to the line of a battle, and the Rebel yells were coming out of the woods, and shouted: "Officers to the rear! Officers to the rear!" Then every officer gets behind the line of private soldiers, and the higher the officer's rank the farther behind he goes. Not because he is any less 935 brave, but because the laws of war require that.

And yet he shouted, "I, with my shining sword"—In that house there sat the company of my soldiers who had carried that boy across the Carolina rivers that he might not wet his feet. Some of them had gone far out to wet his feet. Some of them had gone
940 far out to get a pig or a chicken. Some of them had gone to death under the shell-swept pines in the mountains of Tennessee, yet in the good man's speech they were scarcely known. He did refer to them, but only incidentally. The hero of the hour was this boy. Did the nation own him anything? No, nothing then and nothing now. Why was he the hero? Simply because that man fell into that same human error—that this boy was great
945 because he was an officer and these were only private soldiers.

Oh, I learned the lesson then that I will never forget so long as the tongue of the bell of time continues to swing for me. Greatness consists not in the holding of some future office, but really consists in doing great deeds with little means and the accomplishment of vast purposes from the private ranks of life. To be great at all one must be great here,
950 now, in Philadelphia. He who can give to this city better streets and better sidewalks, better schools and more colleges, more happiness and more civilization, more of God, he will be great anywhere. Let every man or woman here, if you never hear me again, remember this, that if you wish to be great at all, you must begin where you are and what you are, in Philadelphia, now. He that can give you to his city any blessing, he who can be a good
955 citizen while he lives here, he that can make better homes, he that can be a blessing whether he works in the shop or sits behind the counter or keeps house, whatever be his life, he who would be great anywhere must first be great in his own Philadelphia.

FAITH, REASON AND THE UNIVERSITY: MEMORIES AND REFLECTIONS

POPE BENEDICT XVI

UNIVERSITY OF REGENSBURG

SEPTEMBER 12, 2006

This lecture by Pope Benedict XVI caused an international uproar when one of his references to Islam was taken out of context and reported around the world.

Your Eminences, Your Magnificences, Your Excellencies, Distinguished Ladies and Gentlemen,

It is a moving experience for me to be back again in the university and to be able once again to give a lecture at this podium. I think back to those years when, after a
5 pleasant period at the Freisinger Hochschule, I began teaching at the University of Bonn. That was in 1959, in the days of the old university made up of ordinary professors. The various chairs had neither assistants nor secretaries, but in recompense there was much direct contact with students and in particular among the professors themselves. We would meet before and after lessons in the rooms of the teaching staff. There was a lively
10 exchange with historians, philosophers, philologists and, naturally, between the two theological faculties. Once a semester there was a *dies academicus*, when professors

from every faculty appeared before the students of the entire university, making possible a genuine experience of *universitas*—something that you too, Magnificent Rector, just mentioned—the experience, in other words, of the fact that despite our specializations which at times make it difficult to communicate with each other, we made up a whole, working in everything on the basis of a single rationality with its various aspects and sharing responsibility for the right use of reason—this reality became a lived experience. The university was also very proud of its two theological faculties. It was clear that, by inquiring about the reasonableness of faith, they too carried out a work which is necessarily part of the "whole" of the *universitas scientiarum*, even if not everyone could share the faith which theologians seek to correlate with reason as a whole. This profound sense of coherence within the universe of reason was not troubled, even when it was once reported that a colleague had said there was something odd about our university: it had two faculties devoted to something that did not exist: God. That even in the face of such radical scepticism it is still necessary and reasonable to raise the question of God through the use of reason, and to do so in the context of the tradition of the Christian faith: this, within the university as a whole, was accepted without question.

    I was reminded of all this recently, when I read the edition by Professor Theodore Khoury (Münster) of part of the dialogue carried on—perhaps in 1391 in the winter barracks near Ankara—by the erudite Byzantine emperor Manuel II Paleologus and an educated Persian on the subject of Christianity and Islam, and the truth of both. It was presumably the emperor himself who set down this dialogue, during the siege of Constantinople between 1394 and 1402; and this would explain why his arguments are given in greater detail than those of his Persian interlocutor. The dialogue ranges widely over the structures of faith contained in the Bible and in the Qur'an, and deals especially with the image of God and of man, while necessarily returning repeatedly to the relationship between—as they were called—three "Laws" or "rules of life": the Old Testament, the New Testament and the Qur'an. It is not my intention to discuss this question in the present lecture; here I would like to discuss only one point—itself rather marginal to the dialogue as a whole—which, in the context of the issue of "faith and reason", I found interesting and which can serve as the starting-point for my reflections on this issue.

    In the seventh conversation (διάλεξιζ—controversy) edited by Professor Khoury, the emperor touches on the theme of the holy war. The emperor must have known that surah 2,256 reads: "There is no compulsion in religion". According to some of the experts, this is probably one of the suras of the early period, when Mohammed was still powerless and under threat. But naturally the emperor also knew the instructions, developed later and recorded in the Qur'an, concerning holy war. Without descending to details, such as the difference in treatment accorded to those who have the "Book" and the "infidels", he addresses his interlocutor with a startling brusqueness, a brusqueness that we find unacceptable, on the central question about the relationship between religion and violence in general, saying: "Show me just what Mohammed brought that was new, and there you will find things only evil and inhuman, such as his command to spread by the sword the faith he preached." The emperor, after having expressed himself so forcefully, goes on to explain in detail the reasons why spreading the faith through violence is

55   something unreasonable. Violence is incompatible with the nature of God and the nature of the soul. "God", he says, "is not pleased by blood—and not acting reasonably (σύν''' λόγω) is contrary to God's nature. Faith is born of the soul, not the body. Whoever would lead someone to faith needs the ability to speak well and to reason properly, without violence and threats. . . . To convince a reasonable soul, one does not need a strong arm,

60   or weapons of any kind, or any other means of threatening a person with death. . . ."

     The decisive statement in this argument against violent conversion is this: not to act in accordance with reason is contrary to God's nature. The editor, Theodore Khoury, observes: For the emperor, as a Byzantine shaped by Greek philosophy, this statement is self-evident. But for Muslim teaching, God is absolutely transcendent. His will is not

65   bound up with any of our categories, even that of rationality. Here Khoury quotes a work of the noted French Islamist R. Arnaldez, who points out that Ibn Hazm went so far as to state that God is not bound even by his own word, and that nothing would oblige him to reveal the truth to us. Were it God's will, we would even have to practise idolatry.

     At this point, as far as understanding of God and thus the concrete practice of

70   religion is concerned, we are faced with an unavoidable dilemma. Is the conviction that acting unreasonably contradicts God's nature merely a Greek idea, or is it always and intrinsically true? I believe that here we can see the profound harmony between what is Greek in the best sense of the word and the biblical understanding of faith in God. Modifying the first verse of the Book of Genesis, the first verse of the whole Bible, John

75   began the prologue of his Gospel with the words: "In the beginning was the λόγος". This is the very word used by the emperor: God acts, σύνλόγω, with *logos*. *Logos* means both reason and word—a reason which is creative and capable of self-communication, precisely as reason. John thus spoke the final word on the biblical concept of God, and in this word all the often toilsome and tortuous threads of biblical faith find their culmi-

80   nation and synthesis. In the beginning was the *logos*, and the *logos* is God, says the Evangelist. The encounter between the Biblical message and Greek thought did not happen by chance. The vision of Saint Paul, who saw the roads to Asia barred and in a dream saw a Macedonian man plead with him: "Come over to Macedonia and help us!" (cf. *Acts* 16:6–10)—this vision can be interpreted as a "distillation" of the intrinsic

85   necessity of a rapprochement between Biblical faith and Greek inquiry.

     In point of fact, this rapprochement had been going on for some time. The mysterious name of God, revealed from the burning bush, a name which separates this God from all other divinities with their many names and simply asserts being, "I am", already presents a challenge to the notion of myth, to which Socrates' attempt to vanquish and

90   transcend myth stands in close analogy. Within the Old Testament, the process which started at the burning bush came to new maturity at the time of the Exile, when the God of Israel, an Israel now deprived of its land and worship, was proclaimed as the God of heaven and earth and described in a simple formula which echoes the words uttered at the burning bush: "I am". This new understanding of God is accompanied by a kind of

95   enlightenment, which finds stark expression in the mockery of gods who are merely the work of human hands (cf. *Ps* 115). Thus, despite the bitter conflict with those Hellenistic rulers who sought to accommodate it forcibly to the customs and idolatrous cult of the

Greeks, biblical faith, in the Hellenistic period, encountered the best of Greek thought at a deep level, resulting in a mutual enrichment evident especially in the later wisdom literature. Today we know that the Greek translation of the Old Testament produced at Alexandria—the Septuagint—is more than a simple (and in that sense really less than satisfactory) translation of the Hebrew text: it is an independent textual witness and a distinct and important step in the history of revelation, one which brought about this encounter in a way that was decisive for the birth and spread of Christianity. A profound encounter of faith and reason is taking place here, an encounter between genuine enlightenment and religion. From the very heart of Christian faith and, at the same time, the heart of Greek thought now joined to faith, Manuel II was able to say: Not to act "with *logos*" is contrary to God's nature.

In all honesty, one must observe that in the late Middle Ages we find trends in theology which would sunder this synthesis between the Greek spirit and the Christian spirit. In contrast with the so-called intellectualism of Augustine and Thomas, there arose with Duns Scotus a voluntarism which, in its later developments, led to the claim that we can only know God's *voluntas ordinata*. Beyond this is the realm of God's freedom, in virtue of which he could have done the opposite of everything he has actually done. This gives rise to positions which clearly approach those of Ibn Hazm and might even lead to the image of a capricious God, who is not even bound to truth and goodness. God's transcendence and otherness are so exalted that our reason, our sense of the true and good, are no longer an authentic mirror of God, whose deepest possibilities remain eternally unattainable and hidden behind his actual decisions. As opposed to this, the faith of the Church has always insisted that between God and us, between his eternal Creator Spirit and our created reason there exists a real analogy, in which—as the Fourth Lateran Council in 1215 stated—unlikeness remains infinitely greater than likeness, yet not to the point of abolishing analogy and its language. God does not become more divine when we push him away from us in a sheer, impenetrable voluntarism; rather, the truly divine God is the God who has revealed himself as *logos* and, as *logos*, has acted and continues to act lovingly on our behalf. Certainly, love, as Saint Paul says, "transcends" knowledge and is thereby capable of perceiving more than thought alone (cf. *Eph* 3:19); nonetheless it continues to be love of the God who is *Logos*. Consequently, Christian worship is, again to quote Paul—"$\lambda o \gamma \iota \kappa \eta \ \lambda \alpha \tau \rho \varepsilon \iota \alpha$", worship in harmony with the eternal Word and with our reason (cf. *Rom* 12:1).

This inner rapprochement between Biblical faith and Greek philosophical inquiry was an event of decisive importance not only from the standpoint of the history of religions, but also from that of world history—it is an event which concerns us even today. Given this convergence, it is not surprising that Christianity, despite its origins and some significant developments in the East, finally took on its historically decisive character in Europe. We can also express this the other way around: this convergence, with the subsequent addition of the Roman heritage, created Europe and remains the foundation of what can rightly be called Europe.

The thesis that the critically purified Greek heritage forms an integral part of Christian faith has been countered by the call for a dehellenization of Christianity—a call which has more and more dominated theological discussions since the beginning of the modern age. Viewed more closely, three stages can be observed in the programme of dehellenization: although interconnected, they are clearly distinct from one another in their motivations and objectives.

145   Dehellenization first emerges in connection with the postulates of the Reformation in the sixteenth century. Looking at the tradition of scholastic theology, the Reformers thought they were confronted with a faith system totally conditioned by philosophy, that is to say an articulation of the faith based on an alien system of thought. As a result, faith no longer appeared as a living historical Word but as one element of an overarching

150 philosophical system. The principle of *sola scriptura*, on the other hand, sought faith in its pure, primordial form, as originally found in the biblical Word. Metaphysics appeared as a premise derived from another source, from which faith had to be liberated in order to become once more fully itself. When Kant stated that he needed to set thinking aside in order to make room for faith, he carried this programme forward with a radicalism that

155 the Reformers could never have foreseen. He thus anchored faith exclusively in practical reason, denying it access to reality as a whole.

    The liberal theology of the nineteenth and twentieth centuries ushered in a second stage in the process of dehellenization, with Adolf von Harnack as its outstanding representative. When I was a student, and in the early years of my teach-

160 ing, this programme was highly influential in Catholic theology too. It took as its point of departure Pascal's distinction between the God of the philosophers and the God of Abraham, Isaac and Jacob. In my inaugural lecture at Bonn in 1959, I tried to address the issue, and I do not intend to repeat here what I said on that occasion, but I would like to describe at least briefly what was new about this second stage of

165 dehellenization. Harnack's central idea was to return simply to the man Jesus and to his simple message, underneath the accretions of theology and indeed of hellenization: this simple message was seen as the culmination of the religious development of humanity. Jesus was said to have put an end to worship in favour of morality. In the end he was presented as the father of a humanitarian moral message. Fundamentally,

170 Harnack's goal was to bring Christianity back into harmony with modern reason, liberating it, that is to say, from seemingly philosophical and theological elements, such as faith in Christ's divinity and the triune God. In this sense, historical-critical exegesis of the New Testament, as he saw it, restored to theology its place within the university: theology, for Harnack, is something essentially historical and therefore strictly scientific. What

175 it is able to say critically about Jesus is, so to speak, an expression of practical reason and consequently it can take its rightful place within the university. Behind this thinking lies the modern self-limitation of reason, classically expressed in Kant's "Critiques", but in the meantime further radicalized by the impact of the natural sciences. This modern concept of reason is based, to put it briefly, on a synthesis between Platonism

180 (Cartesianism) and empiricism, a synthesis confirmed by the success of technology. On the one hand it presupposes the mathematical structure of matter, its intrinsic rationality, which makes it possible to understand how matter works and use it efficiently: this basic premise is, so to speak, the Platonic element in the modern understanding of nature.

On the other hand, there is nature's capacity to be exploited for our purposes, and here only the possibility of verification or falsification through experimentation can yield decisive certainty. The weight between the two poles can, depending on the circumstances, shift from one side to the other. As strongly positivistic a thinker as J. Monod has declared himself a convinced Platonist/Cartesian.

This gives rise to two principles which are crucial for the issue we have raised. First, only the kind of certainty resulting from the interplay of mathematical and empirical elements can be considered scientific. Anything that would claim to be science must be measured against this criterion. Hence the human sciences, such as history, psychology, sociology and philosophy, attempt to conform themselves to this canon of scientificity. A second point, which is important for our reflections, is that by its very nature this method excludes the question of God, making it appear an unscientific or pre-scientific question. Consequently, we are faced with a reduction of the radius of science and reason, one which needs to be questioned.

I will return to this problem later. In the meantime, it must be observed that from this standpoint any attempt to maintain theology's claim to be "scientific" would end up reducing Christianity to a mere fragment of its former self. But we must say more: if science as a whole is this and this alone, then it is man himself who ends up being reduced, for the specifically human questions about our origin and destiny, the questions raised by religion and ethics, then have no place within the purview of collective reason as defined by "science", so understood, and must thus be relegated to the realm of the subjective. The subject then decides, on the basis of his experiences, what he considers tenable in matters of religion, and the subjective "conscience" becomes the sole arbiter of what is ethical. In this way, though, ethics and religion lose their power to create a community and become a completely personal matter. This is a dangerous state of affairs for humanity, as we see from the disturbing pathologies of religion and reason which necessarily erupt when reason is so reduced that questions of religion and ethics no longer concern it. Attempts to construct an ethic from the rules of evolution or from psychology and sociology, end up being simply inadequate.

Before I draw the conclusions to which all this has been leading, I must briefly refer to the third stage of dehellenization, which is now in progress. In the light of our experience with cultural pluralism, it is often said nowadays that the synthesis with Hellenism achieved in the early Church was an initial inculturation which ought not to be binding on other cultures. The latter are said to have the right to return to the simple message of the New Testament prior to that inculturation, in order to inculturate it anew in their own particular milieux. This thesis is not simply false, but it is coarse and lacking in precision. The New Testament was written in Greek and bears the imprint of the Greek spirit, which had already come to maturity as the Old Testament developed. True, there are elements in the evolution of the early Church which do not have to be integrated into all cultures. Nonetheless, the fundamental decisions made about the relationship between faith and the use of human reason are part of the faith itself; they are developments consonant with the nature of faith itself.

And so I come to my conclusion. This attempt, painted with broad strokes, at a critique of modern reason from within has nothing to do with putting the clock back to the time before the Enlightenment and rejecting the insights of the modern age. The positive aspects of modernity are to be acknowledged unreservedly: we are all grateful for the marvellous possibilities that it has opened up for mankind and for the progress in humanity that has been granted to us. The scientific ethos, moreover, is—as you yourself mentioned, Magnificent Rector—the will to be obedient to the truth, and, as such, it embodies an attitude which belongs to the essential decisions of the Christian spirit. The intention here is not one of retrenchment or negative criticism, but of broadening our concept of reason and its application. While we rejoice in the new possibilities open to humanity, we also see the dangers arising from these possibilities and we must ask ourselves how we can overcome them. We will succeed in doing so only if reason and faith come together in a new way, if we overcome the self-imposed limitation of reason to the empirically falsifiable, and if we once more disclose its vast horizons. In this sense theology rightly belongs in the university and within the wide-ranging dialogue of sciences, not merely as a historical discipline and one of the human sciences, but precisely as theology, as inquiry into the rationality of faith.

Only thus do we become capable of that genuine dialogue of cultures and religions so urgently needed today. In the Western world it is widely held that only positivistic reason and the forms of philosophy based on it are universally valid. Yet the world's profoundly religious cultures see this exclusion of the divine from the universality of reason as an attack on their most profound convictions. A reason which is deaf to the divine and which relegates religion into the realm of subcultures is incapable of entering into the dialogue of cultures. At the same time, as I have attempted to show, modern scientific reason with its intrinsically Platonic element bears within itself a question which points beyond itself and beyond the possibilities of its methodology. Modern scientific reason quite simply has to accept the rational structure of matter and the correspondence between our spirit and the prevailing rational structures of nature as a given, on which its methodology has to be based. Yet the question why this has to be so is a real question, and one which has to be remanded by the natural sciences to other modes and planes of thought—to philosophy and theology. For philosophy and, albeit in a different way, for theology, listening to the great experiences and insights of the religious traditions of humanity, and those of the Christian faith in particular, is a source of knowledge, and to ignore it would be an unacceptable restriction of our listening and responding. Here I am reminded of something Socrates said to Phaedo. In their earlier conversations, many false philosophical opinions had been raised, and so Socrates says: "It would be easily understandable if someone became so annoyed at all these false notions that for the rest of his life he despised and mocked all talk about being—but in this way he would be deprived of the truth of existence and would suffer a great loss". The West has long been endangered by this aversion to the questions which underlie its rationality, and can only suffer great harm thereby. The courage to engage the whole breadth of reason, and not the denial of its grandeur—this is the programme with which a theology grounded in Biblical faith enters into the debates of our time. "Not to act reasonably, not to act with

logos, is contrary to the nature of God", said Manuel II, according to his Christian under-   270
standing of God, in response to his Persian interlocutor. It is to this great *logos*, to this
breadth of reason, that we invite our partners in the dialogue of cultures. To rediscover it
constantly is the great task of the university.

Of the total number of 26 conversations ($\delta\iota\acute{\alpha}\lambda\varepsilon\xi\iota\zeta$ Khoury translates this as "controversy") in the
dialogue (Entretien), T. Khoury published the 7th controversy with footnotes and an extensive
introduction on the origin of the text, on the manuscript tradition and on the structure of the dialogue, together with brief summaries of the controversies not included in the edition; the Greek
text is accompanied by a French translation: "Manuel II Paléologue, Entretiens avec un Musulman.
7th edition", *Sources Chrétiennes* n. 115, Paris 1966. In the meantime, Karl Förstel published in
Corpus Islamico-Christianum (*Series Graeca* ed. A. T. Khoury and R. Glei) an edition of the text
in Greek and German with commentary: "Manuel II. Palaiologus, Dialoge mit einem Muslim", 3 vols.,
Würzburg-Altenberge 1993–1996. As early as 1966, E. Trapp had published the Greek text with an
introduction as vol. II of *Wiener byzantinische Studien*. I shall be quoting from Khoury's edition.

On the origin and redaction of the dialogue, cf. Khoury, pp. 22–29; extensive comments in this
regard can also be found in the editions of Förstel and Trapp.

Controversy VII, 2 c: Khoury, pp. 142–143; Förstel, vol. I, VII. Dialog 1.5, pp. 240–241. In the Muslim
world, this quotation has unfortunately been taken as an expression of my personal position, thus
arousing understandable indignation. I hope that the reader of my text can see immediately that this
sentence does not express my personal view of the Qur'an, for which I have the respect due to the
holy book of a great religion. In quoting the text of the Emperor Manuel II, I intended solely to draw
out the essential relationship between faith and reason. On this point I am in agreement with Manuel
II, but without endorsing his polemic.

Controversy VII, 3 b–c: Khoury, pp. 144–145; Förstel vol. I, VII. Dialog 1.6, pp. 240–243.

It was purely for the sake of this statement that I quoted the dialogue between Manuel and his
Persian interlocutor.

In this statement the theme of my subsequent reflections emerges.

Cf. Khoury, p. 144, n. 1.

R. Arnaldez, *Grammaire et théologie chez Ibn Hazm de Cordoue*, Paris 1956, p. 13; cf. Khoury, p. 144.
The fact that comparable positions exist in the theology of the late Middle Ages will appear later in
my discourse.

Regarding the widely discussed interpretation of the episode of the burning bush, I refer to my book
Introduction to Christianity, London 1969, pp. 77–93 (originally published in German as *Einführung
in das Christentum*, Munich 1968; N.B. the pages quoted refer to the entire chapter entitled
"The Biblical Belief in God"). I think that my statements in that book, despite later developments in
the discussion, remain valid today.

Cf. A. Schenker, "L'Écriture sainte subsiste en plusieurs formes canoniques simultanées", in
*L'Interpretazione della Bibbia nella Chiesa. Atti del Simposio promosso dalla Congregazione per la
Dottrina della Fede*, Vatican City 2001, pp. 178–186.

On this matter I expressed myself in greater detail in my book *The Spirit of the Liturgy*, San Francisco,
2000, pp. 44–50.

Of the vast literature on the theme of dehellenization, I would like to mention above all: A. Grillmeier,
"Hellenisierung-Judaisierung des Christentums als Deuteprinzipien der Geschichte des kirchlichen
Dogmas", in idem, *Mit ihm und in ihm. Christologische Forschungen und Perspektiven*, Freiburg
1975, pp. 423–488.

Newly published with commentary by Heino Sonnemans (ed.): *Joseph Ratzinger-Benedikt XVI, Der Gott des Glaubens und der Gott der Philosophen. Ein Beitrag zum Problem der theologia naturalis*, Johannes-Verlag Leutesdorf, 2nd revised edition, 2005.

Cf. 90 c–d. For this text, cf. also R. Guardini, *Der Tod des Sokrates*, 5th edition, Mainz-Paderborn 1987, pp. 218–221.

Source: © Copyright 2006—Libreria Editrice Vaticana. Used by permission.

DISCUSSION STARTERS

What about "Acres of Diamonds" do you think made it so wildly popular in its day? In what sense does the speaker, Russell Conwell, himself enact the characters in his stories? In the Pope's lecture, how would you rewrite or rephrase the section that caused so much controversy to head off possible misunderstanding?

BIBLIOGRAPHY

Bligh, Donald A. *What's the Use of Lectures?* San Francisco: Jossey-Bass, 2000.

Arguing that "lecturing is an art," Englishman Donald Bligh provides a comprehensive analysis of the lecture as a teaching method and the most thorough discussion of how to succeed in lecturing available today.

McKeachie, Wilbert J., & Marilla Svinicki. *Teaching Tips: Strategies, Research, and Theory for College and University Teachers*, 12th edition. Boston: Houghton Mifflin, 2005. Chapter Five, *How to Make Lectures More Effective*.

McKeachie provides a practical, common sense approach to academic lecturing.

Ray, Angela G. *The Lyceum and Public Culture in the Nineteenth Century United States*. East Lansing: Michigan State University Press, 2005.

In the first chapter of this book, Ray recounts the history of the Lyceum Movement in the nineteenth century, showing how it evolved from an emphasis on culture and learning to commercial entertainment.

Wilson, Woodrow. "An Old Master." *Selected Literary and Political Papers of Woodrow Wilson*, Vol. 3. New York: Grosset & Dunlap, 1927, pp. 3–24.

At the turn of the twentieth century, when he was president of Princeton University, Woodrow Wilson was lamenting the apparent demise of good academic lecturing. In this essay, the "old master" is the philosopher and lecturer *par excellence*, Adam Smith (1723–1790). Wilson describes Smith's vast knowledge as well as his brilliant style, concluding that he was "in the highest sense, interesting."

Speaking Processes

Speaking from a Manuscript

ASSIGNMENT

Present a manuscript speech of one of the types of speeches discussed in Part One of this book.

COMMENTARY

Although there are no hard statistics to prove it, it is safe to assume that most of the speeches given in the United States on any given day, whether in business, civic, religious, or educational settings, are delivered extemporaneously. In other words, the speeches are prepared and then given conversationally from notes. Manuscript speeches, those written out and then delivered word for word from the written text, are less common, but are often given in the most important speaking situations. Inexperienced speakers sometimes mistakenly believe that manuscript speeches are easier to give than extemporaneous speeches. This is true in a way. Almost anyone can stand in front of an audience and read words off a piece of paper. The communication that results, however, is hardly a speech. It is more like words read off a piece of paper. As Dartmouth University speech professor James Winans colorfully put it, "A speech is not merely an essay standing on its hind legs."

Most standard public speaking textbooks advise using a manuscript when "careful wording is required." What situations call for such careful wording? When your speech might be subject to extensive press coverage is one such situation requiring thoughtful composition. Legal settings also come to mind. If your words might be brought to bear on a civil or criminal proceeding or even be introduced as evidence in court, you cannot be too careful in what you say. Similarly, speeches given in the midst of various kinds of negotiations need to be carefully worded. Another setting where a manuscript would be advisable is when audience emotions are running high and where even a slight extemporaneous misstep could easily provoke a negative reaction. Finally, use a manuscript when time constraints are severe. You should know exactly how long a manuscript speech will take to deliver.

Good speakers do not take lightly the difference between an essay and a manuscript speech. Manuscript speeches require what is sometimes called "oral style." This means we must write like we talk. Most of us do not write like we talk. We write like we write and as we have been educated to write, following the conventions of written prose. That is why an essay read to an audience does not sound like a speech. Very few people naturally write like they talk. Such writing is a learned skill developed with practice. Here are a few qualities of oral style:

- Oral style sits loose to the rules of grammar. This does not mean that it is ignorantly ungrammatical, but that the rules are loosely applied. For example, sentence fragments—clauses lacking a subject or predicate—might be used. Contractions are also more natural to spoken discourse than written.
- Oral style has a more limited vocabulary. Our reading vocabulary is nearly always more extensive than our speaking vocabulary. Manuscript speaking sticks with the words common to oral discourse.
- Oral style features various types of repetition. What would be considered redundancy in a written composition seems natural in spoken communication.
- Oral style employs personal pronouns. Unlike a writer addressing a "universal audience," a speaker, face to face with live human beings, can speak directly and personally.

What follows is an example of the difference between essay prose style and oral style. The next paragraph is taken from a critical discussion of President John F. Kennedy's inaugural speech and deals with the speech's length.

> One of the first things that strikes the reader is the relative brevity of the speech—1343 words, which at the normal rate for public address would take between nine and ten minutes to deliver. When the President wrote this speech he could not have known that the "live" audience for the speech would be standing in the biting cold that followed a heavy snowstorm in the Washington area on the day before the inauguration. So the President had not made his speech brief out of consideration for his wind-chilled audience. In preparing the speech, however, he might have taken into consideration that it would be delivered at the end of some lengthy preliminary speech-making. But perhaps the consideration that mainly determined the brevity of the speech was the traditional nature of inaugural addresses. As we have observed, inaugural addresses usually deal in broad, undeveloped generalities. Principles, policies, and promises are enunciated without elaboration.[1]

Here is the same paragraph rewritten to incorporate some of the qualities of oral style mentioned earlier.

> One of the striking things about this speech is how short it is. 1343 words. At a normal rate of delivery, it would only be about nine or ten minutes long. Why so short? Did the president cut it short because of the freezing weather? Probably not. He couldn't have known ahead of time that a big snowstorm was going to hit DC on the day before. Did he prepare a short address because he realized that

---

[1]"John F. Kennedy's Inaugural Address," *The New Yorker 36* (Feb. 4, 1961):23–24.

it would be given after lots of other speeches? Maybe. But the most likely reason the speech was short was something we've already talked about. The nature of inaugural speeches. They're usually about generalities, not specifics. You don't get much elaboration on principles, policies and promises in an inaugural.

The secret of good manuscript speaking is delivering the speech exactly as it is written without appearing to be reading. This is why it is often claimed that preparing to deliver a manuscript speech is more demanding than preparing for an extemporaneous presentation. If you over-rehearse the speech, it will come across as a memorized recitation. If you under-rehearse, you will look down at the text too much and appear to be reading. So not only is writing a manuscript speech difficult, delivering it is also fraught with potential problems. When preparing a manuscript, use a large type font and a spacious page layout. Make notations to yourself on the manuscript such as where to pause or what to emphasize, and use the same manuscript that was used in rehearsal to deliver the speech. Practice until you get to the point where you are completely familiar and comfortable with your ideas, words, and the very pieces of paper you will carry to the podium.

CLASSICAL CONCEPT: WRITING AND SPEAKING

Many speeches have come down to us from antiquity in written form. Obviously, classical orators wrote down their speeches for publication, but it is hard to know if they actually gave whole speeches from a written text with manuscript in hand. Probably not, but they were acutely aware of the connection between speaking and writing as illustrated in this passage from Cicero's *De Oratore*.

One of the dialogue's main characters, L. Licinius Crassus, argues that many speakers gain little from practicing delivering their speeches.

This mistake is due to their having heard it said that it is by speaking that men as a rule become speakers. But that other adage is just as true—that by speaking badly men very easily succeed in becoming bad speakers . . . though there is a value in plenty of extempore[2] speaking, it is still more serviceable to take time for consideration, and to speak better prepared and more carefully. But the chief thing is what, to tell the truth, we do least (for it needs great pains which most of us shirk)—to write as much as possible. The pen is the best and most eminent teacher of eloquence, and rightly so. For if an extempore and casual speech is easily beaten by one prepared and thought-out, this latter in turn will assuredly be surpassed by what has been written with care and diligence. The truth is that . . . all the thoughts and expressions, which are the most brilliant in their several kinds, must need flow up in succession to the point of our pen; then too the actual marshalling and arrangement of words is made perfect in the course of writing. . . . These are the things which in good orators produce applause and admiration; and no man will attain these except by long and large practice in writing, however ardently he many have trained himself in those off-hand declamations. *(I, 149–152)*

---

[2]A better translation would be "impromptu." The comparison is between impromptu speaking—speaking without any advanced preparation—and extemporaneous speaking, which depends on preparation but is not written out, and speaking from a fully written text.

Example | **133**

Do you think Crassus overstates the value of writing? Is the discipline of writing as challenging as he claims?

EXAMPLE

Address

By

C. Everett Koop, MD, ScD

Surgeon General

of the

U. S. Public Health Service

and

Deputy Assistant Secretary of Health

U. S. Department of Health and Human Services

Presented to the National Religious Broadcasters

Washington, D.C.

February 2, 1987

1

(GREETINGS TO HOSTS, GUESTS, FRIENDS, ETC.)

I'M PLEASED TO COME BEFORE YOU ONCE AGAIN TO RENEW AN OLD AND
VALUED FRIENDSHIP AND TO SHARE MY THOUGHTS WITH YOU.

YOU AND I HAVE HAD MANY SERIOUS MOMENTS TOGETHER OVER THE PAST
FEW YEARS. WE HAVE, FOR EXAMPLE, CONFRONTED TOGETHER THE PROFOUND
MORAL AND ETHICAL QUESTIONS RAISED BY "BABY DOE."

YOU WERE UNDERSTANDING THEN...AND YOU SUPPORTED ME.

AND TOGETHER...WE WERE <u>RIGHT</u>.

WE CONFRONTED TOGETHER THE ISSUE OF PORNOGRAPHY IN AMERICAN
LIFE. WE DARED TO SPEAK AGAINST THE HARM THAT SUCH TRASH VISITS UPON
THE COMMUNITY AND UPON THE FAMILY.

Example | **135**

2

AGAIN, WHEN OTHERS STEPPED BACK...YOU STEPPED FORWARD.

YOU UNDERSTOOD THE ISSUE...AND YOU SUPPORTED ME.

AND TOGETHER...<u>WE WERE RIGHT</u>.

EVER SINCE THE PRESIDENT MADE ME THE COUNTRY'S SURGEON GENERAL, I'VE BEEN NO STRANGER TO CONTROVERSY.

THROUGHOUT THIS TIME, HOWEVER, YOUR ASSOCIATION HAS BEEN A SUPPORT AND A COMFORT.

AND TODAY, I NEED THAT SUPPORT AND THAT COMFORT ONCE MORE.

3

THE NEW ISSUE WE FACE...<u>TOGETHER</u>...IS THE ISSUE OF AIDS.   WHAT IS
IT?   AND WHAT SHOULD WE DO ABOUT IT?

SO MUCH HAS BEEN WRITTEN AND SAID ABOUT AIDS THAT I WON'T TAKE
THE TIME TO GO OVER IT ALL AGAIN.

INSTEAD, LET ME EMPHASIZE JUST A FEW KEY POINTS FROM MY OWN
PERSPECTIVE AS YOUR SURGEON GENERAL.

AIDS IS A MYSTERIOUS, CONTAGIOUS DISEASE THAT IS <u>SPREADING</u>.   THE
NUMBER OF VICTIMS IS DOUBLING IN LITTLE MORE THAN A YEAR.   AS OF A
YEAR AGO, FOR EXAMPLE, WE HAD HAD A TOTAL OF 16,000 CASES OF AIDS
REPORTED TO THE AUTHORITIES SINCE THE FIRST REPORTS WERE MADE IN JUNE
OF 1981.

Example | **137**

4

TODAY THAT OVERALL TOTAL IS <u>30,000</u>. OVER HALF OF THOSE VICTIMS
HAVE DIED OF THE DISEASE. AND THE REST APPARENTLY <u>WILL</u>.

BY THIS TIME NEXT YEAR WE WILL HAVE ADDED OVER <u>23,000</u> NEW CASES
OF AIDS. AND BY THE END OF 1990 MY COLLEAGUES IN THE PUBLIC HEALTH
SERVICE PREDICT THAT <u>A QUARTER OF A MILLION PEOPLE</u> WILL HAVE
CONTRACTED AIDS.

MAKE NO MISTAKE ABOUT IT. AIDS IS SPREADING AMONG MORE AMERICANS
...AND IT IS <u>KILLING</u> MORE AMERICANS.

AFTER LOOKING AT ALL THE INFORMATION WE NOW HAVE, MY BOSS, DR.
OTIS R. BOWEN, THE SECRETARY OF HEALTH AND HUMAN SERVICES, LIKENED THE
SPREADING AIDS SITUATION TO THE ARRIVAL AND SPREAD OF SMALLPOX AND THE
BUBONIC PLAGUE IN EUROPE SEVERAL CENTURIES AGO.

5

AND THERE ARE, UNFORTUNATELY, MANY SIMILARITIES. LIKE THOSE
HELPLESS EUROPEANS, WE ALSO DO NOT HAVE A CURE FOR THIS SPREADING,
LETHAL DISEASE. I'M SURE YOU'VE READ ABOUT THIS OR THAT DRUG BEING
TESTED ON AIDS PATIENTS, AND THE MEDIA HAVE GIVEN MUCH COVERAGE TO ONE
DRUG, A.Z.T., THAT SEEMS TO PROLONG THE LIVES OF SOME AIDS VICTIMS
DYING OF PNEUMOCYSTIS CARINII PNEUMONIA.

BUT I'M AFRAID THAT'S ALL IT DOES...<u>PROLONG</u> SOME LIVES, NOT SAVE
THEM.

PEOPLE ALWAYS ASK, "DR. KOOP, WHEN WILL WE HAVE AN EFFECTIVE
VACCINE AVAILABLE?" AND I HAVE TO TELL THEM THAT I DON'T SEE ONE IN
THE FORESEEABLE FUTURE. WE'RE STILL IN THE VERY FIRST STAGES OF
VACCINE DEVELOPMENT, A PROCESS THAT TAKES YEARS.

Example | **139**

6

AND I HAVE TO REMIND PEOPLE THAT WE CAN'T HAVE A TRULY EFFECTIVE
VACCINE UNTIL WE KNOW EXACTLY WHAT WE'RE FIGHTING...AND THAT'S
SOMETHING WE STILL DON'T KNOW.

THE AIDS VIRUS ITSELF IS STILL A MYSTERY.

WE DO, HOWEVER, KNOW HOW IT GETS PASSED FROM PERSON TO PERSON.
IT IS PASSED EITHER IN BLOOD OR IN SEMEN.

THIS TRAIT EXPLAINS, FOR EXAMPLE, WHY AIDS HAS BEEN SO PREVALENT
AMONG HOMOSEXUAL AND BISEXUAL MEN AND AMONG DRUG ABUSERS WHO BORROW
INTRAVENOUS NEEDLES FROM OTHER ADDICTS WHO HAVE AIDS.

BUT LATELY WE'VE BEEN SEEING A RISE IN THE REPORTS OF AIDS
OCCURRING AMONG HETEROSEXUAL MEN AND WOMEN WHO ARE NOT I.V. DRUG
ABUSERS. IN FACT, THEIR HETEROSEXUAL ACTIVITY ITSELF SEEMS TO BE
THEIR ONLY COMMON RISK FACTOR.

7

AS OF LAST WEEK, ABOUT 4 PERCENT OF ALL AIDS REPORTS INVOLVED
HETEROSEXUAL MEN AND WOMEN.

ON THE FACE OT IT, 4 PERCENT IS NOT MUCH.   HOWEVER, WE SEEM TO BE
LOOKING AT A SHARPLY RISING CURVE.

WHILE THE OVERALL NUMBERS OF AIDS CASES WILL PROBABLY INCREASE
ABOUT 9-FOLD OVER THE NEXT FIVE YEARS, THE NUMBER OF AIDS CASES
INVOLVING HETEROSEXUALS WILL INCREASE ABOUT 20-FOLD.   AND THAT'S
SIGNIFICANT, I THINK YOU'LL AGREE.

UNTIL RECENTLY, WE'VE BEEN BEAMING VIRTUALLY ALL OUR INFORMATION
AND EDUCATION EFFORTS AT HOMOSEXUAL AND BISEXUAL MEN AND DRUG ABUSERS.
THEY SEEMED TO BE THE ONES WHOSE LIVES WERE AT MOST RISK AND, THERE-
FORE, THE INFORMATION WAS LITERALLY LIFE-SAVING FOR SOME OF THEM.

Example | **141**

8

I'VE BEEN DISAPPOINTED -- TO SAY THE LEAST -- AT THE FACT THAT SO
MANY OF MY FELLOW CITIZENS ENGAGE WILLINGLY AND KNOWINGLY IN SEXUAL
AND DRUG-TAKING PRACTICES THAT RISK THEIR OWN LIVES AND THE LIVES OF
OTHERS.

BUT MY DISAPPOINTMENT IS HARDLY THE ISSUE HERE. AS THE SURGEON
GENERAL OF THE U.S. PUBLIC HEALTH SERVICE, IT'S MY JOB TO WAGE ALL-OUT
WAR AGAINST <u>DISEASE</u>...AND NOT AGAINST PEOPLE.

I BELIEVE I AM A MORAL PERSON. BUT I'M <u>NOT</u> A MORAL PERSON
BECAUSE I AM A DOCTOR. THAT'S BACKWARDS.

I BECAME A DOCTOR BECAUSE I AM A MORAL PERSON. MY PERSONAL DEDI-
CATION TO HEALING AND TO CARING FOR OTHERS LED ME TO MEDICINE AND,
JUST A FEW YEARS AGO, LED ME TO ACCEPT THE PRESIDENT'S INVITATION TO
BE THE COUNTRY'S SURGEON GENERAL.

9

I HAVE BEEN TESTED BY "BABY DOE" AND BY ORGAN TRANSPLANTS AND BY
FAMILY VIOLENCE AND BY THE DISEASES OF THE AGING...BY A DOZEN OR MORE
ISSUES IN WHICH PERSONAL ETHICS AND MORALITY CAN BECOME ENTWINED WITH
MATTERS AFFECTING THE PUBLIC HEALTH. I BELIEVE I'VE COME THROUGH
THOSE ISSUES, HAVING SERVED MY PRESIDENT AND MY COUNTRY WELL.

BUT THEY WERE JUST TRAINING-GROUNDS FOR AIDS.

NOW, ONCE AGAIN, THE COUNTRY IS CONFRONTED BY A HEALTH MATTER
THAT IS LIFE-THREATENING. AND...ONCE AGAIN...I'VE BEEN ASKED TO PLAY
A LEADERSHIP ROLE. IN THAT ROLE, I MUST SPEAK TO MY FELLOW AMERICANS
PRIMARILY AS A HEALTH OFFICER.

AND WITH THIS ISSUE OF AIDS, I MUST...YES, ONCE AGAIN...COME DOWN
ON THE SIDE OF DOING WHATEVER I CAN TO SAVE HUMAN LIFE. AND I ASK
EVERY AMERICAN...I ASK EACH ONE OF YOU HERE THIS AFTERNOON...TO JOIN
ME IN THIS FUNDAMENTALLY MORAL CRUSADE AGAINST A BRUTAL, HUMILIATING,
AND FATAL DISEASE.

Example **143**

10

WHAT CAN WE DO? WE'RE NOT ALL SCIENTISTS AND BRILLIANT RESEARCHERS. SO, WHAT CAN WE REALLY DO?

THE MOST IMPORTANT THING WE CAN DO IS TO TELL THE AMERICAN PEOPLE THE FACTS ABOUT AIDS AND WHAT THEY CAN DO TO PROTECT THEMSELVES FROM IT AND TO PREVENT IT FROM SPREADING ANY FURTHER.

I HOPE YOU ALL READ MY REPORT ON AIDS. IF YOU HAVEN'T, PLEASE GET OUT A PENCIL AND TAKE DOWN THIS ADDRESS FOR YOUR COPY.

AIDS...POST OFFICE BOX 14252...WASHINGTON, D.C....20044

OR PICK UP THE PHONE AND CALL AREA CODE 301...443-0292.

LET ME REPEAT THAT FOR YOU:

AIDS...POST OFFICE BOX 14252...WASHINGTON, D.C....20044

OR CALL AREA CODE 301...443-0292.

11

IT'S IMPORTANT THAT YOU READ IT. I PUT DOWN IN THAT REPORT, IN PLAIN ENGLISH, THE NATURE OF THE THREAT WE ARE FACING AND JUST WHAT EACH OF US MUST DO TO ESCAPE ITS LETHAL GRASP.

TOTAL ABSTINENCE FROM ALL SEXUAL RELATIONS IS ONE ANSWER, BUT IT IS TOTALLY UNREALISTIC. AND IN ANY CASE, I'M NOT READY TO GIVE UP ON THE HUMAN RACE QUITE YET...AND I'M AFRAID THAT'S THE LOGICAL END OF SUCH ADVICE.

YES, IF YOU'RE YOUNG AND YOU HAVEN'T YET ACHIEVED A MUTUALLY FAITHFUL, MONOGAMOUS RELATIONSHIP -- WHAT THIS AUDIENCE CALLS "MARRIAGE" -- THEN YOU SHOULD BY ALL MEANS TAKE THE BEST POSSIBLE PRECAUTIONS AGAINST DISEASE BY ABSTAINING. PERIOD. THAT'S MY ADVICE TO YOUNGSTERS AND I DON'T THANK THERE'S ANY BETTER ADVICE YOU CAN GIVE.

Example | **145**

12

IF YOU'RE AN ADULT AND HAVE A FAITHFUL AND LOVING PARTNER -- AND YOU ARE ONE YOURSELF -- THEN SEXUALITY IS A PART OF THAT LOVING RELATIONSHIP AND THERE IS NO NEED FOR ABSTINENCE.

BUT PEOPLE DO GROW UP AND BECOME ADULTS...AND MANY ADULTS, FOR WHATEVER REASONS, DO NOT FIND A FULFILLING AND FAITHFUL, MONOGAMOUS RELATIONSHIP.

THAT'S TOO BAD...BUT I DON'T WANT THEM TO DIE BECAUSE OF IT.

IF THEY'RE GOING TO HAVE SEXUAL RELATIONS WITH FIRST SOMEONE AND THEN ANOTHER ONE, I MAY NOT FEEL VERY GOOD ABOUT THAT, BUT OF FAR MORE PUBLIC HEALTH CONSEQUENCE IS THE FACT THAT THEY SHOULD CARRY ON THAT LIFESTYLE IN THE MOST RESPONSIBLE MANNER POSSIBLE.

THE MORAL "BOTTOM LINE" FOR ME -- AND I'M SURE IT IS FOR YOU AS WELL -- IS THAT I HOPE THEY LIVE AND I MUST DO WHATEVER I CAN TO HELP THEM LIVE.

13

AND RIGHT NOW, WITHOUT A VACCINE AND WITHOUT MUCH ELSE TO GO ON, I, AS A PUBLIC HEALTH OFFICIAL, CAN ONLY ADVISE THE USE OF A CONDOM FROM START TO FINISH.

WILL THIS PROVIDE 100 PERCENT PERFECT PROTECTION? NO, AND I DON'T KNOW ANYTHING HERE ON EARTH THAT DOES.

BUT OF THE VERY FEW THINGS AVAILABLE RIGHT NOW, THE CONDOM IS THE BEST WE'VE GOT.

THIS, THEN, IS THE THREE-PART MESSAGE I'VE BEEN RELAYING TO THE AMERICAN PEOPLE SINCE OCTOBER 22:

Example | **147**

14

FIRST, IF YOU DON'T KNOW WHAT YOU'RE DOING...DON'T DO IT.
ABSTAIN.

SECOND, YOUR BEST POSSIBLE DEFENSE AGAINST THIS DISEASE -- AND
AGAINST A GREAT DEAL MORE IN THIS WORLD -- IS A FAITHFUL, MONOGA-
MOUS RELATIONSHIP. IF YOU'VE GOT IT...KEEP IT.

AND THIRD, IF YOU'RE AN ADULT WHO UNDERSTANDS YOUR OWN SEXUALITY
BUT YOU JUST HAVEN'T FOUND THAT MAGICAL MONOGAMOUS PARTNER YET,
THEN PLEASE BE CAREFUL AND, AMONG OTHER THINGS, USE A CONDOM FROM
START TO FINISH.

15

LET ME AGAIN EMPHASIZE THAT WE'RE TALKING ABOUT A DISEASE THAT NOW THREATENS EVERYBODY...EVERYWHERE.

IT IS NO LONGER PRIMARILY A DISEASE ATTACKING THE HOMOSEXUAL COMMUNITIES OF SAN FRANCISCO, LOS ANGELES, AND NEW YORK CITY.

NOT ANY MORE.

NOW, OTHER CITIES AND STATES ARE SHOWING A RISE IN CASES, TOO. THE SAME CITIES, SMALL AND LARGE, IN WHICH YOU BROADCAST YOUR MESSAGES OF DEVOTION EVERY DAY.

<u>HOUSTON</u> HAD 345 CASES LAST YEAR...

<u>DALLAS</u> HAD 208...

<u>ATLANTA</u> HAD 185...

Example | **149**

16

BOSTON HAD 155 LAST YEAR, ALSO...

COLORADO REPORTED 167 NEW CASES...

OHIO HAD 173...

AND ARKANSAS HAD 40 NEW CASES LAST YEAR.

ALL 50 STATES, THE DISTRICT OF COLUMBIA, PUERTO RICO, GUAM, THE TRUST TERRITORIES...ALL HAVE BEEN TOUCHED BY AIDS.

WE COULD ALREADY SEE THIS DEVELOPMENT OCCURRING, WHEN PRESIDENT REAGAN ASKED ME -- BACK IN FEBRUARY OF 1986 -- TO PULL TOGETHER EVERYTHING WE KNEW ABOUT AIDS AND PUT IT IN THAT PLAIN-ENGLISH REPORT TO THE AMERICAN PEOPLE...THE ONE I MENTIONED A MOMENT AGO.

17

I MET WITH INDIVIDUALS AND GROUPS FROM ACROSS THE SPECTRUM OF SOCIETY...

GROUPS LIKE THE NATIONAL EDUCATION ASSOCIATION AND THE NATIONAL P.T.A....

THE NATIONAL COUNCIL OF CHURCHES AND THE CHRISTIAN LIFE COMMISSION OF THE SOUTHERN BAPTIST CONVENTION...

THE SYNAGOGUE COUNCIL OF AMERICA AND THE NATIONAL CONFERENCE OF CATHOLIC BISHOPS...

I TALKED WITH THE NATIONAL COALITION OF BLACK AND LESBIAN GAYS AND THE WASHINGTON BUSINESS GROUP ON HEALTH.

I MET WITH THE REPRESENTATIVES OF LOCAL, COUNTY, AND STATE AND TERRITORIAL HEALTH OFFICIALS, ALSO...26 GROUPS IN ALL.

Example | **151**

18

THEY WERE ALL EXTRAORDINARILY CANDID. AND EACH ONE ALSO PLEDGED TO HELP GET MY REPORT INTO THE HANDS OF EVERY AMERICAN.

AFTER 8 MONTHS OF LISTENING AND WRITING, I DELIVERED MY REPORT TO THE CABINET AND TO THE PRESIDENT. IT WAS ACCEPTED...AND I RELEASED IT ON OCTOBER 22, 1986.

LADIES AND GENTLEMEN, I WANT TO ASSURE YOU THAT AT <u>NO</u> TIME DID <u>ANYONE</u> SUGGEST A LITTLE CHANGE HERE OR A LITTLE CHANGE THERE. THE FINAL REPORT I RELEASED WAS THE EXACT SAME REPORT THAT I PERSONALLY WROTE BETWEEN FEBRUARY AND SEPTEMBER OF LAST YEAR.

AND I CAN FURTHER ASSURE YOU THAT SINCE THAT TIME I HAVE HAD <u>NO</u> MISGIVINGS ABOUT ANYTHING IN THAT REPORT.

IT'S TRUE. AND IT STANDS.

19

BUT, AS I SAY, <u>NOTHING</u> AND <u>NOBODY</u> IS PERFECT. SO, IF I HAD TO DO IT OVER AGAIN, I'D PROBABLY BE JUST A LITTLE BIT CLEARER ON PAGE 5, ON THAT PAGE OF THE REPORT I WROTE THAT "EDUCATION ABOUT AIDS SHOULD START IN EARLY ELEMENTARY SCHOOL AND AT HOME..." AND SO ON.

YOU CAN'T TEACH A CHILD ANYTHING ABOUT AIDS UNLESS HE OR SHE HAS SOME BASIC SEXUAL EDUCATION. SO CLEARLY, EDUCATION ABOUT HUMAN SEXUALITY SHOULD COME FIRST AND THUS PROVIDE THE NECESSARY CONTEXT FOR THE SPECIFIC MATERIAL ABOUT AIDS THAT SHOULD COME ALONG LATER.

IN GENERAL MY 32-PAGE REPORT HAS HAD OVERWHELMING APPROVAL AND ACCEPTANCE. BUT IT DOES CONTAIN 92 WORDS ON SEX EDUCATION. AND THOSE 92 WORDS BECAME THE FOCAL POINT OF THE MEDIA COVERAGE OF THE REPORT... AND OF MUCH BICKERING AND CRITICISM, TOO.

ODDLY ENOUGH, MY MOST VOCAL CRITICS HAVE BEEN OF A VERY CONSERVA-TIVE PERSUASION -- AS AM I.

Example | **153**

20

BUT THESE CRITICS HAVE PRESENTED <u>THEIR OWN</u> WORST POSSIBLE INTER-
PRETATIONS OF THE REPORT AND THEN THEY'VE HELD <u>ME</u> UP AS THE ONE
RESPONSIBLE FOR THESE WORST-CASE SCENARIOS.

HOWEVER, I'VE BEEN ATTACKING SEX EDUCATION CURRICULA THAT JUST
TEACH TECHNIQUE AND DON'T MENTION RESPONSIBILTY OR MORALITY...AND I
TOOK THAT POSITION BEFORE SOME OF MY CRITICS KNEW THERE <u>WAS</u> SUCH A
THING AS SEX.

WHEN YOU SPEAK OF SEX EDUCATION, YOU OUGHT TO KEEP A FEW THINGS
IN MIND. FOR EXAMPLE...

21

    *   WE HAVE ONLY A FEW YEARS OF GRACE TO HELP A YOUNG CHILD UNDERSTAND HIS OR HER SEXUALITY BEFORE THE ONSET OF PUBERTY.

    *   ALSO, A PARENT SHOULD HANDLE THIS EDUCATION OF THE CHILD, BUT EXPERIENCE HAS SHOWN THAT A PARENT CAN NEVER BE THE EXCLUSIVE EDUCATOR. THE <u>BEST</u> EDUCATOR...THE <u>EDUCATOR OF CHOICE</u>...YES, OF COURSE. BUT THE <u>EXCLUSIVE</u> EDUCATOR, I DOUBT THAT.

    I WISH WE <u>COULD</u> SAY THAT PARENTS WHO WANT TO CAN BE IN TOTAL CONTROL OF A CHILD'S SEX EDUCATION. BUT WE KNOW THAT CHILDREN DO LEARN ABOUT SEX FROM MANY UNSTRUCTURED AND UNPLANNED EXPERIENCES, INCLUDING THE VIEWING OF MOVIES AND TELEVISION AND FRIENDSHIPS WITH OTHER CHILDREN.

Example | **155**

22

SOME RESEARCH WAS RECENTLY DONE ON THIS MATTER BY MICHIGAN STATE UNIVERSITY. THE RESEARCHERS FOUND, FOR EXAMPLE, THAT A LARGE NUMBER OF 9TH- AND 10TH-GRADE GIRLS WATCH BETWEEN 1 AND 2 HOURS OF SOAP OPERAS EVERY DAY AFTER SCHOOL.

AND WHAT ARE THEY VIEWING? THE RESEARCHERS REPORT THAT, AMONG OTHER THINGS, SEXUAL INTERCOURSE BETWEEN UNMARRIED PARTNERS IS SHOWN OR DISCUSSED ON MID-DAY SOAP OPERAS ON AN AVERAGE OF 1.56 TIMES AN HOUR.

IN THE EVENING, A LARGER NUMBER OF 9TH- AND 10TH-GRADE GIRLS AND BOYS WATCH 3 TO 4 HOURS OF TELEVISION. ON THOSE PRIME-TIME EVENING SHOWS, ACTS OF UNMARRIED INTERCOURSE ARE SHOWN OR DISCUSSED ON AN AVERAGE OF ONCE AN HOUR.

23

THE SAME RESEARCHERS ALSO FOUND THAT OVER 60 TO 70 PERCENT OF THOSE 9TH- AND 10TH-GRADERS SAW THE TOP 5 "R"-RATED FILMS, IN WHICH SEXUAL INTERCOURSE BETWEEN UNMARRIED PARTNERS OCCURRED ON THE AVERAGE OF <u>8 TIMES PER FILM</u>.   IN THE WORST FILMS, IT OCCURRED <u>15</u> TIMES.

AMERICA'S CHILDREN DON'T LIVE IN A VACUUM, AND, THEREFORE, WE ALL MUST WORK TOGETHER -- PARENTS, EDUCATORS, AND RELIGIOUS AND COMMUNITY LEADERS -- TO HELP OUR CHILDREN GROW UP AND COPE WITH THE REAL WORLD OF PLEASURE AND DANGER.

*   SOMETHING ELSE WE NEED TO KEEP IN MIND, IN THIS MATTER OF SEX EDUCATION.

WHEN A CHILD COMES HOME FROM SCHOOL AND TALKS ABOUT SOME CONTRO-VERSIAL IDEA THAT WAS PRESENTED, MOST PARENTS DON'T PANIC...EVEN THOSE PARENTS WHO HAVE STRONG FEELINGS ON THE MATTER.

Example | **157**

24

NO.   THOSE PARENTS SIT DOWN AND PASS ON TO THEIR CHILDREN -- IN
POSITIVE TERMS -- WHAT THEIR FEELINGS AND THEIR STANDARDS ON THE
MATTER MAY BE.

WHY CAN'T PARENTS ACT THE SAME WAY WHEN THEIR CHILDREN RAISE
QUESTIONS ABOUT SEX?

I THINK THEY SHOULD.   BUT "SHOULD" AND "COULD" ARE TWO DIFFERENT
MATTERS.

MANY PARENTS ARE SIMPLY NOT COMFORTABLE ENOUGH WITH THEIR OWN
SEXUALITY TO TALK ABOUT IT FREELY EVEN WITH A SPOUSE.   AND THEY CONVEY
THAT SAME DISCOMFORT TO THEIR CHILDREN, RIGHT AT THE TIME WHEN THE
CHILDREN NEED STRONG PARENTAL GUIDANCE...OR SOME POSITIVE DIALOGUE ON
THE MATTER...OR SIMPLY SOME HONEST AND COMPLETE ANSWERS TO THEIR
QUESTIONS.

25

A CHILD WILL SENSE THIS DISCOMFORT AND WILL BACK AWAY FROM THE
SUBJECT...AND AN OPPORTUNITY FOR THE PARENTS WILL BE LOST.

SEX EDUCATION -- WHICH I'D RATHER CALL "HEALTH AND HUMAN DEVELOP-
MENT" -- CAN PROBABLY BE TAUGHT BEGINNING IN KINDERGARTEN AND FIRST
GRADE. AND HERE I'M SPEAKING OF A CURRICULUM THAT ANSWERS THE COMMON,
EVERYDAY QUESTIONS RAISED BY YOUNG CHILDREN, QUESTIONS SUCH AS "WHERE
DO BABIES COME FROM?"

THIS KIND OF EDUCATION CAN AND SHOULD BE NON-THREATENING...IT CAN
TEACH GOOD VALUES...IT CAN HELP DEVELOP THE CHILD'S OWN SENSE OF
PERSONAL RESPONSIBILITY...AND IT CAN STRENGTHEN THE CONCEPT OF "THE
FAMILY."

Example | **159**

26

THIS KIND OF SEX EDUCATION SHOULD UNFOLD ACCORDING TO THE
DEVELOPMENTAL AGE OF CHILDREN AND TO THEIR DIFFERENT LEVELS OF AWARE-
NESS AND CURIOSITY. I DON'T SEE ANY REASON TO CLING TO A RIGID
SCHEDULE BASED ON CHRONOLOGICAL AGE.

IF THE CURRICULUM IS WELL-PLANNED AND THOUGHTFULLY CARRIED OUT,
THEN IT WILL BE POSSIBLE TO BRING TO THE ATTENTION OF THE CHILDREN THE
FACTS ABOUT SEXUALLY TRANSMITTED DISEASE -- AND AIDS IN PARTICULAR --
ALONG ABOUT THE JUNIOR HIGH SCHOOL YEARS...THE YEARS OF EARLY
ADOLESCENCE.

SOME UNINFORMED, INACCURATE, AND LESS-THAN-HONEST CRITICS OF MY
POSITION BELIEVE THAT WHAT I'VE JUST SAID IS TANTAMOUNT TO THE MOST
HEINOUS OF ACTIVITIES. THEY SAY IT MEANS, FOR EXAMPLE, AND I'M
QUOTING NOW...

27

"...SPONSORING HOMOSEXUALLY-ORIENTED CURRICULA..."

"...TEACHING BUGGERY IN THE 3RD GRADE..."

OR "...PROVIDING CONDOMS TO 8-YEAR-OLDS..."

ISN'T THAT AWFUL STUFF? OF COURSE IT IS.

AND THEY CHARGE THAT, BY ADVOCATING A STRONG, HONEST, AND FAMILY-
CENTERED APPROACH TO SEX EDUCATION IN ORDER TO SAVE THE LIVES OF OUR
YOUNG PEOPLE, I HAVE THEREFORE "DEPARTED THE FAITH" -- WHATEVER THAT
MEANS -- OR I'VE "GONE OVER TO THE OTHER SIDE" -- WHEREVER <u>THAT</u> IS.

THIS IS A PERSONAL MATTER, SO LET ME GET PERSONAL, FOR A MOMENT.

Example | **161**

28

AS YOU KNOW, I'VE CARRIED A LOT OF WATER FOR POLITICAL CONSERVA-
TIVES...AND SOME OF THEM HAVE TURNED OUT TO BE FAIR-WEATHER FRIENDS.

AND TO THAT MEMBER·OF THE RELIGIOUS RIGHT WHO WROTE THAT THE
NOISE I HEAR IS FRANCIS SCHAEFFER ROLLING OVER IN HIS GRAVE...I SAY
THAT THE NOISE I HEAR IS MORE LIKELY HIS APPLAUSE.

YOU, AS CHRISTIANS, WILL CONTINUE TO BE TESTED BY TREMENDOUS
QUESTIONS THAT ARISE FROM THE TURMOIL OF CURRENT EVENTS. THESE
QUESTIONS MAKE YOU EXAMINE AND RE-EXAMINE WHO YOU ARE AND WHAT YOU
STAND FOR.

THIS IS NOT AN AGE FOR THE FAINT OF HEART...OR OF SOUL.

ONE OF THOSE QUESTIONS INVOLVES HOMOSEXUALITY. YOU CAN'T AVOID
IT, IF YOU'RE GOING TO DISCUSS AIDS.

29

IF YOU REGARD HOMOSEXUAL BEHAVIOR AS SIN, PLEASE REMEMBER THAT ONE OF YOUR FUNDAMENTAL TEACHINGS HAS BEEN TO "SEPARATE THE SIN FROM THE SINNER."

YOU MAY HATE THE SIN...BUT YOU ARE TO LOVE THE SINNER.

AND LET ME REPEAT AGAIN THE CRUX OF OUR BATTLE...IT IS A BATTLE AGAINST A <u>DISEASE</u>, <u>NOT</u> AGAINST PEOPLE.

AND HERE'S ANOTHER QUESTION THAT CAN TEST YOU. YOU WILL HEAR A LOT ABOUT "SAFE SEX" AND HOW THIS OR THAT TECHNIQUE IS A WAY OF CONTAINING THE AIDS EPIDEMIC.

BUT THE SAFEST APPROACH TO SEXUALITY FOR ADULTS IS TO CHOOSE EITHER ABSTINENCE OR FAITHFUL MONOGAMY. IN THE ABSENCE OF SUCH A CHOICE, THEN AN INDIVIDUAL MUST BE WARNED TO USE THE PROTECTION OF A CONDOM -- FROM START TO FINISH -- IN SEXUAL INTERCOURSE.

Example | **163**

30

AND THERE'S A THIRD QUESTION THAT WE MUST FACE.

A LARGE NUMBER OF TRULY INNOCENT PEOPLE ARE BEING INFECTED BY THE AIDS VIRUS AND THEY ARE GOING TO DIE. WHO ARE THEY? THEY ARE...

THE WIVES OF BISEXUAL MEN...

THEY ARE THE SPOUSES OF I.V. DRUG USERS...

THEY'RE THE WIVES AND HUSBANDS OF PROMISCUOUS SPOUSES.

AND I'M AFRAID WE MUST ALSO COUNT THE BABIES BORN TO I.V. DRUG USERS OR OTHERWISE INFECTED MOTHERS. THEY ARE BEING ABANDONED AND ARE DYING ALONE IN HOSPITAL NURSERIES.

THEY ARE THE MOST INNOCENT VICTIMS OF ALL.

31

I'VE GONE INTO SOME DETAIL HERE BECAUSE I KNOW YOU ARE GENUINELY CONCERNED ABOUT THESE MATTERS. BUT I HOPE I HAVE GIVEN YOU SOME NEW FOOD FOR THOUGHT.

I HOPE THAT, WHEN YOU NEXT HEAR THE TERM "SEX EDUCATION," YOU WON'T JUST JUMP TO THE CONCLUSION THAT IT MEANS SOME CRACK-BRAINED CURRICULUM THAT HAS GOTTEN OFF THE TRACK. AND I HOPE YOU WON'T CONSIDER IT TO BE A CURRICULUM THAT -- BY DEFINITION -- CAN ONLY TEACH TECHNIQUE WITHOUT MENTIONING RESPONSIBILITY OR MORALITY.

NOT SO. THINK INSTEAD, IF YOU WILL, ABOUT SOME OF THE THINGS I'VE MENTIONED HERE THIS AFTERNOON.

AND LASTLY, WHEN AIDS INTRUDES ON SOME ASPECT OF YOUR OWN LIVES, PLEASE REMEMBER THAT THE SICK AND THE DYING REQUIRE OUR CARE AND OUR COMPASSION, NO MATTER HOW THE ILLNESS WAS CONTRACTED.

Example | **165**

32

NOW, YOU'VE BEEN A VERY GOOD AND PATIENT AUDIENCE AND I WILL
CLOSE MY REMARKS WITH A LITTLE PERSONAL RECOLLECTION.

A FEW YEARS AGO, FRANCIS SCHAEFFER AND I WERE TOURING THE
COUNTRY, SPEAKING OUT AGAINST ABORTION, AND PRESENTING OUR FILM,
"WHATEVER HAPPENED TO THE HUMAN RACE."

I CAN TELL YOU THAT WE WERE FREQUENTLY VERY DISCOURAGED BY THE
RESPONSE OF MANY EVANGELICALS. THEY DREW THEIR SKIRTS ABOUT THEM AND
SHUNNED THE ISSUE OF ABORTION.

IN DUE TIME THEY'VE COME AROUND AND HAVE BECOME ACTIVISTS IN THE
PRO-LIFE MOVEMENT.

DISCUSSION STARTERS

In the Commentary section, several suggestions are made as to when a manuscript speech might be necessary. Which of these factors do you think applied to the surgeon general in this situation? What do you see in this manuscript that tends to personalize the speaker's message?

BIBLIOGRAPHY

Crocker, Lionel. "Speaking Without Notes." *Today's Speech* 8, no. 2 (Apr. 1, 1960):3–8.

> Prof. Crocker takes the side opposite manuscript speaking. He asserts, "Many a speaker would make himself more effective if he would only train himself to throw away his notes." Is it true that speaking notes somehow "come between" a speaker and audience and make speech-making harder?

Storytelling

ASSIGNMENT

Tell a story from your own ethnic, family, or cultural tradition. The tradition you choose may originate outside the United States, or it may be distinctly American.

COMMENTARY

Narrative is as old as human communication itself. Some would argue that all communication is narrative. Sometimes in public speaking a whole speech might be constructed as one narrative (see Conwell's "Acres of Diamonds" in Chapter 8). More often, narratives or anecdotes[1] appear within speeches to support an argument in persuasion, to illustrate an idea in informative speaking, or to magnify a virtue in ceremonial speeches. The effect of stories is often emotional. Obviously, the recitation of facts, data, and statistics has little power to move an audience emotionally. A well-told story, on the other hand, has considerable potential to provoke emotion.

Anecdotes appearing in speeches can be sorted into four basic types. Personal anecdotes are things that have happened to the speaker himself or herself. Contemporary stories reflect events from recent times, the kinds of things we hear about in the news of the day. Historical anecdotes come from the past, say, before the speaker's birth. Finally, fictional stories come from fables, novels, TV shows, movies, and all the other sources of print and broadcast fiction, present and past.

Regardless of what type they are, all stories seem to be based on a common narrative structure. Stories begin with the introduction of some sort of conflict or plot. The conflict then develops by creating suspense about its outcome. The suspense builds up to a point of climax or resolution of the conflict. Then the story winds down to a conclusion. One problem associated with the use of anecdotes in speaking is the failure of speakers to transform incidents into anecdotes. In other

---

[1]For our purposes, narratives shall refer to longer stories and anecdotes to shorter ones.

words, it is seldom compelling to merely tell what happened. What happened must be constructed with conscious effort to appropriately develop conflict, suspense, and resolution.

A properly structured story will likely feature more than one of the following characteristics:

- *Specific details.* There's an old saying that "specificity is the soul of credibility." It is also the soul of good storytelling. Specific rather than abstract language, physical and psychological details, descriptions of people, appeals to the senses, and the inclusion of facts combine to create and sustain interest in stories.
- *Interest factors.* Stories incorporate things that people find interesting like competition, money, sex, death, celebrity, secrets, the future, novelty, and so on.
- *Dialogue.* When stories relate conversations between people, speakers can use vocal and nonverbal cues to say the exact words of characters.
- *Humor.* When appropriate to the speaker's objectives, stories may include humor in the form of hyperbole, puns, irony, and the like.

In January 1991, the U.S. Senate engaged in a notably vigorous and eloquent debate on the authorization of military force prior to the first Gulf war. In the course of the debate, Senator Alan Dixon of Illinois spoke in favor of a minority position that would have allowed American airpower to be used against Iraq without a ground invasion of Kuwait. In his speech, Senator Dixon told the following story:

> And later in the day, yesterday, the President of the United States [George H. W. Bush] called me and asked me to vote for this resolution. I said, "Can't we work out a compromise by which some of us could stand in support of you by use of air power without committing our ground forces there?" And he made no such commitment.
>
> Now, let me tell you something. My dear friend and young Congressman, Jerry Costello, from my home 21st Congressional District in Illinois has a boy on the ground there in Kuwait in the 82nd Airborne.
>
> My best friend and neighbor lost his son as a lance corporal in Vietnam. Mr. President, I was a young State Senator in Illinois in those years. I was trying a lawsuit and I went home to my house to get a medical file for my lawsuit, and while I was there the doorbell rang. I came down the steps and opened the door to my house. There stood a Marine major in resplendent formal uniform and a Marine sergeant, and they asked for my friend. They said, "He is not home next door." I knew what that meant, Mr. President. I told them where his place of business was, and they went there.
>
> When my friend had emotionally recovered, to some extent, he later told me that he was sitting in his office and he saw that Marine major and that Marine sergeant walking through his place of business, and he jumped up from his desk and he ran to the door and he said, "My God, they have killed my son. My God, they have killed my son."
>
> Mr. President, sanctions and talks can work if we are diligent and we assiduously pursue that course, but if they do not, massive air power in a matter of days can bring this villain to his knees to sue for peace.[2]

---

[2]*Authorizing Use of U.S. Armed Forces Pursuant to U.N. Security Council Resolution*, 102nd Cong., 1st sess., *Congressional Record—Senate* 137, no. 8:369–404. Dixon's speech appears on p. 373.

This anecdote illustrates several ideas about stories discussed earlier. Senator Dixon uses the story as evidence in a persuasive speech. He is involved in this story, but only as a bystander. So we would classify the story more a contemporary anecdote than a personal one. Notice how the structure of the story builds to a climax. The suspense of the story does not revolve around whether the young marine was killed in Vietnam. We are told that fact at the outset. The point of the story is our heartbreaking reaction to the tragedy of death in war. Notice also the attention to detail: "a medical file for my lawsuit," "resplendent, formal uniform." In the video recording of this speech, Senator Dixon can be heard using his voice forcefully and emotionally to convey the dialogue, especially of the bereaved father.

Obviously, there was no place for humor in Senator Dixon's story. But there was a note of irony or ambiguity that helped advance his argument against a costly ground invasion of Kuwait. When the father shouts, "They've killed my son!" to whom is he referring? The Viet Cong? The Marine Corps? The politicians who supported the Vietnam War? This is Dixon's point. When soldiers die in battle, someone bears responsibility for it. This is an argument against the Senate giving hasty or premature authorization for an invasion. Dixon and others wanted to see if aerial warfare by itself would be sufficient to defeat Iraq before sending in ground troops. Dixon's story of the fallen marine advances his argument with emotional proof—exactly what you would expect a story in a persuasive speech to do.

CLASSICAL CONCEPT: PATHOS

In addition to rational proof (logos) and speaker credibility (ethos), classical rhetoricians identified emotional proof or pathos as critical to persuasive discourse. Today the emotions are usually thought of negatively as being irrational. For the ancients, however, the emotions were seen to reflect reasonable psychological motivations. Aristotle begins his discussion of emotion by pointing out how important it is for a speaker "to entertain right feelings towards his hearers; and also that his hearers themselves should be in just the right frame of mind (*Rhetoric*, II, 1)." During the 2008 presidential campaign, both candidates were often criticized on the basis of emotion. Barack Obama was taken to task for being overly cool, detached, and unflappable, while John McCain was said to be reactive and given to excess emotion. Both candidates generated strong emotional responses from the electorate.

Rather than seeing emotion as something "out of control," classical rhetoricians taught that the awareness and use of the emotions were speaking skills that could be developed through observation and experience. According to Cicero, the common emotions are identifiable: "the emotions which eloquence has to excite in the minds of the tribunal, or whatever other audience we may be addressing, are most commonly love, hate, wrath, jealousy, compassion, hope, joy, fear or vexation . . ." (*De Oratore*, II, 206). Aristotle spends considerable time analyzing a list of emotions (II, 2–11). Furthermore, speakers must determine if the situation is right for an emotional appeal. For Cicero, emotional "fireworks should not be used in petty matters, or with men of such temper that our eloquence can achieve nothing in the way of influencing their minds" (II, 205).

Cicero has one of his characters declare, "For men decide far more problems by hate, or love, or lust, or rage, or sorrow, or joy, or hope, or fear, or illusion, or some other inward emotion, than by reality, or authority, or any legal standard, or judicial precedent, or statute" (*De Oratore*, II, 178). Do you agree with this sweeping assertion?

EXAMPLE

STATEMENT TO THE CREDENTIALS COMMITTEE

FANNIE LOU HAMER
DEMOCRATIC NATIONAL CONVENTION

In 1964, a dissident and racially integrated delegation of Democrats from Mississippi tried to unseat the regular party and segregated delegation at the Democratic National Convention. A member of the dissident delegation, Fannie Lou Hamer, told her story at a Credentials Committee hearing at the Convention. Hamer's speech is in narrative form and is clearly connected to a type of religious rhetoric called testifying. People who testify simply tell what happened to them. The climax of this story occurs near the end when Hamer says, "I was in jail when Medgar Evers was murdered." We know from the outset that Hamer survived her ordeal. Reference to Evers, however, reveals the true nature of the conflict. Her story is not about mere harassment; it reveals itself to be a hor-rific life-and-death struggle over the simple right to vote. The stark, matter-of-fact simplicity of the story carries a profound emotional power.

Mr. Chairman, and to the Credentials Committee, my name is Mrs. Fannie Lou Hamer, and I live at 626 East Lafayette Street, Ruleville, Mississippi, Sunflower County, the home of Senator James O. Eastland, and Senator Stennis. It was the 31st of August in 1962 that eighteen of us traveled twenty-six miles to the county courthouse in Indianola to try to
5 register to become first class citizens. We was met in Indianola by policemen, Highway Patrolmen, and they only allowed two of us in to take the literacy test at the time. After we had taken this test and started back to Ruleville, we was held up by the City Police and the State Highway Patrolmen and carried back to Indianola where the bus driver was charged that day with driving a bus the wrong color.
10 After we paid the fine among us, we continued on to Ruleville, and Reverend Jeff Sunny carried me four miles in the rural area where I had worked as a timekeeper and sharecropper for eighteen years. I was met there by my children, who told me the plantation owner was angry because I had gone down tried to register. After they told me, my husband came, and said the plantation owner was raising Cain because
15 I had tried to register. And before he quit talking the plantation owner came and said, "Fannie Lou, do you know did Pap tell you what I said?" And I said, "Yes, sir." He said, "Well I mean that." Said, "If you don't go down and withdraw your registration, you will have to leave." Said, "Then if you go down and withdraw," said, "you still might have to

Example 171

go because we're not ready for that in Mississippi." And I addressed him and told him and said, "I didn't try to register for you. I tried to register for myself." I had to leave that same night. 20

On the 10th of September 1962, sixteen bullets was fired into the home of Mr. and Mrs. Robert Tucker for me. That same night two girls were shot in Ruleville, Mississippi. Also, Mr. Joe McDonald's house was shot in. And June the 9th, 1963, I had attended a voter registration workshop; was returning back to Mississippi. Ten of us was traveling by 25 the Continental Trailway bus. When we got to Winona, Mississippi, which is Montgomery County, four of the people got off to use the washroom, and two of the people to use the restaurant, two of the people wanted to use the washroom. The four people that had gone in to use the restaurant was ordered out. During this time I was on the bus. But when I looked through the window and saw they had rushed out I got off of the bus to 30 see what had happened. And one of the ladies said, "It was a State Highway Patrolman and a Chief of Police ordered us out."

I got back on the bus and one of the persons had used the washroom got back on the bus, too. As soon as I was seated on the bus, I saw when they began to get the five people in a highway patrolman's car. I stepped off of the bus to see what was happening 35 and somebody screamed from the car that the five workers was in and said, "Get that one there." And when I went to get in the car, when the man told me I was under arrest, he kicked me.

I was carried to the county jail and put in the booking room. They left some of the people in the booking room and began to place us in cells. I was placed in a 40 cell with a young woman called Miss Ivesta Simpson. After I was placed in the cell I began to hear sounds of licks and screams. I could hear the sounds of licks and horrible screams. And I could hear somebody say, "Can you say, 'yes, sir,' nigger? Can you say 'yes, sir'?" And they would say other horrible names. She would say, "Yes, I can say 'yes, sir.'" So, well, say it. She said, "I don't know you well enough." They beat 45 her, I don't know how long. And after a while she began to pray, and asked God to have mercy on those people.

And it wasn't too long before three white men came to my cell. One of these men was a State Highway Patrolman and he asked me where I was from. And I told him Ruleville. He said, "We are going to check this." And they left my cell and it wasn't too 50 long before they came back. He said, "You are from Ruleville all right," and he used a curse word. And he said, "We're going to make you wish you was dead."

I was carried out of that cell into another cell where they had two Negro prisoners. The State Highway Patrolmen ordered the first Negro to take the blackjack. The first Negro prisoner ordered me, by orders from the State Highway Patrolman, for me to lay 55 down on a bunk bed on my face. And I laid on my face, the first Negro began to beat me. And I was beat by the first Negro until he was exhausted. I was holding my hands behind me at that time on my left side, because I suffered from polio when I was six years old.

After the first Negro had beat until he was exhausted, the State Highway Patrolman ordered the second Negro to take the blackjack. The second Negro began to beat and 60 I began to work my feet, and the State Highway Patrolman ordered the first Negro who

had beat to sit on my feet to keep me from working my feet. I began to scream and one white man got up and began to beat me in my head and tell me to hush. One white man my dress had worked up high he walked over and pulled my dress. I pulled my dress
65   down and he pulled my dress back up. I was in jail when Medgar Evers was murdered.

All of this is on account of we want to register, to become first class citizens. And if the Freedom Democratic Party is not seated now, I question America. Is this America, the land of the free and the home of the brave, where we have to sleep with our telephones off of the hooks because our lives be threatened daily, because we want to live
70   as decent human beings, in America?

Thank you.

Source: Statement to the Credentials Committee at the Democratic National Convention (1964) by Fannie Lou Hamer. Copyright (c) 1964. Reprinted with permission of Charles McLaurin, Fannie Lou Hamer Statue Committee. Information on National Black United Fund (NBUF) can be found at the website, www.nbuf.org. For more information on FLHSC and the legacy of Mrs. Hamer please visit www.fannielouhamer.info.

DISCUSSION STARTERS

How does this story illustrate the old saying that "specificity is the soul of credibility?"

BIBLIOGRAPHY

Fisher, Walter R. "Narration as a Human Communication Paradigm: The Case of Public Moral Argument." *Communication Monographs* 63 (1996):1–28.

Fisher goes beyond the classical idea of narrative as one of several rhetorical techniques to argue that a "narrative paradigm" can be seen at work as a fundamental structure of all human communication.

On Camera Speaking

ASSIGNMENT

Select a speech assignment from one of the chapters in this book and present it on camera. Present only the video recording to the class.

COMMENTARY

Technological advances in recent years have made video productions of all kinds ubiquitous. In an age when everyone is a TV producer, we may think we are capable to video record whatever we want to. However, video speaking in leadership contexts is a far cry from the pratfall clips of funniest home videos, webcam stunts, or YouTube entertainments. Serious pursuits require more than point-and-shoot cell phones. Speaking on video is an important component of political campaigns, useful in business, and often employed by religious organizations. Savvy public speakers understand that the same principles of effective communication like organization, preparation, and substance apply just as much to video as to live audience speeches. At the same time they realize that video presentations are not the same as live speeches. Serious speech communication via video technology creates several special considerations for public speakers.

One thing video speakers need is a vivid imagination. In video speaking, the audience you want to address exists in your imagination. When recording, a little red light on a small machine is the only audience you see. The real audience for your speech is in your mind. Speakers are often advised to strike a casual or conversational style in video delivery because we often imagine the video audience as sitting in a living room at home. Television is a notoriously casual or cool medium, but that does not always mean a video recording will be viewed in casual circumstances. Video can be watched in a variety of contexts: on a computer screen while sitting on an airplane, on a TV while lying in bed, or at a meeting in an auditorium with five hundred other people. When you imagine your audience in a video presentation, try to take into account who will watch and under what circumstances.

These factors must be integrated into the nature and content of your message to achieve the best approach to the unseen audience.

Live video speakers must be on time. When a machine dictates ten minutes, it means ten minutes, not ten minutes and twenty seconds. Richard Nixon was a pioneer in the use of TV for politics, but in his famous Checkers speech (discussed in Chapter 2), he was tripped up by time constraints. When the thirty minutes of airtime he had purchased were up, he was cut off in mid-sentence just as he tried to tell people what to do to express their support for him. Just the opposite is true for taped video speakers. Make time to shoot numerous takes. Also, when recording, you can ignore mistakes and gaffs and leave them to editing, if it is available.

Video speakers have to look good. Cameras, especially high-definition ones, can do close-ups that reveal far more than any live audience could get close enough to see. Every baseball fan has seen the TV close-ups that enable him or her to count the nose hairs of pitchers and batters. Eight years after the Checkers speech, Richard Nixon was ambushed by the demands of video production when he appeared in the very first televised presidential debates in desperate need of a shave. The color and contrast of both skin and clothing must be attended to by video speakers. By all means, use makeup if you can (men included!). Studio lighting is bright and can be very hot. Not only can makeup soften glare, it can also hide perspiration. You should not be seen sweating on camera. Avoid patterned clothing and the colors red, black, and white. Make sure nonverbal elements such as hairstyle and wardrobe correspond naturally to the content and purpose of the speech. Obviously, business presentations are made in business attire, not cutoffs and T-shirts. Finally, and sad to say, even though it is cruel and ought to be resisted, people who are less than good looking by social and cultural norms might, if given the choice, consider carefully whether to make video presentations.

Speaking for video requires extraordinary control. Since cameras magnify the smallest gestures and facial expressions, related nonverbal communication factors can be even more important for video speeches than live audience presentations. As a result, video speakers must control delivery factors and learn how to vary delivery in subtle ways. In regard to movement, the basic rule of thumb is to hold still. Movement must be purposeful and limited. Large gestures are appropriate for the podium and big audiences, but for the small screen use small gestures.

Finally, the best advice for public speakers who use the television medium is to remember that all media are not the same. Don't assume that if it worked for a live audience it will also be successful on the screen or vice versa. In classical times communication media were limited, first to the spoken word, then including written communication. Today the modern communication environment encompasses a great variety of media requiring multiple skills of successful communicators.

CLASSICAL CONCEPT: AUDIENCES

When compared to Los Angeles County, California, or Queens County, New York, as we know them, the classical Greek city-states appear to be very demographically homogeneous. Nevertheless, Aristotle saw what he regarded as important differences among the mostly male members of Athenian audiences. We can read

Example | **175**

his audience analysis as a kind of "psychological profiling" in which he tries to figure out the interests, needs, and reactions of various groups (*Rhetoric* II, 12–17).

For example, Aristotle discusses the ages of audience members, observing that young men tend to "look at the good side rather than the bad, not having yet witnessed many instances of wickedness." Old men, however, "lack confidence in the future; partly through experience—for most things go wrong, or anyhow turn out worse than one expects. . . ." In addition to age, Aristotle directs speakers to take into account the social status of their hearers. These factors include birth or family background, wealth, and power. Someone from humble and impoverished origins will have a different take on life from someone from a rich and powerful family.

We might criticize Aristotle's audience analysis as being based on nothing more than common sense or stereotypes. In a way, both charges are true. Keep in mind, however, that stereotypes do not fall out of the sky, but are often based on shared perceptions and experiences. What gives stereotypes a bad name is that our perceptions and experiences are often limited or skewed. Also, applying general observations to a particular person is almost always unfair and foolish. Even so, it is also foolish to completely discount the value of common sense in figuring out how to address particular audiences.

Speakers today are likely to encounter audience diversity far beyond anything Aristotle could have imagined. Gender, race, ethnicity, language, religion, economic status, and many other factors, along with age and social status, create huge challenges to rhetorical communication. The "diversity sensitivity" we strive for is vitally important, but not altogether new. Aristotle would probably enthusiastically endorse our efforts to do what he tried to do, and that is to "pay attention to your audience."

EXAMPLE

Richard Nixon's 1952 Checkers speech is a notable example of a major political speech in the early days of television. Watch the video (Educational Video Group at www.evgondemand.com) of the whole speech from the standpoint of television speaking. From observation, how do you think TV production standards have changed over the years? What does Nixon do in the speech that we might avoid today? What does he do that still works on TV?

BIBLIOGRAPHY

Brown, Lillian, & Edwin Newman. *Your Public Best: The Complete Guide to Making Successful Public Appearances in the Meeting Room, on the Platform and on TV*. New York: Newmarket Press, 2002.

This book discusses the basics of appearing on TV along with other related topics, including media relations, tips on public speaking, and how to "dress for success." It is a particularly useful handbook on the topic of TV appearances.

Rhetorical Styles

ASSIGNMENT

Develop and deliver two versions of the same speech. Strategize a way to change the purpose of the speech resulting in a change of style, but not of overall topic or content. Or, as an alternative, give two speeches on closely related, but not identical, topics on the same day but with a different purpose for each speech. This is a difficult assignment. Study the examples given carefully to understand the differences and similarities you are trying to articulate.

COMMENTARY

Defining rhetorical or literary style is notoriously difficult. In the classic writing manual *Elements of Style*, E. B. White describes it as well, and more colorfully, than anyone else. He says that style is what "ignites a certain combination of words, causing them to explode in the mind."[1] Cicero would probably agree with White, but he would also argue that the explosion caused by style could be gauged and controlled according to the purposes of a speaker who knows how to properly set the charge. Like the other classical rhetoricians, Cicero was intensely interested in style and wrote about it extensively. His taxonomy of style has had great influence throughout the history of rhetorical theory and may still serve as a starting point for thinking about speaking style.

Cicero saw a connection between the purpose of a speech and the style adopted by the speaker. Speakers aiming to teach an audience could adopt a low or plain style, while those seeking to move the audience would use a grand style. In between these poles was a middle style designed for occasions when the goal was to please. In his dialogue *Orator*, Cicero describes the plain style as "restrained." It does not show off the talent of the speaker, but is perceived to be down to earth, so much

---

[1]William Strunk, Jr., & E. B. White, *Elements of Style*, 4th edition, New York: Longman, 2000, p. 66.

so that ordinary people who hear it "are sure that they can speak in that fashion," even though it is much harder than it sounds (*Orator*, 76). The plain style employs maxims and metaphors but avoids excessively metaphorical language (80–82). For Cicero, the middle style "is fuller and somewhat more robust than the simple style" (91). Connecting delivery to style, he observes that the middle style is more verbally charming than physically animated (91). The middle style is a "highly colored and polished style in which all the charms of language and thought are intertwined" (96).

Finally, the grand style is what we might call over-the-top oratory. It is "magnificent, opulent, stately and ornate . . . the kind of eloquence which rushes along with the roar of a mighty stream, which all look up to and admire, and which they despair of attaining. This eloquence has power to sway men's minds and move them in every possible way" (97). Interestingly, Cicero holds that truly outstanding speakers could be masters of either the plain or middle styles alone. The grand style, however, must be built on proficiency in the other two (98).

In contemporary terms, we would recognize the plain style in a good university lecture. The grand style calls to mind the most famous American speech of the twentieth century, Martin Luther King Jr.'s "I Have a Dream." The middle style is more difficult to conceptualize. One possible example is the 2009 Inaugural Address of President Barack Obama. The inaugural was described by some as subdued and not the soaring oratorical performance Obama is capable of and what many expected.[2] If the president's purpose was to rein in the inflated expectations that were being placed on his administration, then the middle style may have been the appropriate response, especially in light of his emerging pragmatic approach to policy.

Cicero recognized the extraordinary difficulty of one speaker mastering all the various styles, ". . . very few have attained our ideal of being equally successful in all" (*Orator*, 20). An experienced corporate trainer who is lost when asked to give a eulogy and a priest who can deliver fine homilies but botches an after-dinner speech are just two examples of many good speakers who could be outstanding if they mastered a variety of speaking purposes and styles. One way to attain this mastery is to study the relatively rare examples of it we find in rhetorical history. It is hard to imagine a more striking example of the grand and plain styles than Franklin Roosevelt's performance during early March 1933.

Roosevelt gave his memorable first inaugural address at the Capitol on March 4, 1933. Just eight days later he broadcast the first of the famous fireside chats. In both cases, Roosevelt's audience was the American people, nearly all of whom heard the speeches through the medium of radio. Clearly, the inaugural sounds more oratorical than the fireside chat, which seems much more relaxed and conversational. The fundamental difference between the two performances is their purpose. The inaugural can be described as declaratory, a call to arms for the nation to confront the gravest national crisis since the Civil War. The fireside chat, on the other hand, was explanatory, a commonsense discussion of the banking crisis. These differing purposes resulted in ostensibly different styles.

The difference in style between the speeches is seen in a variety of specific factors. The inaugural has allusions to classical literature, especially the Bible

---

[2]See Frank Rich, "No Time for Poetry," *New York Times*, January 25, 2009, WK:10.

("plague of locusts," "money changers," "where there is no vision the people perish," and "ministered unto but to minister"). Grand metaphors are also present. The most prominent is the war metaphor ("convert retreat into advance," "lines of attack," "trained and loyal army," "leadership of this great army," "disciplined attack," "wage a war against the emergency").[3] A common oratorical flourish, anaphora, occurs in the tenth paragraph (It can be helped...). The fireside chat lacks these flourishes. There is little need to speak of war and religion when discussing a person's bank balance.

One difference between the inaugural and the chat may at first seem surprising. We might expect the more oratorical of the compositions to feature longer, more complex sentences. Just the opposite is true. The average length of the first 25 sentences of the inaugural is 19.7 words. (If one 66-word sentence composed of a series of independent clauses joined by semicolons is omitted, the number drops to 17.7). The first 25 sentences of the fireside chat, on the other hand, average 30.6 words. The chat is more expansive, its pace slower in keeping with its purpose of explaining the banking crisis as simply as possible. The structure of the chat is also simple as the president enumerates his points seriatim. The transitions between ideas in the inaugural are more subtle and artful. Finally, extensive use of the second-person pronoun in the fireside chat, virtually absent from the inaugural, conveys personal engagement with the audience.[4]

In his legendary textbook *Speech-making*, James Winans draws attention to another remarkable example of stylistic variation by a noted speaker. In 1830, Daniel Webster prosecuted the trial of John Francis Knapp for the murder of Captain Joseph White. The parallel passages reprinted here are taken from Webster's summation of the case to the jury. Winans observes that the two passages "show how different the same speaker, within the same half hour, dealing with the same set of facts, can sound according to the nature of his purposes."[5] The first passage[6] reconstructs the crime, step by step, according to Winans, to "prove a conspiracy." The second passage reenacts the crime "in order to wipe out any sympathy" for the defendant.[7]

In both passages, Webster uses highly visual language. In the first case, "appearances . . . have a tendency to show" a conspiracy. In the other, the "circumstances . . . clearly in evidence spread out the whole scene." Notice how Webster shifts perspective to observe these appearances. The perspective of the first passage is that of a detached observer, like a detective or prosecutor, reconstructing the crime

[3]See Halford Ross Ryan, "Roosevelt's First Inaugural: A Study of Technique," *Quarterly Journal of Speech* 65, 2 (Apr. 1979):137–149. For the connection of the war metaphor and religious allusions into "holy war," see Suzanne M. Daughton, "Metaphorical Transcendence: Images of the Holy War in Franklin Roosevelt's First Inaugural," *Quarterly Journal of Speech* 79, 4 (Nov. 1993):427–446.

[4]For a contrary view of the Chats see Elvin T. Lim, "The Lion and the Lamb: De-Mythologizing Franklin Roosevelt's Fireside Chats," *Rhetoric & Public Affairs* 6, 3 (Fall 2003):437–464.

[5]James Winans, *Speech-Making*, The McGraw Hill Companies, 1938, p. 18.

[6]Edwin P. Whipple, ed., *The Great Speeches and Orations of Daniel Webster*, Boston: Little, Brown & Co., 1891, pp. 195, 200.

[7]Winans, p. 18.

after the fact. The second description of the same crime puts the audience side by side with the murderer, retracing each step as the crime was committed, like a film-maker who follows along with a handheld camera. Unlike Webster's grand oratory with its expansive and repetitive sentence structure, both of these passages feature straightforward syntax. Also, especially in the second passage, the evocative power of carefully chosen adjectives figures prominently.

How would the two passages by Webster match up with the Ciceronian ideal? The first passage seems clearly enough to be an example of plain style. Even though the second passage has a strong emotional element—a power to move the audience—it is still probably better regarded as an example of middle style rather than grand. For examples of his ability to speak in the grand style, see other Webster speeches such as his 1825 "Bunker Hill Monument" oration. Webster was one of the rare speakers who could command all three Ciceronian styles.

Webster, First Passage

Let me ask your attention, then, in the first place, to those appearances, on the morning after the murder, which have a tendency to show that it was done in pursuance of a preconcerted plan of operation. What are they? A man was found murdered in his bed. No stranger had done the deed, no one unacquainted with the house had done it. It was apparent that somebody within had opened, and that somebody without had entered. There had obviously and certainly been concert and co-operation. The inmates of the house where not alarmed when the murder was perpetrated. The assassin had entered without any riot or any violence. He had found the way prepared before him. The house had been previously opened. The window was unbarred from within, and its fastening unscrewed. There was a lock on the door of the chamber in which Mr. White slept, but the key was gone. It had been taken away and secreted. The footsteps of the murderer were visible, out-doors, tending toward the window. The plank by which he entered the window still remained. The road he pursued had been thus prepared for him. The victim was slain, and the murderer had escaped. Everything indicated that somebody within had co-operated with somebody without. Every thing proclaimed that some of the inmates, or somebody having access to the house, had had a hand in the murder. On the face of the circumstances, it was apparent, therefore, that this was a premeditated, concerted murder; that there had been a conspiracy to commit it.

Webster, Second Passage

The deed was executed with a degree of self-possession and steadiness equal to the wickedness with which it was planned. The circumstances now clearly in evidence spread out the whole scene before us. Deep sleep had fallen on the destined victim, and on all beneath his roof. A healthful old man, to whom sleep was sweet, the first sound slumbers of the night held him in their soft but strong embrace. The assassin enters, through the window already prepared, into an unoccupied apartment. With noiseless foot he paces the lonely hall, half lighted by the moon; he winds up the ascent of the stairs, and reaches the door of the chamber. Of this, he moves the lock, by soft and continued pressure, till it turns on its hinges without noise; and he enters, and beholds his victim before him.

The room is uncommonly open to the admission of light. The face of the innocent sleeper is turned from the murderer, and the beams of the moon, resting on the gray locks of his aged temple, show him where to strike. The fatal blow is given! And the victim passes, without a struggle or a motion, from the repose of sleep to the repose of death! It is the assassin's purpose to make sure work; and he plies the dagger, though it is obvious that life has been destroyed by the blow of the bludgeon. He even raises the aged arm, that he may not fail in his aim at the heart, and replaces it again over the wounds of the poniard! To finish the picture, he explores the wrist for the pulse! He feels for it, and ascertains that it beats no longer! It is accomplished. The deed is done. He retreats, retraces his steps to the window, passes out through it as he came in, and escapes.

CLASSICAL CONCEPT: STYLE

Classical rhetoricians were very interested in the idea of style. One third of Cicero's *De Oratore* (Book III) is devoted to it. In contemporary pop culture, style has commonly been thought of as a way to make an impression through superficial mannerisms or appearances. More recently, some have taken an opposite view, thinking of style as the outward expression of the inner self. Interestingly, this second perspective is actually closer to classical ideas. For the ancients, style grew out of thought and was expressed in the nuts and bolts of language. Style encompassed how language works and how speakers can make language work for their own purposes. Classical discussions of style usually focused on four specific factors: correctness, clarity, appropriateness, and impressiveness. (See Chapter 5 for a discussion of appropriateness or decorum.)

Cicero said that the foundation of oratory was a "faultless and pure Latin diction" (*Brutus* lxxiv, 258). This is what we would call "good English" and involves grammar, spelling, punctuation and related matters. Cicero was a traditionalist who disparaged what he viewed as the decline of good Latin in his time due to "the influx of many impure speakers coming from different places" and "the easily distorted rule of common usage." Most rhetoricians today take the opposite view, seeing correctness as a moving target precisely because of diversity and changing usage. Instead of striving to live up to a bygone standard, speakers today are advised to be sensitive to the standards of correct language that come into play in each rhetorical situation. In many ways this is more difficult than adhering to a set standard.

Clarity has always been highly valued in the rhetorical tradition. It could be argued that the whole point of communication is to be clear. Aristotle claims that "speech which fails to convey a plain meaning will fail to do just what speech has to do" (*Rhetoric* III, 1404b). Diplomats and negotiators can sometimes justify unclear communication, but for almost everyone else every speaking occasion calls for clarity.

Finally, classical rhetoric called for stylistic ornamentation or impressiveness (*Rhetoric* III, 1407b). The Greek words *onkos* or *auxesis* are sometimes thought of as "bombast" or "pomp," but this is not what the ancients had in mind. Impressiveness involves figures of speech like metaphors, which make language vivid or colorful. It may contribute to both clarity and persuasion.

Style, seen in the classical sense as integral to language itself rather than as some sort of ornamental add-on, furthers our understanding of communication.

For example, the rhetorical style of 2008 vice presidential candidate Sarah Palin provoked much discussion and no little derision. Her rhetoric, however, could be seen as an example of classical ornamentation. Her "you betchas," "Joe sixpack," and "hockey-mom" references created the image of a "feisty rustic" that appealed to many voters.

EXAMPLES

Here are the two speeches by President Franklin Roosevelt, discussed earlier: the First Fireside Chat and the 1933 Inaugural Address.

FIRST FIRESIDE CHAT
PRESIDENT FRANKLIN D. ROOSEVELT
THE WHITE HOUSE
WASHINGTON, D.C.
MARCH 12, 1933

My friends:

I want to talk for a few minutes with the people of the United States about banking—to talk with the comparatively few who understand the mechanics of banking, but more particularly with the overwhelming majority of you who use banks for the making of deposits and the drawing of checks. 5

I want to tell you what has been done in the last few days, and why it was done, and what the next steps are going to be. I recognize that the many proclamations from State capitols and from Washington, the legislation, the Treasury regulations, and so forth, couched for the most part in banking and legal terms, ought to be explained for the benefit of the average citizen. I owe this, in particular, because of the fortitude and the 10 good temper with which everybody has accepted the inconvenience and hardships of the banking holiday. And I know that when you understand what we in Washington have been about, I shall continue to have your cooperation as fully as I have had your sympathy and your help during the past week.

First of all, let me state the simple fact that when you deposit money in a bank, the 15 bank does not put the money into a safe deposit vault. It invests your money in many different forms of credit—in bonds, in commercial paper, in mortgages and in many other kinds of loans. In other words, the bank puts your money to work to keep the wheels of industry and of agriculture turning around. A comparatively small part of the money that you put into the bank is kept in currency—an amount which in normal times is wholly 20 sufficient to cover the cash needs of the average citizen. In other words, the total amount of all the currency in the country is only a comparatively small proportion of the total deposits in all the banks of the country.

What, then, happened during the last few days of February and the first few days of March? Because of undermined confidence on the part of the public, there was a 25 general rush by a large portion of our population to turn bank deposits into currency or

gold—a rush so great that the soundest banks couldn't get enough currency to meet the demand. The reason for this was that on the spur of the moment it was, of course, impossible to sell perfectly sound assets of a bank and convert them into cash, except
30   at panic prices far below their real value. By the afternoon of March third, a week ago last Friday, scarcely a bank in the country was open to do business. Proclamations closing them, in whole or in part, had been issued by the Governors in almost all the states. It was then that I issued the proclamation providing for the national bank holiday, and this was the first step in the Government's reconstruction of our financial and economic fabric.

35   The second step, last Thursday, was the legislation promptly and patriotically passed by the Congress confirming my proclamation and broadening my powers so that it became possible in view of the requirement of time to extend the holiday and lift the ban of that holiday gradually in the days to come. This law also gave authority to develop a program of rehabilitation of our banking facilities. And I want to tell our citizens in
40   every part of the Nation that the national Congress—Republicans and Democrats alike— showed by this action a devotion to public welfare and a realization of the emergency and the necessity for speed that it is difficult to match in all our history.

The third stage has been the series of regulations permitting the banks to continue their functions to take care of the distribution of food and household necessities and the
45   payment of payrolls.

This bank holiday, while resulting in many cases in great inconvenience, is affording us the opportunity to supply the currency necessary to meet the situation. Remember that no sound bank is a dollar worse off than it was when it closed its doors last week. Neither is any bank which may turn out not to be in a position for immediate opening. The new
50   law allows the twelve Federal Reserve Banks to issue additional currency on good assets and thus the banks that reopen will be able to meet every legitimate call. The new currency is being sent out by the Bureau of Engraving and Printing in large volume to every part of the country. It is sound currency because it is backed by actual, good assets.

Another question you will ask is this: Why are all the banks not to be reopened at the
55   same time? The answer is simple and I know you will understand it: Your Government does not intend that the history of the past few years shall be repeated. We do not want and will not have another epidemic of bank failures.

As a result, we start tomorrow, Monday, with the opening of banks in the twelve Federal Reserve Bank cities—those banks, which on first examination by the Treasury,
60   have already been found to be all right. That will be followed on Tuesday by the resumption of all other functions by banks already found to be sound in cities where there are recognized clearing houses. That means about two hundred and fifty cities of the United States. In other words, we are moving as fast as the mechanics of the situation will allow us.

On Wednesday and succeeding days, banks in smaller places all through the coun-
65   try will resume business, subject, of course, to the Government's physical ability to complete its survey. It is necessary that the reopening of banks be extended over a period in order to permit the banks to make applications for the necessary loans, to obtain currency needed to meet their requirements, and to enable the Government to make common sense checkups.

Please let me make it clear to you that if your bank does not open the first day you   70
are by no means justified in believing that it will not open. A bank that opens on one of
the subsequent days is in exactly the same status as the bank that opens tomorrow.

I know that many people are worrying about State banks that are not members
of the Federal Reserve System. There is no occasion for that worry. These banks can
and will receive assistance from member banks and from the Reconstruction Finance   75
Corporation. And, of course, they are under the immediate control of the State banking authorities. These State banks are following the same course as the National banks
except that they get their licenses to resume business from the State authorities, and
these authorities have been asked by the Secretary of the Treasury to permit their good
banks to open up on the same schedule as the national banks. And so I am confident   80
that the State Banking Departments will be as careful as the national Government in the
policy relating to the opening of banks and will follow the same broad theory.

It is possible that when the banks resume a very few people who have not recov-
ered from their fear may again begin withdrawals. Let me make it clear to you that the
banks will take care of all needs, except, of course, the hysterical demands of hoard-   85
ers, and it is my belief that hoarding during the past week has become an exceedingly
unfashionable pastime in every part of our nation. It needs no prophet to tell you that
when the people find that they can get their money—that they can get it when they want
it for all legitimate purposes—the phantom of fear will soon be laid. People will again be
glad to have their money where it will be safely taken care of and where they can use it   90
conveniently at any time. I can assure you, my friends, that it is safer to keep your money
in a reopened bank than it is to keep it under the mattress.

The success of our whole national program depends, of course, on the cooperation
of the public—on its intelligent support and its use of a reliable system.

Remember that the essential accomplishment of the new legislation is that it makes   95
it possible for banks more readily to convert their assets into cash than was the case
before. More liberal provision has been made for banks to borrow on these assets at the
Reserve Banks and more liberal provision has also been made for issuing currency on
the security of these good assets. This currency is not fiat currency. It is issued only on
adequate security, and every good bank has an abundance of such security.   100

One more point before I close. There will be, of course, some banks unable to
reopen without being reorganized. The new law allows the Government to assist in making these reorganizations quickly and effectively and even allows the Government to
subscribe to at least a part of any new capital that may be required.

I hope you can see, my friends, from this essential recital of what your Government   105
is doing that there is nothing complex, nothing radical in the process.

We have had a bad banking situation. Some of our bankers had shown themselves
either incompetent or dishonest in their handling of the people's funds. They had used
the money entrusted to them in speculations and unwise loans. This was, of course, not true
in the vast majority of our banks, but it was true in enough of them to shock the people of   110
the United States, for a time, into a sense of insecurity and to put them into a frame of mind
where they did not differentiate, but seemed to assume that the acts of a comparative few

had tainted them all. And so it became the Government's job to straighten out this situation and do it as quickly as possible. And that job is being performed.

115 I do not promise you that every bank will be reopened or that individual losses will not be suffered, but there will be no losses that possibly could be avoided; and there would have been more and greater losses had we continued to drift. I can even promise you salvation for some, at least, of the sorely presses banks. We shall be engaged not merely in reopening sound banks but in the creation of more sound banks through

120 reorganization.

It has been wonderful to me to catch the note of confidence from all over the country. I can never be sufficiently grateful to the people for the loyal support that they have given me in their acceptance of the judgment that has dictated our course, even though all our processes may not have seemed clear to them.

125 After all, there is an element in the readjustment of our financial system more important than currency, more important than gold, and that is the confidence of the people themselves. Confidence and courage are the essentials of success in carrying out our plan. You people must have faith; you must not be stampeded by rumors or guesses. Let us unite in banishing fear. We have provided the machinery

130 to restore our financial system, and it is up to you to support and make it work.

It is your problem, my friends, your problem no less than it is mine.

Together we cannot fail.

FIRST INAUGURAL ADDRESS

PRESIDENT FRANKLIN D. ROOSEVELT

WASHINGTON, D.C.

MARCH 4, 1933

President Hoover, Mr. Chief Justice, my friends:

This is a day of national consecration. And I am certain that on this day my fellow Americans expect that on my induction into the Presidency, I will address them with a candor and a decision which the present situation of our people impels.

5 This is preeminently the time to speak the truth, the whole truth, frankly and boldly. Nor need we shrink from honestly facing conditions in our country today. This great Nation will endure, as it has endured, will revive and will prosper.

So, first of all, let me assert my firm belief that the only thing we have to fear is fear itself—nameless, unreasoning, unjustified terror which paralyzes needed efforts to con-

10 vert retreat into advance. In every dark hour of our national life, a leadership of frankness and of vigor has met with that understanding and support of the people themselves which is essential to victory. And I am convinced that you will again give that support to leadership in these critical days.

In such a spirit on my part and on yours we face our common difficulties. They con-

15 cern, thank God, only material things. Values have shrunk to fantastic levels; taxes have risen; our ability to pay has fallen; government of all kinds is faced by serious curtailment of income; the means of exchange are frozen in the currents of trade; the withered

leaves of industrial enterprise lie on every side; farmers find no markets for their produce; and the savings of many years in thousands of families are gone. More important, a host of unemployed citizens face the grim problem of existence, and an equally great number 20 toil with little return. Only a foolish optimist can deny the dark realities of the moment.

And yet our distress comes from no failure of substance. We are stricken by no plague of locusts. Compared with the perils which our forefathers conquered, because they believed and were not afraid, we have still much to be thankful for. Nature still offers her bounty and human efforts have multiplied it. Plenty is at our doorstep, but a gener- 25 ous use of it languishes in the very sight of the supply.

Primarily, this is because the rulers of the exchange of mankind's goods have failed, through their own stubbornness and their own incompetence, have admitted their failure, and have abdicated. Practices of the unscrupulous money changers stand indicted in the court of public opinion, rejected by the hearts and minds of men. 30

True, they have tried. But their efforts have been cast in the pattern of an outworn tradition. Faced by failure of credit, they have proposed only the lending of more money. Stripped of the lure of profit by which to induce our people to follow their false leadership, they have resorted to exhortations, pleading tearfully for restored confidence. They only know the rules of a generation of self-seekers. They have no vision, and when there 35 is no vision the people perish.

Yes, the money changers have fled from their high seats in the temple of our civilization. We may now restore that temple to the ancient truths. The measure of that restoration lies in the extent to which we apply social values more noble than mere monetary profit.

Happiness lies not in the mere possession of money; it lies in the joy of achieve- 40 ment, in the thrill of creative effort. The joy, the moral stimulation of work no longer must be forgotten in the mad chase of evanescent profits. These dark days, my friends, will be worth all they cost us if they teach us that our true destiny is not to be ministered unto but to minister to ourselves, to our fellow men.

Recognition of that falsity of material wealth as the standard of success goes hand 45 in hand with the abandonment of the false belief that public office and high political position are to be valued only by the standards of pride of place and personal profit; and there must be an end to a conduct in banking and in business which too often has given to a sacred trust the likeness of callous and selfish wrongdoing. Small wonder that confidence languishes, for it thrives only on honesty, on honor, on the sacredness of obliga- 50 tions, on faithful protection, and on unselfish performance; without them it cannot live.

Restoration calls, however, not for changes in ethics alone. This Nation is asking for action, and action now.

Our greatest primary task is to put people to work. This is no unsolvable problem if we face it wisely and courageously. It can be accomplished in part by direct recruit- 55 ing by the Government itself, treating the task as we would treat the emergency of a war, but at the same time, through this employment, accomplishing great—greatly needed projects to stimulate and reorganize the use of our great natural resources.

Hand in hand with that we must frankly recognize the overbalance of population in our industrial centers and, by engaging on a national scale in a redistribution, endeavor 60 to provide a better use of the land for those best fitted for the land.

Yes, the task can be helped by definite efforts to raise the values of agricultural products, and with this the power to purchase the output of our cities. It can be helped by preventing realistically the tragedy of the growing loss through foreclosure of our
65 small homes and our farms. It can be helped by insistence that the Federal, the State, and the local governments act forthwith on the demand that their cost be drastically reduced. It can be helped by the unifying of relief activities which today are often scattered, uneconomical, unequal. It can be helped by national planning for and supervision of all forms of transportation and of communications and other utilities that have a defi-
70 nitely public character. There are many ways in which it can be helped, but it can never be helped by merely talking about it.

We must act. We must act quickly.

And finally, in our progress towards a resumption of work, we require two safeguards against a return of the evils of the old order. There must be a strict supervision of all
75 banking and credits and investments. There must be an end to speculation with other people's money. And there must be provision for an adequate but sound currency.

These, my friends, are the lines of attack. I shall presently urge upon a new Congress in special session detailed measures for their fulfillment, and I shall seek the immediate assistance of the 48 States.
80 Through this program of action we address ourselves to putting our own national house in order and making income balance outgo. Our international trade relations, though vastly important, are in point of time, and necessity, secondary to the establishment of a sound national economy. I favor, as a practical policy, the putting of first things first. I shall spare no effort to restore world trade by international economic readjustment;
85 but the emergency at home cannot wait on that accomplishment.

The basic thought that guides these specific means of national recovery is not nationally—narrowly nationalistic. It is the insistence, as a first consideration, upon the interdependence of the various elements in and parts of the United States of America— a recognition of the old and permanently important manifestation of the American spirit
90 of the pioneer. It is the way to recovery. It is the immediate way. It is the strongest assurance that recovery will endure.

In the field of world policy, I would dedicate this Nation to the policy of the good neighbor: the neighbor who resolutely respects himself and, because he does so, respects the rights of others; the neighbor who respects his obligations and respects the
95 sanctity of his agreements in and with a world of neighbors.

If I read the temper of our people correctly, we now realize, as we have never realized before, our interdependence on each other; that we cannot merely take, but we must give as well; that if we are to go forward, we must move as a trained and loyal army willing to sacrifice for the good of a common discipline, because without such discipline
100 no progress can be made, no leadership becomes effective.

We are, I know, ready and willing to submit our lives and our property to such discipline, because it makes possible a leadership which aims at the larger good. This, I propose to offer, pledging that the larger purposes will bind upon us, bind upon us all as a sacred obligation with a unity of duty hitherto evoked only in times of armed strife.

With this pledge taken, I assume unhesitatingly the leadership of this great army of our people dedicated to a disciplined attack upon our common problems. 105

Action in this image, action to this end is feasible under the form of government which we have inherited from our ancestors. Our Constitution is so simple, so practical that it is possible always to meet extraordinary needs by changes in emphasis and arrangement without loss of essential form. That is why our constitutional system has 110 proved itself the most superbly enduring political mechanism the modern world has ever seen.

It has met every stress of vast expansion of territory, of foreign wars, of bitter internal strife, of world relations. And it is to be hoped that the normal balance of executive and legislative authority may be wholly equal, wholly adequate to meet the unprecedented 115 task before us. But it may be that an unprecedented demand and need for undelayed action may call for temporary departure from that normal balance of public procedure.

I am prepared under my constitutional duty to recommend the measures that a stricken nation in the midst of a stricken world may require. These measures, or such other measures as the Congress may build out of its experience and wisdom, I shall 120 seek, within my constitutional authority, to bring to speedy adoption.

But, in the event that the Congress shall fail to take one of these two courses, in the event that the national emergency is still critical, I shall not evade the clear course of duty that will then confront me. I shall ask the Congress for the one remaining instrument to meet the crisis—broad Executive power to wage a war against the emergency, as 125 great as the power that would be given to me if we were in fact invaded by a foreign foe.

For the trust reposed in me, I will return the courage and the devotion that befit the time. I can do no less.

We face the arduous days that lie before us in the warm courage of national unity; with the clear consciousness of seeking old and precious moral values; with the clean 130 satisfaction that comes from the stern performance of duty by old and young alike. We aim at the assurance of a rounded, a permanent national life.

We do not distrust the—the future of essential democracy. The people of the United States have not failed. In their need they have registered a mandate that they want direct, vigorous action. They have asked for discipline and direction under leader- 135 ship. They have made me the present instrument of their wishes. In the spirit of the gift I take it.

In this dedication—In this dedication of a Nation, we humbly ask the blessing of God. May he protect each and every one of us. May he guide me in the days to come.

BIBLIOGRAPHY

Carpenter, Ronald H. *Choosing Powerful Words: Eloquence That Works*. Boston: Allyn & Bacon, 1999.

Professor Carpenter provides a handbook for speakers and speechwriters that is both popular in approach and firmly grounded in the rhetorical tradition.

Advanced Listening: The Speech about a Speech

ASSIGNMENT

Attend a live public speech presented in a leadership situation. For instance, you might hear the main speaker at an association meeting, or a politician addressing a civic group, or a scholar making a special presentation on campus. (Your instructor will provide further parameters for an acceptable venue.) The speech you attend should be at least twenty minutes long and not a panel presentation or discussion program. Prepare a three to five minute critique in which to share what you learned about public speaking from the speech you attended. What did the speaker you observed do right? What were the problems with the speech? Consider content, organization, delivery, management of the space and audience, and any other relevant factors. Do not summarize the speaker's topic. Report on the content of the speech only in the sense of critique, such as how the material was organized or the relevance and effectiveness of the support.

Most speeches will have many high points and low points, and you won't be able to cover them all in a few minutes. Focus on a few things that you think will be most beneficial for your audience to learn. If the speaker had an especially interesting way of making an argument, handling a problem, and interacting with the audience, share that. Tell us if the speaker neglected something important or could have handled something more effectively. Keep your focus on what your audience can learn from what you observed.

COMMENTARY

Most public speaking textbooks include a section on the process of listening, commonly discussed as types or phases of listening.[1] Beyond the mechanics of hearing and comprehension, the phases of listening often include empathic listening, which involves an open-mindedness to what is being communicated. Appreciative listening refers to the aesthetic dimension of communication, the appreciation of eloquence, for example. Critical listening engages the mind in careful logical analysis of what is communicated. Finally, constructive listening occurs when a listener actively seeks personal growth through the application of what is heard. It is in connection with this sort of constructive listening that yet another level of listening is open to people who aspire to be good public speakers.

What we mean by "advanced listening" is learning to listen to speeches as a speaker. Even the most prolific public speakers find themselves in the audience more often than not. Often a speaker-in-the-audience will simply want to enjoy the chance to be an audience member, listening appreciatively or critically to what is said. However, not infrequently, the speaker-in-the-audience will assume the role of critical observer of the speech and speaking situation. In these cases, the listener might be said to be positioned "in the balcony," or in the audience, but not of it. It's the same way an art photographer might view the photographs composed by others or a classical composer might listen to someone else's symphony. What's the difference between this type of audience member and others? The photographer or composer brings a heightened capacity for appreciation—and critique—to his or her responses to the works of others. Accomplished public speakers bring the same kind of enhanced awareness when they listen to speeches. They listen for more than sound bites, funny stories, familiar information or opinions, viewpoints they don't like, or information they can use—the kinds of things typical audience members may be attuned to.

What exactly should an aspiring speaker focus on when listening to others speak? Everything about a speech comes into play, but there are a few factors you might especially want to focus on when listening to a speaker as a speaker.

- *Relationship to the audience.* One of the first things to observe when attending a speech is not the speaker but the audience. Simple observation can give you a read on audience demographics. Race, age, ethnicity, and even economic class might be evident to an astute observer. Don't let false stereotypes lead you to unwarranted certainty about these factors, but don't ignore them either. Beyond demographics, see if you can get a read on the audience's mood, whether or not people seem to know each other or whether there is some common interest among them. Based on your observation of the audience, can you predict the approach the speaker may take toward the speech's length, supporting material, or tone? Given the speech topic and occasion, how would the nature of this particular audience influence you if you were giving the speech?

---

[1]Michael Osborn et al., *Public Speaking*, 8th edition, Upper Saddle River, NJ: Allyn & Bacon, 2008, pp. 74–76.

- *Structure.* All speeches start at exactly the same point—with something that we would call an introduction. The introduction can be very short, a phrase or sentence, or a long discussion. Even a nonverbal action or gesture can introduce a speech. Eventually an introduction ends as the speaker moves on to other material or narrative elements. Obvious or subtle, the break between the introduction and what follows and the subsequent moves between ideas are the speech's transitions. By keeping track of transitions, experienced listeners are able to reconstruct the movement of a speech in their minds or written notes. From transitions the structure of discourse emerges. Clear speech organization can take many forms—rational or narrative, inductive or deductive—but in all cases it makes the task of listening easy. Poor structure makes listening difficult. Be careful, however, of writing off a speech that is ostensibly disorganized. Disorganization itself may be telling or, although not likely, even strategic.

- *Selection of material.* Out of the storehouse of everything he or she has known, read, seen, experienced, or imagined, a speaker draws material to talk about. What a speaker decides to include in a discourse depends on many factors such as the purpose of the speech, the makeup of the audience, the time available, and whether the material can be found or remembered. When listening to a speech and thinking like a speaker, interrogate the speaker's choices of what to say. Where did the speaker come up with this material? Is the material appropriate for this situation, especially in light of the speech's purpose and audience? Are there any logical or emotional liabilities that come with using this material? Can you think of alternative material you would use if speaking on the same topic?

- *Delivery.* One of the great advantages of being present for a speech when it's given is the opportunity to directly experience the speaker's delivery. This experience is impossible when reading speeches or watching recordings. In the nineteenth century, elocutionists tried to codify the meaning of nonverbal cues with the idea that discrete movements or gestures consistently communicated the same emotions or attitudes. More recent research into nonverbal communication indicates that the elocutionists were on to something, but that it is much more subtle and complex than anyone imagined. When attending a speech, listen to and observe carefully what the combination of spoken language and nonverbal performance seems to be saying to you. (Familiarity with the literature on nonverbal communication and its connection to public speaking will surely help you in this.) Both listening and observation are important. Pay attention to both obvious delivery issues like voice volume and subtle factors such as tenseness in the muscles of a speaker's hand or face. Delivery might be said to fail when a combination of obvious and subtle factors leads to a perceived disconnect between the content and delivery of the speech.

- *The whole.* The tendency when critiquing a speech is to break it up into its constituent parts and analyze each part on its own. As a speaker, however, you should know that a speech is more than the sum of its parts. Speakers don't give speeches in bits and pieces, and what most audiences carry away from a speech is an overall impression—the memory of a discrete event.

In summary judgment then, considered as a whole, do you think the speech was all it could or should have been? Did the speaker make the most of what he or she had to work with? Making this judgment, one way or the other, will help you determine what you, as a speaker, can learn from being in the audience.

CLASSICAL CONCEPT: IMITATION

The idea of imitating the skills and practices of others may seem strange to us who live in a culture that values individualism and individual expression. We tend to see imitation as a poor substitute for creativity. At the same time, most of us realize that we can enhance our own abilities by simply being around people who have skills we aspire to. Does this just happen by chance? Do we learn from others as their abilities somehow rub off on us? The classical rhetoricians believed that the skills of the accomplished could be learned by the aspiring, but only through deliberate strategies of what came to be called *imitatio*. Cicero's *De Oratore* says that not only must a prospective writer or speaker have a liberal education, enthusiasm, natural ability, and knowledge of rhetorical theory, but he or she should also select "the most accomplished writers and orators for study and imitation" (*De Oratore*, III, 125).

Methods of imitation became important elements of education from classical times through the Renaissance. "Imitating exercises consisted either of copying some type of *form* within the original, but supplying new content; or, of copying the *content* of the original, but supplying a new form. The intention was to provide a kind of literary and rhetorical apprenticeship by which the best modes of expression from the best models could be appropriated in a regulated, graduated fashion."[2]

Various approaches to imitation are possible, from the very simple to more involved exercises. At the simplest level one might copy a speech word for word (by hand, not on a machine), or read the speech aloud to get a sense of its rhythm, sounds, and pace.[3] One of Cicero's characters, Crassus, claims he tried to imitate the form of a great speaker by changing the words of his speeches. He didn't think this worked because the speaker being imitated had already used the most artful terminology. Changing the words led only to less eloquence. As an alternative exercise, Crassus took fine Greek language speeches and translated them into the best Latin he could think of (*De Oratore*, I, 154–155).

We may think imitation is a sign of lack of originality or, perhaps, as the saying goes, the sincerest form of flattery. Understanding imitation as a way of learning, however, is both an ancient and extraordinarily practical approach. In addition to having a favorite pop star, pro athlete, or actor, people who want to

---

[2]"Imitation," *Silva Rhetoricae*, http://rhetoric.byu.edu/

[3]See Sharon Crowley and Debra Hawhee, *Ancient Rhetorics for Contemporary Students*, 4th edition, New York: Pearson Education, 2009, pp. 321–325. Crowley and Hawhee provide many examples and instructions for imitation exercises.

be good public speakers probably have two or three speakers they admire and whom they could imitate to good advantage.

ASSIGNMENT VARIATION

As a variation on the assignment given earlier, attend a live speech event with another student from your class. Develop your report speeches independently of one another. After your presentations, compare your responses to the speech. What accounts for the differences in your evaluations?

BIBLIOGRAPHY

Tompkins, Paula S. "Rhetorical Listening and Moral Sensitivity." *The International Journal of Listening* 23 (2009):60–79.

Tompkins discusses the ethical component of listening and argues that listening must encompass all the various dimensions of a rhetorical encounter.

Basic Public Speaking Course Redux

In all likelihood, if you are studying advanced public speaking, you have probably taken a basic or introductory public speaking course sometime in the past. Depending on the type of introductory course you took and how long ago you took it, you may need to brush up on some of the basic principles of public speaking. What follows is a summary made up of seven basic principles of public speaking. Included under each principle are Terms to Know and Questions to Consider. Following these is a list of Sources to Consult. Use this material on your own or at the direction of your instructor to review and refresh your memory of your previous studies.

ARRANGEMENT

Terms to Know

Internal Preview: Speaker's statement that forecasts the remaining arguments in a presentation, typically offered after the first main point has been developed. Using an internal preview helps the audience to understand the organization of a speech more easily.

Internal Summary: Speaker's statement of what has been covered thus far in a presentation, offered before he or she makes concluding remarks. Using an internal summary helps the audience to grasp and recall the main points of a speech more easily.

Outlines: Outlines are akin to blueprints for a speech. They follow the established pattern of standard outline format, including indentation and a consistent plan of symbolization. Outlines offer speakers the opportunity to visualize the structure of their intended remarks and to identify those areas that need more evidence, elaboration, and the like. The two primary kinds of outlines are:

Preparation Outline—A detailed outline that is created during the development of a speech. It includes the speech title, the thesis or specific purpose of the address, the central idea of the speech, the introduction, main points, subpoints, connectives, and the conclusion of the address.

Speaking Outline—A relatively abbreviated outline that is used to assist a speaker's memory during an extemporaneous speech. It employs standard outline format, but is typically composed of key words, partial phrases, and delivery cues. This type of outline is sometimes called a key word or key phrase outline.

Parts of a Speech: Speeches are most often composed of three basic parts: the introduction, the body, and the conclusion. The basic characteristics of each are:

Introduction—The opening section of a speech that gains the attention of the audience, prepares the audience to deal with the topic at hand, establishes speaker credibility, promotes common ground, and provides a logical orientation to the presentation through the use of a preview.

Body—The longest and primary section of a speech that develops the main arguments that the speaker wishes to advance, offers sound evidence in support of those arguments, and demonstrates how the audience should interpret the evidence consistent with the speaker's goals.

Conclusion—The ending section of a speech that provides the audience with a sense of closure or completion. Conclusions typically summarize what has been discussed, personalize the issues for the audience, recenter the topic within a broader context, and—especially for persuasive discourses—articulate an ending appeal or inducement to action.

Patterns of Organization: Speeches are often organized according to specific patterns that suit the topic of discussion, the speaker's purpose, and the speaking situation. There are five common patterns of organization. They are:

Causal Order—Organization according to a cause to effect relationship or according to the reverse, an effect to cause relationship. Causal order is sufficiently flexible to work well with informative or persuasive presentations.

Chronological Order—Organization according to a pattern of time, usually moving by minutes, hours, days, years, centuries, and so forth, from the past to the present or even to the future. Reverse chronological order begins in the present and moves backward in time. This pattern of organization works well with informative presentations.

Problem–Solution Order—Organization according to two main sections, the first of which outlines the existence and severity of a problem, and the second of which offers a useful solution to that problem. This pattern of organization is best suited to persuasive or motivational presentations.

Spatial Order—Organization according to a directional pattern, so that the main ideas in the speech are arrayed from left to right, top to bottom, east to west, inside to outside, and the like. Spatial order is particularly useful for speeches or presentations where visualization is desired. This pattern of organization is best suited to informative presentations.

Topical Order—Organization according to the subtopics associated with a particular subject, where each subtopic becomes a main point within the speech. Topical order works with subjects that are sufficiently idiosyncratic as to preclude the use of other forms of organization. This pattern of organization is malleable and thus works well for almost all kinds of presentations and speaking purposes.

Questions to Consider

- At www.americanrhetoric.com, choose one of the first ten speeches from the Top 100 Speeches of the Twentieth Century and outline it. First, identify the introduction and conclusion, and then list the main headings or points. Keep in mind that the "great speeches" often have artful transitions making underlying structure less obvious.
- Examine two political campaign speeches given by the same candidate over a two- or three-month period. Identify the sections of the two speeches that seem to deal with the same content or issues. Do these sections appear in the same order in both speeches? Are they arranged differently for various audiences and purposes? How does rearranging these sections change the meaning or the emphases of the speeches?

AUDIENCE

Terms to Know

Audience: Those persons who are exposed to the speaker's message. Audiences may be characterized in a number of ways. Accomplished speakers adjust their remarks to accommodate these characteristics. Some ways of categorizing audiences are:

Apathetic Audience—Those persons who do not care or who do not hold an opinion about the subject of the speaker's presentation.

Believing Audience—Those persons who support the viewpoint of the speaker about the subject under discussion.

Constructed/Created Audience—The audience that the speaker creates by inviting participation with a certain mindset or orientation toward the topic.

Disbelieving Audience—Those persons who do not support the speaker's position about the subject under discussion.

Empirical Audience/Immediate Audience—The audience that is physically present and with whom the speaker interacts directly.

Extended Audience/Mediated Audience—The audience that is not physically present for the speech but which nonetheless reads, watches, or listens to the presentation.

Uninformed Audience—Those persons who do not have previous knowledge about the topic under discussion.

Common Ground: A technique by which a speaker connects himself or herself with the values, beliefs, attitudes, or experiences of the audience. Language theorist Kenneth Burke called this concept "identification," suggesting that it forms the very bedrock of successful persuasion.

Demographic Analysis: An assessment of the pertinent characteristics of an audience. Key characteristics such as age, ethnicity, educational level, income level, sex, sexual orientation, social class, race, religious affiliation, relationship status, and the like, are determined by speakers as they attempt to identify their target audiences and strategize about how to reach them. Often used in combination with psychographic analysis. (*See* Psychographic Analysis.)

Dog-Whistle Rhetoric: When a speaker includes words or phrases in a speech that are likely to be understood by only a very small segment of the audience. Like a high-frequency whistle that can be heard only by dogs.

Feedback: Messages that listeners send to a speaker during the speaking process. Feedback is typically nonverbal communication and may include such behaviors as clapping, nodding in approval or disapproval, laughing, and the like. Skilled public speakers adjust their presentations to accommodate audience feedback.

Psychographic Analysis: An assessment of the psychological orientation of an audience, including a profile of their beliefs, attitudes, and values. Psychographic analysis may yield a reasonable determination about audience members' overall perspective on the world or about their stance on particular topics. Often used in combination with demographic analysis. (*See* Demographic Analysis.)

Questions to Consider

- Read the most recent State of the Union Address. Identify the different target audiences it tries to address. How do the interests of these audiences relate to the interests of the president's political agenda? Do some target audiences need to hear things that others do not?
- On Memorial Day in 1993, President Clinton gave a speech at the Vietnam Veterans Memorial to an audience that included a significant number of hostile, heckling listeners. Locate and read the speech. How did Clinton attempt to build common ground with this audience? What shared beliefs and values did he invoke?

DELIVERY

Terms to Know

Ad-lib: To improvise words, phrases, or gestures that were not originally planned for inclusion in your speech or presentation. From the Latin *ad*—at + *libitum*—pleasure, rather than *obligatus*, meaning bound or obliged. A speaker who ad-libs says things off the cuff, generally for pleasurable effect.

Articulation: Uttering words clearly and distinctly, with a quality of crispness and precision. Misarticulated words frequently involve dropped letters, such as "goin" for "going," or ungrammatical combinations of words, such as "wanna" for "want to."

Eloquence: The quality of speaking in a forceful, moving, or persuasive manner. An eloquent speaker employs appropriate, fluent, polished, and expressive language, bearing in mind the situated nature of his or her remarks. The term comes from the Latin *e*—out + *loqui*—to speak.

Extemporaneous Speech: An address that is prepared with planned content, but neither read nor memorized verbatim. From the Latin *ex*—out + *tempus, temporis*—time, referring to a spontaneous, conversational speaking style. This is the most frequently used form of delivery, in which speakers familiarize themselves with the structure and some phrases of a speech, while stopping short of more formalized modes of presentation.

Fluency: The quality of speaking (or writing) with apparent ease and grace of expression. Polished speakers cultivate fluency in their presentations by attending to the elements of phrasing and other factors of style. The word comes from the Latin, *fluens, fluere*—to flow.

Forum: A setting in which the speaker opens the floor to questions and then responds to them, typically after he or she has finished delivering prepared remarks. In Latin, forum means "place of public discussion," or marketplace. Accomplished speakers frequently encourage discussion of multiple viewpoints during these periods of informal questions and answers.

Impromptu Speech: A speech that is given on the spur of the moment with virtually no time for preparation. Speakers who are suddenly called upon to "say a few words" speak in this manner. Typically, impromptu speeches should be composed of four elements: a statement of the point the speaker is addressing, a statement of the point the speaker wants to advance, support for the point the speaker wants to advance, and a summary of what has been said.

Manuscript Speech: An address that is written out and read to the audience, although it is typically composed in an oral rather than an essay style. Manuscript speaking requires practice and skill so that both the speaker and the presentation seem accessible to the audience.

Memorized Speech: The rarest form of speaking in contemporary culture, the memorized speech is delivered without notes, completely on the basis of recall. A speaker who delivers memorized remarks must take great care to concentrate on connecting with his or her audience, rather than on remembering the words of the speech.

Performance Anxiety: Also called communication apprehension, this is the common feeling of nervousness that speakers experience before and during public speaking. This type of anxiety is normal and largely results from a rush of natural adrenalin, a hormone that helps our bodies achieve peak performance. Accomplished speakers learn to manage performance anxiety by engaging in thorough speech preparation and practice as well as intellectual and emotional comprehension of the speech content.

Presentational Aids: Visual and other aids that assist a speaker with his or her presentation. These may include overheads, PowerPoint packages, handouts, models, and the like. Accomplished speakers enhance their speeches with these aids, but are also prepared to proceed successfully without them, should unforeseen circumstances or mechanical malfunctions arise.

Pronunciation: The accepted benchmark of rhythm and sound for words in a specific language. Speakers should take care to use proper pronunciation, as it can enhance credibility.

Vocalized Pause: A break in talking during which the speaker fills the silence between his or her words by uttering vocalizations such as "er," "ah," or "um." Vocalized pauses should be avoided as much as possible because they tend to reflect negatively on the speaker's intelligence and level of preparedness.

Vocal Variety: The vocal components of speech delivery that speakers employ to affect the meaning of the words they say and to engage the audience hearing those words. Common verbal elements of delivery include:

Inflection—The use of pitch to emphasize certain points or to create a certain mood.

Pauses—Brief periods of silence or hesitations in the flow of a speaker's delivery.

Pitch—The highness or lowness of a speaker's voice.

Rate—The speed with which a speaker talks.

Volume—The loudness of a speaker's voice.

Questions to Consider

- Watch a recording of Martin Luther King Jr.'s I Have a Dream speech. Can you tell where in the speech Dr. King seems to stop using his prepared manuscript and begins to speak more extemporaneously? Notice the change in the speaker's rate from the beginning of the speech until its end. What effect does this have?

- Go to www.americanrhetoric.com and select a speech that interests you and that has both a written transcript and an audio or a video recording. Read the speech from transcript and note your reactions to it: do you agree with the speaker? Do you think it's a good speech? Now, without looking at the transcript, listen or watch the recording of the speech. Does hearing or seeing it change your reaction? How?

GENRE

Terms to Know

Keynote Address or Keynote Speech: The primary or main speech at a meeting. The keynote address is one of the highly featured events of a meeting or conference, typically delivered at the opening session, at a banquet, or at a closing session to which all attendees are invited. Keynote speeches are frequently given by highly qualified speakers or celebrities and relate often to the overall theme of the meeting.

Narrative: A depiction of events told in dramatic fashion, sometimes referred to as a story or an anecdote. A story is a longer narrative, while an anecdote is a shorter narrative. Narratives are compelling because they create a sense of drama for the audience, are easily remembered, and are structured according to established forms.

Types of Speeches: Aristotle identified three major kinds of speeches that were prevalent in his day. A forensic speech was given in court and had to do with lawsuits or guilt and innocence. In the Greek city-states, court proceedings were common, citizens served as their own lawyers, and a jury could have hundreds of members. A deliberative or persuasive speech was typically given in the assembly and involved persuading the citizens to a course of action such as levying taxes or building a ship. Finally, an epideictic or ceremonial speech was one called for by an occasion such as an anniversary or a patriotic holiday. In terms of temporal action, forensic speeches deal with the past, determining what happened. A deliberative speech is concerned with the future, what to do next, while an epideictic speech focuses on the present occasion to affirm and celebrate cultural values. Aristotle's genres have proven resilient and are still frequently used to classify speeches today.

Questions to Consider

- Review the first twenty-five speeches from the Top 100 Speeches of the Twentieth Century at www.americanrhetoric.com. Identify the genre of each speech. Is it deliberative (persuasive), ceremonial (given for an occasion), or forensic (legal)?
- Some speeches are rhetorical hybrids, possessing characteristics of two genres. Find a speech that fits this description and explain which sections of the speech fulfill one function (e.g., deliberative) and which sections of the speech fulfill a second function (e.g., ceremonial). Explain what effect this combination of genres has on the form and content of the address.

PERSUASION/ARGUMENTATION

Terms to Know

Boomerang Effect: The opposite outcome from what the speaker intends. Persuasive messages, in particular, may boomerang if the speaker's arguments and appeals are too overwhelming for the audience to accept.

Burden of Proof: The obligation assumed by a persuasive speaker who attempts to prove that change from a current program or policy is needed. The speaker must convince his or her audience that the proposed change represents an improvement over the status quo.

Credibility: Audience perception of the speaker's qualifications to speak. Also called speaker credibility or ethos, credibility typically involves an assessment of competence, character, and dynamism. Speakers attempt to enhance their credibility by appearing intelligent, knowledgeable, sincere, and highly engaged in the subject at hand.

Evidence: Materials that are used to support a speaker's claim, to prove or to disprove an argument. Evidence consists of three major kinds of supporting materials. They are:

Examples—A specific case that is employed to illustrate or to depict a group of people, certain conditions, experiences, ideas, and the like. Examples may be short (brief example) or long (extended example) or fictitious (hypothetical example).

Statistics—Numerical data that are employed to quantify the speaker's claims. Because audiences are frequently more literate than they are numerate, care should be taken to work with numbers to achieve clear understanding. Statistics are frequently judged by whether they are reliable and representative, among other things.

Testimony—Direct quotations or paraphrases of statements that are deployed to support a point. Testimony is often compelling to an audience because it buttresses the speaker's claims with outside sources of information. Types of testimony include: "expert testimony," given by individuals who are recognized authorities in their occupations; "eye witness testimony," given by individuals who were present at a particular event; and "peer testimony," given by ordinary people who possess firsthand knowledge or experience with an issue.

Fallacies in Argument: Fallacies are errors in reasoning that invalidate arguments or propositions. Common fallacies include:

Absurd Extreme Fallacy—An error in reasoning that extends an argument to the point that it appears groundless or ridiculous. Also called a *reductio ad absurdum* fallacy.

Against the Person Fallacy—An error in reasoning in which the negative character of one's opponent is claimed as sufficient cause to dismiss that person's argument. Also called an *ad hominem* fallacy.

Appeal to Ignorance Fallacy—An error in reasoning that claims that something is true because it has not been disproven. Also called an *ad ignorantiam* fallacy.

Appeal to Pity Fallacy: A relevance-based error in reasoning in which the speaker asks his or her audience to render judgment on the basis of emotion rather than on the basis of evidence or logic. The term is applied to nearly all types of emotional appeals and is also called an *ad misericordiam* fallacy.

Appeal to Tradition Fallacy—An evidence-based error in reasoning in which the speaker asserts that the status quo is preferable to any new approaches or ideas that may be suggested.

Bandwagon Fallacy—An error in reasoning that claims that because something is popular, it is also correct, desirable, or good. Also called an *ad populum* fallacy.

Begging the Question—Also called circular reasoning, a claim-based error in reasoning that asserts that something is true because it is true or that something is true because the validity of the conclusion is self-evident. Also called *petitio principii* fallacy.

Division Fallacy—An error in reasoning in which the speaker alleges that what is true of the whole is also true of parts of the whole.

False Cause Fallacy—An error in reasoning that claims that there is a causal relationship between two events simply because one followed the other chronologically. Also called a *post hoc ergo proper hoc* fallacy or simply a post hoc fallacy, the Latin translation means "after this, therefore because of this."

False Dilemma Fallacy—Also called an either-or fallacy, an error in reasoning in which the speaker offers only two choices even though other viable alternatives exist.

Hasty Generalization Fallacy—An error in reasoning in which the speaker forms a conclusion based on an insufficient number of cases or examples. Also called a *secundum quid* fallacy.

Red Herring Fallacy—An error in evidential reasoning in which the speaker distracts his or her audience with irrelevant issues or arguments.

Slippery Slope Fallacy—An error in reasoning in which the speaker claims that one event will inevitably lead to another event, without demonstrating the logical relationship between them.

Straw Man or Straw Figure Fallacy—An error in reasoning that arises when the speaker articulates an opposing claim in a much weaker form than is fair, and then, having misrepresented the opposition's position, demolishes the inadequate argument easily.

Modes of Proof: Aristotle outlined three kinds of artistic proof, which he called the modes of proof. Typically used in conjunction, these three forms of artistic proof constitute the primary ways in which speakers support and prove their arguments. (*See* Proof *and* Artistic Proof.) The three modes of proof are:

Ethos—Ethical proof, arising from the character and credibility of the speaker. (*See* Source Credibility.)

Pathos—Pathetic or emotional proof, arising from an appeal to sentiment.

Logos—Logical proof, arising from the articulation and analysis of factual materials such as evidence, testimony, and statistics.

Monroe's Motivated Sequence: A sequence of five steps that was developed in the 1930s by Alan Monroe, a communication professor at Purdue University, for organizing a persuasive speech. The motivated sequence is best suited to policy addresses, but it may be adapted to virtually any type of informative or persuasive presentation. Following the process of human problem solving, the five steps in the sequence are:

Attention Step—Secure the attention of the audience by demonstrating the significance of the topic, relating the subject to their needs and interests and arousing listener curiosity.

Need Step—Demonstrate a significant problem with the status quo and prove its existence thoroughly. Insist that the audience understand the need for change, priming them to listen for a solution to the problem.

Satisfaction Step—Provide the audience with the solution to the problem, offering sufficient details about the proposed policy and how it will work.

Visualization Step—Ask the audience to picture the benefits that will follow from the plan you have proposed. Use vivid imagery to describe the beneficial outcomes that will accrue from your plan.

Action Step—Tell the audience what they can do to help enact the policy you have proposed. Be directive and inspirational about what actions your listeners can take and the outcomes they can produce.

Polysemic: Capable of generating more than one understanding or of being interpreted in multiple ways. Messages that say different things to different sections of an audience are said to be polysemic. Polysemy is often cultivated in persuasive messages.

Proof: A sufficient marshalling of evidence to achieve belief on the part of the audience. The level of proof that a speaker is required to provide in his or her speech will vary according to the situation, the audience, and the topic under discussion. As Aristotle stated in his book *The Rhetoric*, there are two broad categories of proof: artistic and inartistic.

Artistic Proof—Artful in the sense that the speaker finds or generates the information that is employed to prove his or her argument. Artistic proof is composed of evidence, testimony, statistics, and the like. (*See also* Modes of Proof.)

Inartistic Proof—Lacking in artfulness because the speaker finds it in the natural world and applies it to his or her argument.

Propositions: Theses that are common to argumentation. A speaker or writer may advance a proposition of fact, policy, or value.

Proposition of Fact—Asserts that something does or does not exist or that something is true or untrue.

Proposition of Policy—Argues for or against a particular plan or course of action.

Proposition of Value—Asserts the morality/immorality, rightness/wrongness, or worth/lack of worth of something.

Rhetoric: Following Aristotle's definition of the term, rhetoric is the art of discovering in any situation the available means of persuasion. As opposed to contemporary definitions of "mere rhetoric" as trickery or bombast, this classical definition of the word implies the informed and thoughtful decisions that speakers make in adapting their arguments to audience needs, attitudes, and values.

Questions to Consider

- Select one editorial or opinion column from a recent edition of a major newspaper or political blog and analyze its argument. Identify the central or most important claim of the argument. Is it a claim of fact, value, or policy?

Describe the reasons and evidence for the claim. What is the ratio of rational versus emotional appeal in the argument?

■ Recall the most compelling argument you have heard recently, whether for a product, idea, political candidate, and so on. What mode of proof did this argument rely on the most? What effect did this have on your openness to the argument? Do you think reliance on another mode of proof would have strengthened or weakened this argument?

PREPARATION/RESEARCH

Terms to Know

Canons of Rhetoric: Developed by the Roman statesman and orator, Marcus Tullius Cicero, the canons of rhetoric or the "five arts of public speaking" constitute the five essential elements of public discourse, offering guidance for effective speechmaking. The canons of rhetoric are:

Invention—The getting of ideas or arguments for a speech. Both topic choice and selection of arguments are parts of the inventional process.

Disposition (Arrangement)—The organization of ideas and arguments in the speech. Elements of disposition include an introduction, a body, and a conclusion. The ordering of major arguments in a speech is also a matter of disposition.

Style—The language choices employed by the speaker. Style should be suited to the situation and should be compelling to the listener.

Delivery—The physical aspects of giving a speech, including such elements as vocal quality, gestures, and posture.

Memory—Called the "lost canon," memory involves methods of recalling or remembering the speech. Pneumonic devices, once popular among speakers who memorized their speeches, fall into this category.

Deep Web: A part of the World Wide Web that is made up of specialized databases that are not always accessible by traditional search engines. Skilled public speakers know how to access these sources of information, such as those housed by the U.S. government. Common points of access for the deep web include: www.completeplanet.com, www.geniusfind.com, www.incywincy.com, www.newsvoyager.com, and www.usa.gov.

Fair Use: Doctrine in copyright law that permits a speaker to use limited excerpts of an author's work, provided that credit is given to the source of the information. Failure to credit the source of one's information constitutes plagiarism.

Purpose: The purpose of a speech or presentation is the reason that the speaker is speaking. Purposes may be general or specific.

General Purpose—The broad goal of a speech, usually to inform, persuade, or commemorate.

Specific Purpose—A precise statement, usually in infinitive form, that says what the speaker wishes to accomplish as a result of his or her presentation.

Rhetorical Situation: Term invented by rhetorical theorist and critic Lloyd Bitzer, a communication professor at the University of Wisconsin, to describe the elements that coalesce in a situation where rhetoric is required to address issues or to solve problems. The rhetorical situation is composed of three equally important elements to which the speaker must adapt. They are:

Exigence—A flaw, defect, or need in the situation that is capable of being modified by discourse.

Audience—The group of auditors who are capable of effecting the situation.

Constraints—The barriers that the speaker must overcome, either arising from the situation itself or from the predispositions of the audience or both.

Thesis Statement: A one-sentence articulation of the purpose of a speech or presentation. A thesis statement should be concrete, phrased in declarative form, relevant to the speaking occasion, and limited to a single distinct idea.

Questions to Consider

- Pick a term from politics or current events and run a simple Google search for the term. Run the search again in Google Advanced, only this time vary the site or domain of the search. First, try the .gov domain, and then try .org domain. Now search the same term in Google Scholar. How do the results of these searches differ?
- Use the following Web references to answer these questions: *Who said?* "The most potent weapon in the hands of the oppressor is the mind of the oppressed." www.bartleby.com/quotations. *When was it passed?* The Lilly Ledbetter Fair Pay Act. http://thomas.loc.gov/. *Which countries have declining population rates?* www.prb.org/. *How do you pronounce "Mahmoud Ahmadinejad?"* http://names.voa.gov

STYLE

Terms to Know

Connectives: Words, phrases, or sentences that serve as links or bridges between ideas in a speech.

Discriminatory Language: Word choices that are ageist, classist, heterosexist, racist, or sexist in orientation. Accomplished speakers consciously employ language that does not offend or discriminate against particular groups of people, that is respectful, and that is inclusive.

Stylistic Features: Style refers to the language choices that a speaker makes to convey his or her ideas in the best manner possible for the situation and the audience. (*See* Canons of Rhetoric.) There are many recognized stylistic features, including the following:

Alliteration—Starting words or phrases with the same consonants.

Assonance—Starting words or phrases with the same vowel sounds.

Antithesis—Pairings of words or phrases that set them in opposition to each other.

Analogy—A comparison of the similarities between two things. Analogies may be either literal (where there is a real basis in fact for the comparison) or figurative (where the comparison is done for effect only, lacking any substantive likeness in appearance, form, or kind.) The word comes from the Latin, *ana*—according to + logos—proportion.

Onomatopoeia—Words that sound like they mean or that imitate the action which they perform. The word comes from Greek and Latin, *onoma*—name + *poiein*—to make, thus meaning "name-making."

Parallelism/Parallel Structure—Similar arrangement of a series or a pair of words, phrases, or sentences.

Personification—Giving an inanimate object personal or life-like qualities.

Metaphor—A figure of speech in which one object is likened to another by referring to it as if it were that other object. The word comes from the Greek *meta*—beyond, over + *pherein*—to carry, meaning to transfer qualities of one thing to another to illustrate their similarities.

Repetition—Saying the same word or phrase multiple times. Speakers often repeat what must be remembered.

Questions to Consider

- Choose three complex or technical terms from your academic major or a course you are currently taking. Write a paragraph for each term in which you define and explain it for an audience to which it is completely unfamiliar. Make sure your explanation is clear, accurate, and comprehensive.
- Go to www.whitehouse.gov and read a recent statement or speech by the president. Take note of the speech's inclusive language choices such as pronouns like we, our, and us. What impact do these words have on you as you read the speech? Do these choices succeed in uniting the speaker and the audience?

SOURCES TO CONSULT

The best source to consult when reviewing public speaking is a college-level public speaking textbook. If you don't have the text from your introductory public speaking course, get another one and save it for future reference. In addition to a college text, the following sources offer a wealth of material to help you review the basics of public speaking and the foundations of rhetorical study.

American Rhetoric. www.americanrhetoric.com/

This popular website has hundreds of speeches in print, audio, and video format. Review basic information about rhetoric at the "For Scholars" tab and check out the "News and Information Index" for useful links.

Audacity. http://audacity.sourceforge.net/

Audacity is free, open-source software used for recording and editing sounds. Use it to easily listen to your own voice, practice pronunciations, and edit out verbal fillers, and for many other practical voice applications.

Booth, Wayne C., Gregory G. Colomb, and Joseph M. Williams. *The Craft of Research*, 3rd edition. Chicago: University of Chicago Press, 2008.

This is the best guide available for understanding the research process. It explains the questions that should be asked and answered to conduct research from a scholarly perspective. Use it for understanding how to research a speech fully.

Brouwer, Daniel C., and Robert Asen. *Public Modalities: Rhetoric, Culture, Media, and the Shape of Public Life*. Tuscaloosa: University of Alabama Press, 2010.

The authors examine the role of rhetoric in contemporary culture, recognizing the complexity of mediated forms of public communication, in particular.

Campbell, Karlyn Kohrs, and Kathleen Hall Jamieson. "Form and Genre in Rhetorical Criticism: An Introduction." In *Form and Genre: Shaping Rhetorical Action*. Falls Church: Speech Communication Association, 1978. Also appears in *Readings in Rhetorical Criticism*, 3rd edition. Carl R. Burgchardt, Ed. State College: Strata Publishing, Inc., 2005.

This is by far the best short introduction to the topic of rhetorical genre. The authors explain how constellations of elements contribute to the formation of distinct genres and also articulate how combinations of rhetorical genres may coalesce to create rhetorical hybrids.

Crowley, Sharon, and Debra Hawhee. *Ancient Rhetorics for Contemporary Students*, 4th edition. New York: Pearson Longman, 2009.

The basic concepts of public speaking and rhetoric are covered from the classical perspective. Whole chapters are devoted to all the major classical topics including style; delivery; arrangement; and logical, ethical, and pathetic proof.

Goman, Carol Kinsey. *The Silent Language of Leaders: How Body Language Can Help—or Hurt—How You Lead*. San Francisco: Jossey-Bass, 2011.

This book popularizes various aspects of nonverbal communication as it applies to leadership with many applications to public speaking. Remember, speakers lead—leaders speak, and our nonverbal communication speaks louder than we imagine.

Hauser, Gerard A. *Introduction to Rhetorical Theory*, 2nd edition. Prospect Heights, IL: Waveland Press, 2002.

This best-selling textbook covers rhetorical theory and its applications and is very useful for understanding the origins of public speaking principles and practices.

Heinrichs, Jay. *Thank You for Arguing: What Aristotle, Lincoln, and Homer Simpson Can Teach Us about the Art of Persuasion.* New York: Three Rivers Press, 2007.

Heinrichs provides an entertaining and irreverent look at persuasion that is actually an erudite handbook grounded in Aristotelian and Ciceronian rhetorical theory. The author offers excellent examples of persuasive techniques and rhetorical figures, complete with a glossary of rhetorical terms and a brief chronology of the history of rhetoric.

Internet Encyclopedia of Philosophy. www.iep.utm.edu/

The encyclopedia has many articles about concepts that are common to rhetoric and philosophy. See, for example, entries on Argument, Evidence, and Fallacies. The latter entry has an alphabetical list of 204 reasoning fallacies!

Jasinski, James, Ed. *Sourcebook on Rhetoric: Key Concepts in Contemporary Rhetorical Studies.* Thousand Oaks: Sage Publications, Inc., 2001.

This book should be in the reference section of your university library. It contains almost 700 pages of short articles discussing the whole range of rhetorical ideas and terminology.

Jones, Gerald Everett. *How to Lie With Charts*, 2nd edition. La Puerta Productions, 2007.

More than a popular expose of unethical visual aids, this book will help you review the principles of effective and ethical visual communication.

Keith, William M., and Christian O. Lundberg, *An Essential Guide to Rhetoric.* New York: Bedford/St. Martins, 2008.

Less than 100 pages, this slim book covers the origins of rhetoric, including Aristotle's types of speaking situations and the construction of persuasive arguments. The volume also considers various methods of organization and stylistic choices. A sample speech is included.

Lanham, Richard A. *A Handlist of Rhetorical Terms*, 2nd edition. Berkeley: University of California Press, 1991.

A substantial alphabetical list of terms is followed by a concise summary of basic classical topics.

Lunsford, Andrea, Kurt H. Wilson, and Rosa A. Eberly, Eds. *The Sage Handbook of Rhetorical Studies.* Thousand Oaks: Sage Publications, 2009.

The handbook is a lengthy compilation of essays that explore nearly all dimensions of rhetorical theory, criticism, and practice for the advanced student.

Park, Douglas B. "The Meanings of 'Audience.'" *College English 44*, 3 (March 1982):247–257. Online www.jstor.org/stable/377012.

Professor Park argues that although "audience" is relatively easy to talk about, upon reflection, it is more complicated than we usually think.

Peters, John Durham. *Speaking Into the Air: A History of the Idea of Communication*. Chicago: University of Chicago Press, 2000.

Peters traces the varied and sometimes conflicting meanings attached to communication and communicative practices throughout history while probing the role of rhetoric in forging connection (and division) in our increasingly pluralistic society.

Rodgers, Janet. *The Complete Voice and Speech Workout: 74 Exercises for Classroom and Studio Use*. New York: Applause Books, 2002.

Although voice training is more common among singers and actors, public speakers can surely benefit from paying more attention to what is traditionally referred to as "voice and diction." This book can be used for self-improvement in this often overlooked dimension of speaking.

Schudson, Michael. *The Good Citizen: A History of American Civic Life*. Cambridge: Harvard University Press, 1998.

Prof. Schudson, a MacArthur Fellow, considers how changes in public communication behaviors relate to our understanding of U.S. democracy and our practice of civic life. A "must read" book for anyone who leads through public speaking and wants to understand contemporary citizenship in all its myriad manifestations.

Silva Rhetoricae: The Forest of Rhetoric. http://rhetoric.byu.edu/

From the first page: "This site is intended to help beginners, as well as experts, make sense of rhetoric, both on the small scale (definitions and examples of specific terms) and on the large scale (the purposes of rhetoric, the patterns into which it has fallen historically as it has been taught and practiced for 2000+ years)."

Strunk, William, Jr., and E. B. White. *The Elements of Style*, 4th edition. New York: Longman, 2000.

This classic is meant for writers, not speakers. Even so, many of its practical guidelines for clear, effective communication apply just as much to speaking as writing.

Torricelli, Robert, and Andrew Carroll, Eds. *In Our Own Words: Extraordinary Speeches of the American Century*. New York: Kodansha International, 1999.

This book contains 160 texts of significant speeches from the twentieth century, many of which are not available on the American Rhetoric site. With speeches arranged by decade, introductory paragraphs offer snapshot views of the rhetorical situations giving rise to each address.

Winans, James A. *Speech-Making*. New York: Appleton-Century Company, 1938.

Dartmouth College speech professor James Winans' public speaking textbook was popular in the middle of the twentieth century. His chapter on delivery, called "Conversing with an Audience," makes the case that public speaking should be viewed as a form of conversation rather than as a kind of theatrical performance. His explanation of "conversational delivery" has proved valuable to generations of speakers.

INDEX

Note: Page numbers followed by "n" indicate footnotes